Clashing Symbols?

A report on the use of flags, anthems and other national symbols in Northern Ireland

by
Clem McCartney
and
Lucy Bryson

The Institute of Irish Studies
for
The Community Relations Council

ACKNOWLEDGEMENTS

When we began this study we anticipated preparing a short report. However, we received such generous help from so many people that we ended up with a great wealth of information, and this sizeable book. A great debt of gratitude is due to all the individuals and organisations who agreed to be interviewed and all the organisations which took the trouble to provide us with material. They are listed in Appendix 1. In addition we were able to use information from the Counteract study on intimidation in the workplace, and many colleagues around the world generously provided information on the situation in their region.

There is one organisation which is not listed in the Appendix, to whom we are extremely grateful. The Linen Hall Library, and Robert Bell in particular, provided us willingly with advice, encouragement and help in finding sources.

Harry Barton, the chronicler of the exploits of Mr Mooney, and his publisher, Blackstaff Press, gave kind permission to reproduce one of Harry's encounters with Mr Mooney which forms a fitting prologue.

We must also thank the Community Relations Council for giving us the incentive and opportunity to undertake the work, and the office staff for their tolerance and help with mailing, copying, taking messages and all the other demands we made. In preparing the book for publication, we are indebted to Dr Brian Walker and Ms Kate Newmann of the Institute of Irish Studies for their assistance.

CONTENTS

PROLOGUE

Younger readers may not remember Mr Mooney, the leprechaun Public Relations Officer of the Queen's Own Loyal Sinn Fein Republican Volunteers whose mission in life was, and presumably still is, to join all militant extremists together to combat moderation and co-operation. Older readers will regret that Harry Barton, the chronicler of his exploits, is no longer sharing his stories with us. But, since flags and anthems can be divisive, there is no better place to start this study than with the time Mr Mooney and his colleagues turned their minds to the problem. We were delighted that Harry gave us permission to use the story because it also gives us a chance to revive a little bit of Mr Mooney for his old friends and introduce him to new readers[1].

As one of the Little People, Mr Mooney's home is underground, inside Drumnagortihacket Mountain in County Derry, to be precise. He comes to the surface, however, for every new round of the Irish Troubles. In April, 1970, he decided that the present Troubles had become worthy of his attention. He climbed up out of that yawning and bottomless crevasse known to political geologists as the Great Divided Community Rift.

At once, with immediate and resounding success, he took the political initiative. I remember clearly the day he told me about it. I remember the smell; I remember the knock on the door. 'Come in, Mr Mooney,' I said.

The door opened and he came in. 'How did you know it was me?' he asked.

He is of the class of Little People known as leprechaun. He is ten thousand years old and he was a drop-out from the start. If he's not wearing an old green tail coat with a faded orange waistcoat, then he's wearing an old orange tail coat with a faded green waistcoat. Either way there's always a petrol bomb in the tail pocket. His political attitude has remained unchanged – utterly polarised, you might say – since the Battle of the Boyne, at which he fought on both sides.

'Of course I knew it was you,' I told him, 'I could smell you coming up the stairs. I could hear the hum of the air-conditioning deepen as it took on the extra load.'

Mr Mooney was very pleased. 'You could?' he said. 'There's achievement for you.'

He had a scroll in one hand and I asked him what it was.

'It's a solemn agreement,' he said. 'I'm about to read it out to you.'

He unrolled it and struck an attitude like a small smelly herald. 'I'll read out the title,' he said: 'A SOLEMN AGREEMENT BETWEEN

THE DIEHARD LOYALISTS AND THE DIEHARD REPUBLICANS.'

'I question the authenticity of this document,' I told him.

'Just let me get on reading it,' said Mr Mooney. 'You'll find it makes great sense.' He began to read. '*Whereas* – You'll note,' he said, 'that it's all set out in proper legal fashion with *whereases* every five words – *Whereas* nobody loves either lot of us poor diehards. *And whereas* there are only a few handfuls of Us, even when you take the two lots of us together. *And whereas* there are over fifty millions of Them, spread out from Cork to Larne, from Cornwall to the Orkneys, wasting their time over unpatriotic and irreligious activities such as bringing up children, or growing food, or building houses, or painting pictures, or playing football, or saying their prayers in whatever fashion suits them. *And whereas* there's not a single one of them who's interested in warming over the old dead battles of the past the way we – both kinds of us – like to do. *And whereas*—'

I interrupted him: 'I'm not sure that I can stand any more of these '*whereases*'.'

'Have patience,' said Mr Mooney. 'There's only one more before I get to the big final '*therefore*'.'

'*Whereas,* if we joined forces we could invent a new toy flag of our own and stop misusing two real ones.'

'*Therefore*, it is hereby resolved that we shall in future constitute one single organisation, this organisation to be known as the Queen's Own Loyal Sinn Fein Republican Volunteers.'

'The Queen's Own what?'

'The Queen's Own Loyal Sinn Fein Republican Volunteers,' said Mr Mooney. 'An organisation that will be open to diehards of all persuasions, just so long as they *are* diehards and don't care what happens to their children.'

I said I had two questions for him. First of all, who will the Volunteers fight if they haven't got each other to beat into the ground? Can they get on without each other? Won't they get very bored?

'They'll have large numbers of worthy enemies,' said Mr Mooney. 'You might say that they'll be out-numbered. Mothers wheeling prams, young soldiers, very old men on their way to the shop on the corner, policemen, small girls with cold noses on their way to school, members of the fire brigade. They'll have enemies on every side.'

'Secondly,' I said. 'What will your new flag look like? I'd like to be able to recognise it when I see it.'

'Thin vertical stripes of Red, White, Green, Orange and Blue,' he said, 'And in the centre, a blood red hand playing a harp. Very tasteful.'

Notes

1   Reprinted from Harry Barton *Yours, Till Ireland Explodes, Mr Mooney* Belfast: Blackstaff Press, 1973 with kind permission of author and publisher. © Harry Barton

INTRODUCTION

Defining the Issues

Controversy over flags and anthems is not a new phenomena, certainly not in Ireland and, in particular, Northern Ireland. However in some ways the issues have become more complex in recent times. Practices which were normal in the past have changed. Others have been challenged. The certainties of the old status quo may or not have been desirable, but they have now gone and the situation is less clear. Flags and decorations have been removed from factory workshops. Does this mean that the flying of a flag or a picture of the monarch on the wall may not be permissible? The recent controversy over the playing of the National Anthem at Queen's University graduations has been watched with interest by supporters and opponents. What are the legal, ethical and community relations implications of such situations? Flags and national anthems are also involved in other issues such as the controversies around parades.

It is in this context that the Community Relations Council decided that it was desirable to examine the current situation to see if there was a body of good practice which met the wishes of all those concerned. In undertaking the work we were aware of the suspicion of some people, in both the nationalist and unionist communities, that the purpose of this study was to undermine in some way the commitment they have to their current symbols. On the contrary, we wanted to understand and try to explain the intensity of feeling which flags and national anthems arouse in some people. We wanted to explore the nature of the phenomena, and to understand the arguments used by people in supporting or opposing the use of flags or anthems in specific circumstances. We were aware that current practice leaves many people dissatisfied and confused because their wishes are not met. In trying to explain the importance of flags and anthems we hope to clarify the issues, which is the first step in finding responses which are broadly acceptable.

Any observer is quickly struck by the multitude of flags and emblems which are displayed with pride by their supporters in Northern Ireland. Many of these cause offence to their opponents. It would have been convenient if we could have limited ourselves to specific examples, say the national flags and anthems of the United Kingdom and the Republic of Ireland. However, there are widely differing views as to what are the contentious issues. One person may wear an emblem thinking it should offend no one, while someone else will find the sight of it insensitive and provocative. Our concern is not with songs or flags in isolation, but with their meaning and

1

implications in the specific circumstances which arise in Northern Ireland. It would therefore have been inappropriate for us to make a decision to put restrictions on what was worthy of attention.

We are concerned with any flag, emblem or anthem which is important to some section of the community, but which, it could be argued, causes offence to others, and equally we are concerned with any flag or anthem which might help to overcome such controversies. In the context of Northern Ireland this could include religious emblems which in a different context would not be considered to have any overt political significance, such as a badge with the inscription 'Jesus Saves' or a Sacred Heart of Jesus badge. At the same time some flags and emblems are more likely to be actual or potential sources of conflict than others, and consequently they will be considered in more detail. They highlight the underlying issues, which can then be related to those symbols which are more peripheral or which only infrequently cause controversy. In the main most emphasis is given to flags and emblems which are often given a formal or ceremonial significance. In Chapter 2 we will discuss in more detail the range of flags and emblems which are significant in Northern Ireland.

The situation with national anthems is simpler. There are fewer anthems to consider. Most obviously there are the national anthems of the United Kingdom and the Republic of Ireland, but again it will be necessary to refer to a small number of other songs, either because they are used in place of the national anthem, or because they are promoted as a substitute for the national anthem. As with flags and emblems we have given most significance to songs which are often used in a ceremonial context. There are many other songs which cause offence to some people or which are a source of pride for others, and Mary McCann is preparing a study of party songs. They give rise to many of the same issues as anthems, but to keep the subject to manageable proportions we have left the reader to make these connections.

Terminology

We have been concerned not to refer to any symbol in a way which may cause offence to those who respect it. At the same time we wanted to use short names for the convenience of the reader. We have called the national anthems of the United Kingdom and of Ireland by their popular titles, 'The Queen' and 'The Soldier's Song'. For the flag of the United Kingdom, we have not used the popular term, 'Union Jack.' The correct title is the Union flag, with no capital letter for the word 'flag', and we have followed this convention. We refer to the flag of the Irish Republic as the Tricolour. We have used a capital 'T', although this is not strictly correct, in order to show we are referring to the Irish Tricolour and not any other three-coloured flag. The flag of the Government of Northern Ireland is often called 'the Ulster flag', but we have called it by its official name, the 'Northern Ireland flag', and kept the name 'Ulster flag' for the provincial flag and to stress the distinction, we often refer to it as the 'Ulster O'Neill flag'.

In writing about the main traditions in Northern Ireland we have used the political terms, nationalist and unionist, rather than the religious categories, Catholic and Protestant, unless we specifically want to speak of the whole community, regardless of political outlook. This seems the most appropriate approach because in much of the study we are talking about responses to flags as political and national objects. The terms 'loyalist' and 'republican' are reserved for the more militant sections of each community, but we have not implied an association with paramilitary groups unless this is made explicit.

The Approach

We appreciated that we needed to look at the subject in a number of different ways. We wanted to know what is happening currently, but we also wanted to know how people feel about it. We needed to understand how, historically, flags came to have their significance, and we wanted to compare the situation in Northern Ireland with elsewhere in the British Isles and other parts of the world. We were interested in the protocol which surrounds the formal use of flags and anthems, but their informal use is often more contentious. We therefore wanted to know something of their use in different social situations. Where there are disputes about flags and anthems, we wanted to know how they have been handled informally and how the situation is regulated legally.

We did not set out to test any particular ideas or theories about the nature of flags and anthems, as this would unnecessarily restrict our discussions to issues which we thought were important. We were more interested to hear what people thought was important and to let ideas and principles about the issues emerge from the lessons of experience. While we tried to be open, it is inevitable that the issues we raised and the questions we asked did reflect some underlying assumptions about the nature of the subject. We were aware of some theoretical perspectives which have influenced our approach. We do not refer to them directly in later chapters as it would have interrupted the flow of the description and analysis, and therefore it may be useful to acknowledge their contribution at this point

We accepted that flags and anthems are important for people and mean something for them. They are a form of communication. They are a kind of language which conveys meanings. When people use them they are indicating something about themselves or about the situation in which they are used. This leads us to think about systems of expression, the study of signs or semiotics and the question of meaning. We did not think it would add to the understanding of flags and anthems to become embroiled in the abstruse arguments between different schools of thought and thinkers on the nature of communication processes, including the more recent controversies between structuralism, modernism, post structuralism, post-modernism, deconstruction and so on. Nor did we think that our readers would appreciate such a discussion.

For our purposes these debates are not important because of the conclusions reached by any particular school of thought, but they help us to identify certain concepts and issues in which they are all interested and which it is important to examine. We do not need to explore the intricacies of theories of linguistic analysis, but the distinction between signifer and signified reminds us of the need to think of the flag or anthem not only as an object (the signifier) but also as a means of representing ideas and concepts (the signified). Is there a fixed relationship between the object and what it represents? Do they always represent the same things or does it depend on the circumstances, which in theoretical terms is the issue of interpretation and meaning?

These issues also raise the question of the people or actors. We need to think of the people who are displaying the flag or playing the anthem. It is clear that people respond to flags and anthems in different ways. Does it matter what are their intentions? And equally we need to think of the people who are aware of the display (the subject) and we have to consider the validity of their understanding of the display. What are the implications of a situation where the display of a flag or the performance of a national anthem is interpreted differently by those who are doing it and by observers? In trying to decide what is the meaning of the display is it more helpful to try to understand the intention behind the display or its impact on observers? Or is there an authoritative meaning which is universal and constant and which arbitrates between different views?

Underlying these questions are another series of more fundamental questions about how people make sense of the world and the complex and difficult realm of hermeneutics. We need to think about the nature of perception and subjectivity. Given that apparently simple events can be and are interpreted and explained very differently by different people, it is difficult to be satisfied with the view that every phenomenon has one inherent transparent meaning. In exploring the different reactions to flags and anthems, we have kept in mind ideas about the relativity of perception and perception as a social act. From this perspective objects and forms of expression are in fact 'signs whose meanings depend on conventions, relationships and systems', according to Jefferson (1986) who goes on to quote Roland Barthes' phrase 'Culture is a language' in the sense that culture consists of signs which are structured and organised like language. Flags and anthems are such cultural signs. From this perspective the flag is just a piece of cloth or the anthem is just a song until people react to it in ways which give it meaning and significance. This idea is common to structuralism, where it holds a central place, and to most of its subsequent detractors and critics.

These ideas are developed at an abstract level which prompt us to explore the way ideas and attitudes develop but do not provide practical analytical frameworks which help us to understand how these processes work and to explain how flags and anthems can become such potent symbols. More useful in this respect is the collaboration of philosophers with sociologists and psychologists on the relation between social discourse and ideology and on attitude formation, including work on the social construction of knowledge (Berger and Luckman, 1967) and discourse analysis (Potter and

Wetherell, 1987). We need to look behind attitudes because 'an attitude is not a thing, it is a process; it is an interaction. It is an interaction involving not only the person and the object, but all other factors which are present in the situation.' (Rabb and Lipset, 1962). More succinctly 'Men must talk about themselves to know themselves' (Berger and Luckman, 1967).

This analysis encourages us to take a critical view of the use of common sense to justify our views. All of us live our life on the basis of assumptions which might more accurately be called illusions which provide a sense of certainty, and common sense is the word we use for your our deepest and fondest illusions. Only as a last resort will we abandon cherished beliefs even when they appear to contradict the evidence of experience. This analysis also directs us to the critical part played by interaction and discussion with neighbours, friends or colleagues in the process through which existing values and beliefs are retained or new experiences grappled with in order to integrate them as far as possible with existing assumptions.

Beliefs and ideas are shared with others and that group of people forms the context or framework of norms, conventions and assumptions through which people interpret what is happening around them and give meaning to their experiences and create symbols to express them. Buckley (1984) refers to a 'shared paradigm which generates descriptions of the social world.' He is writing in the context or a community in Northern Ireland and he cites the siege of Derry as a 'cultural landmark, a point of orientation for all who inhabit the society.' There are many such cultural features in which flags and anthems can play a part.

This leads to the idea of, in Stanley Fish's (1980) phrase, the interpretive community, which is the reference point to which individuals turn when they are trying to make sense of the world around them. Tajfel's social identity theory (Turner and Giles, 1981) provides a perspective which helps us to understand such groups. It reminds us that people are members of a number of such communities in different aspects of their lives, at work, at home, in the neighbourhood and so on.

These communities may hold different and incompatible views, yet most of the time people have the capacity to absorb these contradictions without apparent tension or even without being aware of their existence. The individual's sense of self comes in part from identification with some groups, but it is also based on the sense of difference from other groups. In psychological experiments wearing different jackets can be the basis for groups to develop a sense of difference and groups look for ways to distinguish themselves from others. Flags and anthems can provide one way to emphasise that difference.

In a Northern Ireland context the basis of the interpretative communities is a shared sense of ethnic identity. To understand how these communities function we have to take account of the nature of ethnicity, (see, for example, Enloe 1986) and recognise the role of symbols in expressing and mobilising that identity. In chapter 2 we shall explore in some depth how this is expressed in the different sections and sub-groups of the nationalist and unionist communities in Northern Ireland, to which the individual responds.

We shall see that in many ways each group understands these symbols differently. Where they agree is in the recognition of their importance.

In carrying out this study our general outlook has been comparative. Although we have not been able to study practice in other countries in depth, we have found valuable insights which have helped us to appreciate the situation in Northern Ireland. It has shown that local conventions are not as unusual as some commentators would have us believe; it has shown the dangers in some practices; and it has demonstrated ways in which other communities have used their flags and anthems to contribute to reconciliation.

The wish to combine historical, comparative, social anthropological, legal and other perspectives had obvious implications. Firstly in the time available, we would not be able to examine definitively any one aspect, and in any case others could write more authoritatively on some aspects of the subject. Therefore our aim was to give an overview of the issues as seen from different perspectives and to identify practices which seemed to offer the most hopeful way to manage difficult situations. The second implication was that we needed to use a variety of approaches to obtain information and understand attitudes. The main methods used were a postal survey, in-depth interviews, consultations with experts in various aspects of the subject, and library research. Appendix 1 lists the people we talked to and the individuals and organisations which provided us with information.

We have also had to think carefully how best to integrate the range of information available, because themes recur in different situations both in Northern Ireland and elsewhere. At the same time we wanted to present each aspect of the subject in such a way that it could be read separately from the rest of the report, to facilitate those who are only interested in specific topics.

The report is therefore in three sections. Chapter 1 deals with the social meaning and significance of flags and anthems in different parts of the world, and discusses their origins and form, the protocol which surrounds their use and the implications of breaches of protocol. This section is quite brief and general and there are only passing references to flags and anthems in Northern Ireland. Chapter 2 however is much more detailed and focuses directly on the situation in Northern Ireland, though there are some comparisons to the wider world, where this may be illuminating. It identifies the significant flags and emblems in Northern Ireland, their origins and what they represent to different sections of the community.

The third section, Chapters 3 to 6, examines the impact of flags and anthems in different aspects of daily life and on special occasions with emphasis on the situation in the workplace and problems of public order.

Chapter 7 draws together the different elements and recurring themes. Opinions on how situations can be managed are referred to and a basis for future planning is described.

The Main Themes

In the next chapter we will begin by looking at why flags and anthems are important to some people. But before proceeding to the main part of the report, it may be helpful to list at the beginning some of the themes which will recur in the report.

Flags and anthems are symbols and as such communicate ideas and attitudes.

They are a simplified form of communication and therefore they cannot convey complex information and they can easily become a cause of misunderstanding and controversy.

In Northern Ireland the controversy about symbols is a way of expressing underlying controversies about the constitutional situation and relations between different sections of the community. The symbols are therefore important for people. This strength of feeling needs to be acknowledged and should not be dismissed by anyone concerned about the situation.

The attitudes and feelings of the different sections of the community about flags and anthems are not mirror images of each other. There is therefore a great deal of mutual misunderstanding, which makes it more difficult to resolve issues about flags.

There are wide variations in how people feel about flags and anthems, and also in the intensity of those feelings, and this makes it more difficult to try to balance the concerns of everyone.

Current policies have defused many of the issues, especially about flags in the workplace and public order problems. Nevertheless they have left some uncertainty about administrative discretion in relation to flags. There is also some uncertainty about the current status of the Union flag which is of particular concern to unionists.

Current policies are based on limiting the use of symbols and freedom of expression, but in other areas policy is encouraging expression of cultural identity.

As they have a potential to divide, symbols can contribute to the improvement of relationships.

CHAPTER 1

Flags and Anthems in a Global Context

Why Flags and Anthems are Important[1]

> Flags have practical uses, but their primary function has always been social communication. National flags in particular stimulate the viewer to feel and act in a calculated way. They represent or identify the existence, presence, origin, authority, possession, loyalty, glory, beliefs, objectives, and status of an entire nation. They are employed to honor and dishonor, warn and encourage, threaten and promise, exalt and condemn, commemorate and deny. They remind and incite and defy the child in school, the soldier, the voter, the enemy, the ally, and the stranger. Flags authenticate claims, dramatize political demands, establish a common framework within which like-minded nations are willing to work out mutually agreeable solutions – or postulate and maintain irreconcilable differences that prevent agreements from occurring. It is scarcely possible to conceive of the world, of human society, without flags . . . Because flags constitute explicit self-analysis by nations-states . . . the study of flag history and symbolism may justly claim to be an auxiliary to the social sciences. (Smith 1980)

We can think of examples of flags being used in most of these ways in Northern Ireland, but many people still find it difficult to understand why national flags and symbols matter so much to people. They tend to the view that we should do away with all these things if they cause controversy. It is therefore necessary to say something of what flags, emblems and anthems mean to different people, and to consider why they not only mean different things to different people, but why the intensity of those feelings range from intense commitment to total indifference.

Playing national anthems and displaying flags and emblems has a significance for people in different ways. But they are commonly a symbol of something: a way of expressing attitudes or views and in particular an expression of one's allegiances. In fact we will often use the rather clumsy phrase 'national symbols' as an abbreviation for national flags, emblems and anthems. Flags are a mark of identity: they identify ourselves, they identify others and they provide a sign around which people can gather. A unionist said that people need things to identify with. When someone identifies with a flag you are associating with what the flag represents: a community, shared values, a sense of history and tradition. In a related way they can mark out ownership of territory and property. A unionist politician said that the display of a flag is regarded as a reminder of the state to which the territory belongs.

As well as being a distinguishing mark, they also are a symbol of identity in a more emotional and psychological sense. They are a symbol through which you can express your loyalty and allegiances. 'They give that sense of belonging, like a backbone', as a loyalist said. A republican said it gives a 'wee emotional fix when you see it – a wee lift to the heart.' They represent a common feeling and are 'emotional shorthand for issues of national pride and culture, or simply issues of national importance.'

The phrase 'emotional shorthand' reminds us that they have an immediate direct impact. 'They are instantly recognisable', said a republican. While for a loyalist they are 'an easy visual way to remember our origins', and therefore 'you don't have to talk for hours about your identity.' There is another side to the directness of their impact on us. They are only able to carry simple blunt messages. Even when they are carefully constructed with precisely chosen imagery to convey a detailed message, the full meaning often gets lost or overlooked. A republican said that they are 'the most banal expressions of nationalism.' They become simple representations of group identity: this is our symbol and that is their symbol. We were told that flags and anthems should be used to unite people. They can be unifying symbols, but only for those who want to identify with the group, and they can easily become associated with chauvinist or fascist attitudes towards other groups. Some groups are keen to use national symbols for this very purpose, while it encourages others to avoid them.

They not only express a sense of belonging, but they can play a more active part in encouraging it, particularly when they are used as part of some ceremony. They help to create a sense of occasion and highlight the importance to an event, and in turn they are honoured by being included in a special function. At a more mundane level, anthems help to give form to an event by marking its opening or closing. These ceremonial practices are 'procedures by which a community reminds itself that it is a community', in the words of one unionist. This is more true of anthems, which are most often used in ceremonies and other group situations. They help to encourage group bonding, shared allegiance, pride and loyalty – 'Like a backbone', in the phrase already quoted. For this reason, many organisations institute ceremonies and practices which incorporate flags and emblems. In this sense there is little difference in the social psychology of a multi-national company's use of flags and symbols to promote corporate identity and loyalty in its workers, and the use of colour parties by a national army, or indeed a paramilitary organisation. Of course each organisation will have different purposes and motivation, and the feelings and emotions tapped, and the intensity of the identification will be quite different.

In the corporate world one quality which is considered important is progressiveness and logos and practices will be updated to ensure that the company is in advance of new trends. At national level a very different image is desired, which embodies permanence, continuity and enduring values. The form and style of symbols and of the ceremonies around them evolve over long periods, or in the case of new states, they are copied to create this sense of historical tradition.

The History and Development of Flags

It is not surprising that flags and emblems are associated with allegiance and loyalty, territory and authority in this way. As the *New Encyclopaedia Britannica* (15 edition,vol 4, p812) says, 'originally used mainly in warfare, flags were, and to some extent, remain, insignia of leadership, serving for identification of friend or foe and as a rallying point. They are now also extensively used for signalling, for decoration and for display.' An old Ukrainian proverb says that 'When flags are flying the mind is on [war] trumpets'.

It is not possible to be precise about the development of the *concept* of a flag or anthem as a social symbol, in the sense that they mean more to people than simply a fragment of cloth or a piece of music. They are a social construct, and as such their significance has evolved over time through social processes. In modern times the decision to adopt a flag or anthem is often well documented, but in many cases, the official adoption is only the ratification of a process through which the symbol has already gained general acceptance.

None of the authorities on flags is prepared to be categorical about how flags developed, but one can make some informed speculation from the evidence. The oldest surviving 'flag' recorded in the *Guinness Book of Records* is around 5000 years old, but it is not a flag at all. It was found in Iran and is made of metal. The oldest documentary evidence from China states that in 1122 BC the Emperor had a white flag carried before him (Barraclough, 1971, p1). Other early references to flags, from Greece in the fifth century B.C., Egypt and Assyria, are associated with war.

According to Barraclough 'it is not unreasonable to assume that flags, originating in China, travelled westwards until they arrived in the Middle East, and the Romans, finding them there, adopted them for their own use.' (p2–3) It is also possible that they developed independently in different places, and many non-literate societies may have devised emblems and symbols which served the same functions as flags. The Roman standards or Eagle, carried by each legion, was a symbol of allegiance and a focus of loyalty to be defended. Each legion also carried a 'vexillum', a piece of coloured cloth which appears to have had the function of helped to distinguish each legion from the others.

The need for precise distinguishing marks became more important in the fragmented world of the European Middle Ages. It was important to recognise each individual leader, and it became more difficult when they were encased in armour. The custom of decorating shields with coloured patterns developed, and now some means was needed to ensure that only those entitled to specific colours and designs could use them. The result was the art of heraldry which regulated the system of designing and allocating patterns or coats of arms. These patterns and their colours were used by their owners in other ways, including cloth banners and flags.

The flag of the Roman legion had been associated with a group, a military unit. The eagle standard gave the soldiers a symbol of the Emperor and by extension the Empire, which they served. The coats of arms and flags of the middle ages were associated with an individual, and in time with families. Individuals could express their identification with him and their allegiance and loyalty to him, by wearing his colours.

Kings and powerful nobles also acquired flags and emblems, which took precedence over the flags of less powerful men, and as the ruler was identified with the state, so his personal flag or standard also came to be identified with the state. Normally this was an informal process of social convention, and the flag would change if the ruler was replaced. The greatest need for clear distinguishing marks was at sea, because it was not easy to identity friendly ships when they were away from their home port. Consequently rulers laid down rules to regulate the right to fly flags on ships.

In time, states began to adopt a national flag with a design which was associated with the nation rather than the ruler. The first such flag was adopted by the city state of Genoa, and the Danish flag, from the 13th century, is the oldest flag in continuous use (Barraclough, p8 and 123). A number of nations adopted the flag of a patron saint. The modern idea of the national flag only developed in the eighteenth and nineteenth century, with the growth of the nation state. States, such as the United States of America, gained independence from colonial powers and republics replaced monarchies, as in France. These new states made conscious decisions to create national flags to replace the old flags of the monarchy or the colonial power, and these flags were officially adopted by a legal process. However, although flags in modern times have normally been adopted by a clear process, it does not follow that the reasons for adopting particular colours or symbols is always clear.

The Designs of Flags

Flags are normally a rectangular piece of material, the Nepal flag with two tails being the exception. They can be a plain cloth of one colour, but usually they carry a variety of patterns and symbols, One can often find similarities between the flags in a region. The Nordic flags, for example, are all based on a cross design. Symbols and motifs are copied to show an association with other groups or nations which have used them.

Perhaps colours are the most fundamental element. The origins of flags may in fact be the simple coloured ribbons which were tied to a standard, and today the colours of the national flag are used in decorations as a reminder of the state. Today many flags are simply made up of a series of coloured stripes. Colours have long been associated with particular religions and races, even before they were placed on flags, and certain combinations of colours recur. Green is associated with Muslim states, dating back to the use of green flags by the sons Mohammed. They often incorporate the other Muslim symbols of the star and crescent. The families of the followers of Mohammed chose different colours, green, red, white and black, and these are now the pan-Arab colours, which can be found on the flags of many Arab countries.

Red white and blue are among the most common colours though for different reasons in different parts of the world. They are the pan-Slavic colours and so are found in many East European flags, including the new flag of Russia. States which had an association with either the United States of America or the United Kingdom have adopted flags in those colours.

Colours are often used to symbolise aspects of the nation and the land, but the meanings vary considerably. Black has been used variously to represent the wealth of the county or the soil, or the people. Yellow or gold often means wealth, or more specifically the mineral gold, but yellow also refers to the sun.

A white stripe is often explained as a symbol of unity or peace, and it is found in many flags. But there may be another reason for its prevalence. In heraldic convention, two colours should not be put together and should be separated by a 'metal', that is gold (yellow) or silver (white).

A wide variety of symbols are also incorporated in flags. Stars are common, though again they have a variety of meanings. States in Oceania, especially those associated with the British Commonwealth, have used the pattern of the Southern Cross, or other stars. Brazil incorporates the pattern of constellations which can be seen above Brazil, but as in many other flags the number of stars also represents the constituent provinces or states. The star was a common symbol found on the flags of communist states. When they ceased to be governed by the Communist Party, Yugoslavia (Serbia and Montenegro) simply removed the star and otherwise retained the existing flag in the Slavic colours. Nevertheless the red star symbol of communism does, on occasions, still inspire a very hostile reaction in Bosnian Muslims and Croats who identify it with Belgrade oppression.

The sun is also a favoured motif, either depicted or represented simply by the colour yellow. The sun is incorporated in the flag of Japan, as it is the 'land of the rising sun', whereas it is included in the flag of the Canadian province of British Columbia, since it is the province which faces the setting sun. This is one more example of how the same symbol can mean different things.

Other states have used representational symbols which are associated with the nation. The Cypriot flag is probably the only national flag which provides a map, showing the physical boundaries of the island, though not the political divisions which have occurred since the flag was adopted. Depictions of flora and fauna are common from the maple leave of Canada to the bird of paradise of Papua New Guinea. Others include representations of the nation's wealth such as a nutmeg in the Grenadan flag. Socialist states in particular depicted symbols of work: the hammer and sickle of the Soviet Union, the cogwheel and rice of Burma and so on. The state emblem is also common in the flags of socialist states, but can be found in other flags, sometimes as a distinguishing mark from a similar flag of another country.

Flags can be based on the colours or flags of the previous rulers, as in the Sri Lankan flag, or the ruling party, as in a number of African states. The most obvious example of the symbols of a ruling party becoming the state flags is the Third German Reich. Two flags were used, the Swastika flag of Hitler's National Socialist Party, and a simple striped flag in the same colours, red, white and black, and this shows the problems of having two flags. A German ship, visiting the United States, was boarded and the Swastika was burnt. The United States authority took no action claiming that the national flag had not been touched. To avoid farther confusion about the status of the Swastika, from henceforth it became the only national flag.

The way the elements are combined can also be significant. In the Basque flag, the green background represents the nation, the overlying red cross indicates the struggle for freedom and the white cross placed on top represents hope for the eventual peace and stability of the country. The combination of elements from different traditions can be used to indicate unity and co-operation. The Sri Lanka flag which was adopted after independence in 1978 referred back to the pre-independence Singalese nation, and included symbols of Bhuddism. Shortly afterwards in 1950 it was modified to give more recognition to the other communities in the country by adding stripes of green and orange to represent the minority religious groups of Hindus and Moslems. This aspect of the United Kingdom and Irish flags will be discussed later.

Not all flags are designed to promote harmony. Some are intended to make the statement that the users of the flag are different in some way from another group. A case in point is the adoption of a flag similar to the Nazi Swastika by the right wing movement in South Africa, Afrikaner Weerstands Beweging (AWB), suggesting, whether intentionally or not, that its supporters share the Nazi philosophy of racial purity (see below, p29). When Croatia became independent from Yugoslavia in 1991, it revived the Slavic red white and blue flag with a shield in the middle, the flag which had been used during the republic established under the Nazis in the 1940s. This may have been a way for the people to remember a time when they were independent of Serbia, but for Serbians it was a reminder of the conflict of the 1940s and the atrocities which were committed then. It was unlikely to be seen as a conciliatory gesture.

Perhaps the best example of a flag being adopted to express opposition to another group was in 1956 in the state of Georgia, in the United States of America. At that time the civil rights movement was becoming active, and historic Supreme Court decisions such as Brown v. Board of Education were ruling against segregation. The State Legislature changed its flag to incorporate the battle flag of the Confederacy in the American civil war. The Confederacy favoured slavery and white superiority and attempted to break away from the Union of the United States to protect that type of society. In the 1950s the Georgian legislature was not wishing to reintroduce slavery or secede from the Union . But it was saying something about its opposition to civil rights and its identification with the Confederacy. An alternative argument is that it was changed because the centennial of the Confederacy was coming up (though not for more than five years) and it was in honour of the Confederate war dead. Strangely enough there are no records which show the intention of the Legislature but one Republican, Denmark Groover said at the time 'This will show what we stood for, will stand for and will fight for.' Groover is the only member of the Legislature in 1956 who is still in office and he said in the Legislature in 1993 'I cannot say to you that I personally was in no way motivated by a desire to defy [desegregation] ... I can say in all honesty that my willingness was in large part because that flag symbolized a willingness of a people to sacrifice their all for their beliefs.'

His most recent statement was made in the context of an attempt by the Governor, Zell Miller, to have the flag changed. In his 1993 State of the State address the Governor called on the Legislature to change the flag and 'help me now to give bigotry no sanction, and persecution no assistance.' He backed down in the face of opposition, and although he was arguing that a flag had this kind of power and influence in 1993, one year later he argued that it is not important: 'I'm not going to lead any more parades [to change the flag], now or ever. I did my duty. I think ... [Atlanta Mayor] Bill Campbell phrased it better than I did, and that was that this doesn't affect the daily lives of individuals. I am going to devote my time to working on those things that affect the day-by-day lives of individuals.' But the reason he could not push through the change was because individuals did care very much about the flag, and this left him in danger of not being re-elected over his stand on the issue. (*Atlanta Journal,* 29 January 1994)

The issue has rumbled on and public hearings were called. A number of solutions have been suggested, including a referendum on the issue, flying the Black Liberation flag along with the Confederate flag, or only flying the Confederate flag in April as part of a Confederate history month (*Atlanta Journal* 22.4.1994)

The confederate battle flag has also led to controversy in Alabama recently, a farther reminder that it is not only in Northern Ireland that debates about flags become heated. It flies over the Capitol in Montgomery, Alabama, where the Confederate Congress met during the Civil War. Many Alabamans think that it is the state flag, but in fact the state flag is a reminder of Ireland: a Saint Patrick's Cross.

Recently, the Governor of Alabama, Guy Hunt, lost his office when he was found guilty of embezzlement. His replacement ordered that the battle flag should be removed from the Capital and Court House, and placed on the Southern White House where the President of the Confederacy lived. This proposal brings in not only a question of values but also of protocol. Until this controversy the Confederacy State flag of the Star and Bars flew over the Southern White House, which is correct both in the light of flag protocol and historically. The battle flag would never have been flown over the President's home. The flags were removed but the whole controversy has heightened awareness of the flag issue. For example in one high school, tension was so high recently that armed police were called in. We shall refer to this incident again (p26) , when we discuss how schools deal with controversy about national symbols. At a state level the Governor's decision was contested in the Supreme Court, which supported the decision to remove the flags.

The flag is widely displayed across the Southern part of the United States, and it is incorporated in the state flag of South Carolina and Mississippi, as well as Georgia, and it is flown over the state house in South Carolina. Many Southerners stick the battle flag on their car bumper, which is, of course another historically inaccurate use of the flag. No one believes that this represents a desire to leave the Union. But it does express opposition to some values of the rest of the United States, including support for racism, and a longing for manly, rural, traditional values against the liberal and urban. Some Southerners to-day identify these values with the Confederacy, even though it existed in a very different social climate. On the last day of the Waco siege, when federal authorities surrounded the headquarters of the Branch Dravidian Sect of David Koresh, after they were refused admittance, one of the armoured vehicles was flying a small confederate flag, which was noted with pride by some Southerners as an example of how they were called upon to sort out the nation's problems.

Another twist was given to the use of the Confederate flag by the creation of the New South flag, which was originally designed as part of the promotion for a record by a rap group. It uses the design of the confederate flag but has replaced the red white and blue with green red and black, the colours of the Black Liberation flag, designed at the beginning of the twentieth century by African American activist, Marcus Garvey. It is reminiscent of a flag which is occasionally seen in Northern Ireland. It has the design of the union flag, but the colours are those of the Irish Tricolour, green white and orange. A spokesperson for the record company, who may have a material interest in promoting the New South flag, said 'It's time to move forward and leave the past behind. Transforming the Confederate battle flag with the African-American colours and claiming the victory for black and whites alike is a way to take away the power from the old symbol and what it represents.' (*Atlanta Journal*, 22.4.1994) However the flag has created controversy, especially after a student was banned from school in South Carolina for refusing to remove a shirt which featured the flag (see p26).

The Development of Anthems

The Japanese anthem has words which date back to the ninth century and they are credited with being the oldest words of any national anthem, though at that time it would not have been considered an anthem in the modern sense. The modern concept of the national anthem is a song or tune which has a special status recognised in some formal manner, and which is a focus for national identity and an expression of national loyalty. The *New Encyclopaedia Britannica* (15th edition, vol8, p530) describes it as 'a hymn or song expressing patriotic sentiment and either governmentally authorised as an official national hymn or holding that position by popular feeling.'

This concept, like that of the national flag, is a social construction which has evolved, and there is no authoritative explanation of how this has happened. But again we can speculate.

Like the national flag, the development of this concept is associated with the growth of the nation state in the late 18th and 19th centuries. But its roots are much older. The term 'anthem' applies first and foremost to a piece of sacred music, a song of praise or gladness. The praise and gladness might be for an important person or a secular event, such as a victory in battle, and the anthem could become associated with that person or event. Or again another contribution to the development of the idea of an anthem may be in the tradition of a fanfare to greet the arrival of a distinguished person, a tradition which has continued until the present day. Later came the idea of composing music to greet the arrival of a distinguished person and in time it would have been convenient to play the same music on subsequent occasions, perhaps because it was a particular favourite. In time words were added. The pre-eminence of one anthem may have resulted from the practices and etiquette which surrounded it, and in turn, as it became seen as special, additional protocol would be added.

The next step was the transfer of the focus of the music from the individual to the nation. Philip Hammond (1993) has considered how a piece of music became associated with the national ideal:

> the concept of national music has been universally accepted by numerous politicians throughout the last few centuries since in fact the concept of nationhood itself became the driving force of political advancement. Hence the rise of 'national anthems' which in artistic terms or perhaps not so artistic terms could become a focus of national pride, arrogance, conceit, call it what you will. The British national anthem was the first such musical manifestation of nationhood ... the custom spread widely throughout the nineteenth century and even to this day is used as much as an indication of national identity as say a national costume or a national flag. Indeed flag-waving and anthem singing are indispensable features of any national celebration and are closely linked to the outcome of competition between nations.

The Forms of Anthems

Many societies and nations have a number of special national or patriotic songs. For America we can think of 'God Bless America', of for England there are 'Rule Britannia', 'Land of Hope and Glory' and Blake's 'Jerusalem'. Perhaps in Ireland 'A Nation Once Again' might hold such a place. All of these songs share many of the same qualities as anthems. Some of them are older and might well have become the official anthem. Often it is impossible to discover why one song was chosen over another. A particular song may be chosen because in some way it struck a cord in the national psyche, if we can talk of such a vague concept.

There are some structural requirements which exclude some melodies. It is preferable that it is easy to sing. Therefore a song with too great a range will not be suitable. Songs with a complicated rhythm are also unsatisfactory. As a result the anthem is often a fairly simple melody which will appeal to the widest cross-section of the community. Philip Hammond (1993) quotes Donal Henehan from the *New York Times* in 1976: 'Banality and self-deception are so integral a part of patriotic music'. According to *The New Groves Dictionary of Music*, 'National anthems are rarely noted for their musical quality.' It identifies five types based on their musical characteristics: hymns, marches, operatic anthems, folk anthems and fanfares. It notes that there is a tendency for countries to emulate their neighbours, with the result that there are regional similarities in anthems.

Few of the tunes have features which are associated with music of the country. As we have already mentioned, military marches are common, but that form has little to do with the indigenous musical forms of many nations, especially those in the developing world. It may have more to do with the training of their officer corps in European military colleges. Sweden is one European country whose national anthem is based on a traditional folk melody, and a few Asian countries use indigenous musical forms and instrumentation.

The historical context and events associated with the origins of the anthem may also touch a cord in the nation. This is true of the French anthem, 'The Marseillaise', which had very unprepossessing origins. It was written quickly in one evening in 1792 after the Mayor of Strasbourg had asked a captain of engineers to compose a marching song for the French troops. It became popular with them and the association was established between the song and the Revolutionary Wars.

Eleven countries, including Spain, have anthems without words, so words are not an essential feature. We have already noted that the symbolism on flags can be very imprecise and open to different interpretations. The addition of words to an anthem allow a more defined message to be communicated, but at the same time many people do not know the words of their own anthem or may only know particular phrases which resonate with the mood of the people. And words conjure up very different images and memories. We only have to think of the different images evoked for unionists and nationalists in Ireland by the first three words of the Irish national anthem: 'Soldiers are We'.

Some anthems should only be sung in the indigenous language of the nation. Not surprisingly this convention is an issue where the language is a major distinguishing mark of the nation, or where the language is at risk to a more dominant neighbouring language. Examples are the Welsh, Basque and Irish anthems.

Roy Arbuckle has read the words of most of the world's national anthems and has concluded that there are three main subjects for national anthems. To paraphrase his categories slightly, they are concerned with struggle and war, the land, and loyalty. Sometimes they combine all three. References to war and the struggle for freedom are very common, which indicates the origin of most modern states in revolution or emancipation from colonial rule. Mr. Arbuckle notes that every state which has an anthem referring to war has some current involvement in the use of force. He contrasts the New Zealand anthem which calls on God to protect the nation from war. Even it has a somewhat bellicose third verse ('Lord of battles in thy might, Put our enemies to flight'). The second common theme is more lyrical: an expression of love and identification with the land.

Expressions of loyalty, are a more disparate group to categorise than the other two. In a monarchy, the identity of the nation is associated with the person of the monarch and, as in the case of the United Kingdom, the anthem may be addressed to the monarch. The United States anthem is unusual in that it is addressed to the flag, but, as the pledge of allegiance (p23) says, the flag stands for the Republic. Since anthems are basically hymns of devotion and praise it is not surprising that many national anthems are prayers to God.

The Basque Country demonstrates the problems which can arise in trying to reconcile all the factors and achieve a popular consensus. There are two possible anthems, but each is unacceptable to part of the population. One is very religious in tone while the other is militaristic. The former, without the words, is used at the close down of television transmission.

The New Groves Dictionary of Music suggests that the forms and images in the anthem 'can reveal much about the character of a nation at the time the words were written. The text of an anthem may often have to be revised or modified in the light of political changes within the country or in its relations with its neighbours.' A good example of this is the change in the German anthem after the second world war. Germany had already changed its anthem a number of times, adopting the melody first of the United Kingdom anthem and then in 1922 the Austrian anthem. Before the rise of Hitler, the words were the first verse of a poem by Hoffmann Von Fallerlebus, 'Deutschland, Deutschland, Uber Alles' or Germany over all'. During Hitler's Third Reich this was used together with the Nazi Party song 'Horst Wessel Lied'. After the Second World War the words of the anthem seemed too expansionist in view of the country's occupation of neighbouring countries and subsequent defeat. A simple and appropriate solution was found by adopting the third verse of the Von Fallerlebus poem 'Einigkeit und Recht und Freiheit' or 'Unity and Rights and Freedom'

Finally, in view of the problems which can arise, it is worth remembering that four states manage without an anthem.

Other Symbols

Before going on to look at how people feel about their flags and anthems, we need to remember there are many other symbols which evoke similar feelings. Many states and provinces have national flowers, trees, animals and so on, but they are usually less important symbols of identity. Portraits of religious leaders, the founder of the present regime or the present leader can have a symbolic importance. In many states an official portrait is displayed in public offices. In the Lebanon for example it is possible to identify the group manning a check point from the portraits erected on the hut or nearby.

The language of the people may be an important distinguishing feature of the nation, or, if the language is no longer widely spoken, it may have a symbolic power. This is true of Irish, but also of Welsh and the Basque language and some of the languages of native inhabitants of America.

Physical locations may also evoke similar responses. They may be the ancient sites for council meetings, as with the Tynwald in the Isle of Man. Native peoples in America, Australia and elsewhere have sacred sites connected to the myths of the people, and the failure of the state to understanding their significance has given rise to disputes between native peoples and Governments over mineral rights or other proposed changes (Enloe, 1986). They may be sites where important historic events have taken place as with the agreements reached between the ruler and the people at Runymede in England and the Tree of Gernika in the Basque country. The bridge at Lexington, Massachusetts where the American War of Independence started is one example of a battle sites can also evoke some reverence. In Ireland we have sites that rouse similar passions: the Boyne and the old walled centre of Derry or Londonderry have a special significance for unionists, and the GPO in Dublin has a significance for Irish people which has more to do with the Easter Rising than with the delivery of letters. Although we do not propose to discuss these symbols in detail, we need to remember that they can play a part similar to flags and emblems in strengthening national identity.

Using Symbols and Questions of Protocol

Symbols are there to be used, and as flags and anthems acquired symbolic importance, etiquette and protocol developed to show respect for the flag and anthem and, more importantly, the person or entity which they represented. These rules also governed when and how flags and anthems should be used. Many of these customs and practices are now observed widely across the world, but their origins are lost in the mists of time.

If one did not identify with symbols, it was important to at least show courtesy. *The New Encyclopaedia Britannica* (15th edition, vol 8, p812) notes that 'the royal flag had all the attributes of kingship, being identified with the ruler himself and treated with a similar respect' and it records that in 660 A.D. a minor prince in China was punished for failing to lower his standard before a superior. This basic concept is the origin of many of the modern rules of precedence. Generally most states put their own flag in a pre-eminent position, and in many states no other national flag can be flown unless the national flag is also flown. Respect is also shown in the practice of lowering or dipping a flag when it is carried past another flag or a dignitary. At another level, the flag should not be allowed to touch the ground or treated casually in other ways. They should be folded neatly when not in use, and replaced when they are worn. They should be taken down at dusk and never flown overnight.

In ancient China and India, the loss of the flag in battle was a sign of defeat as much as the loss of the leader. Consequently the leader would rarely expose himself and the flag together and would entrust it to his general. The threat to the flag could be a stimulus to the troops to gather round it and fight harder in its defence, as in the modern phrase 'to rally round the flag'. Lowering of the flag is a sign of surrender, and at sea it was the practice to hoist flags on each mast, in case one mast should be knocked down and that should be taken as a sign of surrender. The phrase 'nailing your colours to the mast' indicates a refusal to even consider surrender, because then the flag can not be taken down. We should not be surprised therefore when people are unhappy and feel vulnerable when their flags and emblems are removed.

Fixed flags or standards came to be used to indicate specific locations associated with the person represented by the flag. This could be his head-quarters in battle, but later it was also placed over his position at ceremonies or flown over his castle or building. This custom is still evident in the practice of flying over a building the standard of the monarch or president when they are present.

Flags are generally used as a sign of territory. In the colonial era, the European powers staked a claim to territory by erecting the flag. Even to-day this has been one answer to the dispute between Ireland and England over the ownership of the island of Rockall. An Englishmen visited the island and erected a Union flag, and two Irishmen have talked of attempting to visit the island and erect the Tricolour. Mountaineers also erect the national flag on mountain summits, but this is a sign of national pride and has no territorial implications.

The first records of flags being used to give signals is also to be found in China and India. The first recorded use of a white flag to signal a truce was in 1542. The way the flag is flown may also give a signal. Most people are aware of the convention that a flag flown at half mast is a sign of mourning and a flag flown upside down is a flag of distress. This last practice may come from the idea that no one would willingly fly a flag wrongly as it would be a sign of disrespect.

Conventions related to national anthems are more specific, because the anthem is only played on specific ceremonial occasions, and so a large body of conventions has not grown up as with flags. The main convention which is found in most cultures is that everyone present should stand to attention while it is played. It is easy to see how that convention came about. We have noted that the origin of anthems may have arisen in music written to honour an important persons or ruler, and his achieve-ments, and it was played when he entered the room. We also know it was expected that those present should stand respectfully when he entered the room. It is not difficult to assume that the custom of standing may have become associated with the music as well as the person. The convention associated with the 'Hallelujah Chorus' is well documented and may pro-vide a parallel to the conventions around national anthems. When Handel's *Messiah* was first performed in Dublin in 1745, King George II was present, and it is well know that he was so moved by the 'Hallelujah Chorus' that he stood up. The rest of the audience stood up as was customary when the king rose, and that led to the custom that the audience always rises when that piece is played.

Conventions are also associated with when the anthem should be played, and these differ form country to country and from time to time. It is not necessary to discuss these variations here and we will discuss later these conventions as they have operated in Northern Ireland.

Social and Cultural Differences in Attitudes to Symbols

Some people do not follow the conventions because they do not feel particularly attached to a group or a nation, and consequently the symbols do not mean much to them. Others feel closely attached to their group or their nation, but they do not find that national symbols are very important. They may feel secure in their identity and do not need symbols to express that feeling. It will be apparent in the next chapter that this was true of a number of the people interviewed for this study. Some of those who hold strong views about the constitutional future of Northern Ireland, including some who would take a militant stand, nevertheless said that they did not care very much about flags and anthems themselves.

A number of Irish nationalists suggested that the ceremonies and rituals which surround national flags are old fashioned and anachronistic, but this does not seem to take account of the continuing observance of these customs in many societies which consider themselves to be progressive and modern. We were also told that young people are not interested. This may be true in peace time when symbols are not contentious, and older people seem more committed to the traditions they represent. But in a situation of conflict, when the symbols are threatened, young people are likely to become very involved with them.

Flags and anthems seem to be more important for those with more right wing political views. This should not be very surprising since we already noted that symbols are only capable of communicating a simple blunt message, which at its most basic distinguishes groups from each other. Right wing groups value patriotism and commitment to the national group for which national flags and anthems give a simple direct expression. They also have a strong belief in order and discipline and national symbols are associated with formal military ceremony. Right wing parties invariably use the national flag in their party symbols and logos.

Sometimes other sections of the community resent this and claim that the right wing have tried to high-jack the national symbols. It then becomes difficult to use the national symbols without appearing to identify with the rightist party. In the United Kingdom on 22 October 1993 John Patton, the Education minister in the Conservative government, itself right of centre, called on the general public to reclaim the national flag from 'skin heads' and use it more widely. In the ensuing debate it was also suggested the portrait of the monarch should be displayed in schools. One reaction was the fear that this approach would be accepting the British National Party's postion.

In Sweden where the growing right wing party has encouraged people to use the flag in their support, but as we will see below, the flag is already widely used by the whole Swedish population. There has been a debate among the rest of the population. Some feel they cannot use the flag any more, but others have taken the opposite view. If everyone uses the flag it will be impossible to claim that everyone is supporting the right wing. This is a good example of how one action can be defused by not making the expected reaction. Much of the controversy about flags is the use of flags to create a reaction by opponents which heightens the controversy.

It is possible to think of factors which might influence the level of commitment to one's own national symbols, and corresponding dislike of the symbols of opponents. For example if a group such as a national group is threatened or its loyalty is tested, it will be more likely to want to use its symbols and will be more sensitive to behaviour which shows disrespect. One person interviewed for the study said 'flag-flying is a reaction, not an action in itself – a reaction to encroachment and threat.'

If a state is new the pride in its new symbols may be stronger. Small states can also be sensitive about how their symbols are treated, as law students from Queen's University found out. They got a shock when they were shot at by the local police in Luxembourg, when they tried to remove a national flag to take home as a souvenir. If a group is involved in a conflict with another group the level of patriotic feeling may be increased and find expression in the use of symbols. All these seem to be examples of situations where a group feels a need to assert its identity. So, the British are considered generally to be patriotic and royalist, but they are very casual about their national symbols, which are among the oldest in the world. But at times such as the Falklands War there was a great deal of flag waving and jingoism, encouraged in part by the popular press which printed large pictures of the Union flag.

But there are many situations which cannot be explained by such reasoning. The commitment to flags and anthems is more striking in some cultures than in others, and it may be best understood as a cultural and social phenomena. It appears that some cultures simply value these symbols because they relate to some quality in the culture and the personalities of the people. Or perhaps it becomes a self perpetuating learned behaviour because it is a pervasive part of the culture in which young people are growing up.

For example in recent times the Nordic states have been peaceful and accommodating in their relations with other states, but they treat their flags very seriously, with care and respect. They are flown as often as possible, and are kept in good condition. Flags are never flown from temporary posts. They are mounted on proper tall flag poles. In Finland there is even a law governing the location of flag poles in the garden. In Sweden it is customary to spend summer weekends and holidays at a summer cottage, and the first thing most families do when they arrive is to hoist the flag. Very few countries or groups which claim to be patriotic and loyal show this kind of attention to the use of the flag, but there is no obvious reason why this attitude should have arisen and persisted in the Nordic countries. It is in situations like this that one relies on the argument that it fits well with the local temperament.

The United States is another nation which puts a great deal of emphasis on its national symbols, but there is no obvious reason why this should be so. It is no longer a new state, though perhaps Americans like to believe that it is. It is not a state under threat, though again Americans often feel that they are threatened, if not physically, then economically and doctrinally. Nevertheless the flag is possibly respected more in the United States than in any other country. There is a national flag day, 14 June. Its national anthem, 'The Star-Spangled Banner', is one of the few which was written in honour of the national flag. The famous war photograph of soldiers raising the flag on Iwo Jimo during the Second World War epitomises the American commitment to the flag and is almost a cultural icon. It has been reproduced on a grand scale in the Marine memorial at Arlington Cemetry.

The flag is not only flown on all public buildings and on many other buildings, but it must be flown at polling stations during elections which is the opposite of the situation in Northern Ireland where a Union flag could be construed as an influence on how people should vote. It also stands in the corner of many offices, all courts of justice and all public school class rooms.

Children must make a pledge of allegiance to it every morning at the beginning of class: 'I pledge allegiance to the flag of the United States of America and to the Republic for which it stands, one Nation under God, indivisible, with liberty and justice for all.' Some groups such as Seventh Day Adventists are exempt from the pledge of allegiance on religious grounds, but it is widely expected that all others will take the pledge.

There is great sensitivity about disrespect for the flag. In 1954 the artist Jasper John created a representation of the flag from hot wax which the Museum of Modern Art considered buying in 1958. However it decided not to acquire it as it might offend patriots.

In this situation it is not surprising that we are more aware of incidents when the United States flag or anthem was treated disrespectfully. We will refer later to the burning of the flag in protest at United States foreign policy and to the black power protests at the Mexican Olympic Games. Sometimes the strength of feeling may be underestimated. In 1992 the Irish singer Sinead O'Connor was unwilling to appear at a concert in New Jersey if the anthem was played. She may not have been prepared for the wave of hostility from young Americans as young people are not normally very interested in national symbols.

Why is the flag so important in America? It was first promoted by an American President who was a native Ulsterman, William McKinley, though the significance of this fact is hard to assess. The pledge of allegiance in the class room is intended to increase respect for the flag in the next generation. The main explanation of the importance of the flag in America is that other states are symbolised by a person or an institution which is above politics, such as the British Monarchy. But no such entity exists in the United States and the flag has become the supreme symbol of the state, with the stripes representing the founding states and the stars the current number of states.

Over the years new rules and conventions have grown up to govern the use of flags, and at the same time there is a trend towards greater informality in public life. This makes it more difficult to know what is appropriate behaviour. When should the flag be flown or the anthem played? Virtually every situation could be an occasion for showing respect or insulting the flag and what it represents. Therefore practices have been codified, mainly to provide guidance on what should happen on formal occasions such as visits by foreign dignitaries or state funerals. These are matters mainly for the state authorities and the military who play a leading role on these occasions. In the United Kingdom they are contained in the detailed *Queen's Regulations (For The Army)*.

For more general use a few states have produced a flags code for 'dignified usage of the flag' by every citizen. The United States produced the first such code in 1923, drawn up at a meeting of sixty-eight patriotic organisations (*Encyclopaedia Americana*, International Edition, 1982, vol11, p353). This code was subsequently ratified by the United States Congress in 1942. Few states have followed suit, and the desire for such a code is likely to be related to the importance of the flag in the local culture. Ireland is one country with a similar code and the United Nations also has a code for the use of its flag, in view of the complications resulting from its special status, different from national flags.

Most states have some form of legal or constitutional protections for the national flag, the United Kingdom being one of the few countries which has no such provisions. Some countries have felt the need to restrict the right to fly other flags. Sometimes this will be covered by the general restrictions on actions which are likely to cause a breach of the peace, but specific laws or rules have been enacted in some countries, especially where the state is challenged by a powerful opposition which uses symbols in a subversive way. Later in this chapter, we refer to the British authorities' attempt to oppose the Indian Congress party flag, and we will discuss in detail the past and current limitations which have existed in Northern Ireland.

In the troubled West Bank of the Jordan and Gaza, even wearing the colours of the Palestine state was a breach of the Military Orders of the Israeli army which was the source of authority. Military Order 101, 'An Order Concerning the Prohibition of Incitement and Adverse Propaganda', 27 August 1967, was interpreted as applying to paintings. In April 1980, for example, Bethlehem University students were prohibited from wearing white T-shirts which had streaks of green black and red because these constitute the colours of the new Palestinian flag.' (Shehadeh, 1985, p. 159) Following the Agreement between the Israeli Government and the Palestinian Liberation Organisation signed on 13 September 1993, the most immediate and potent expression of its impact was the next day when Palestinian flags were flying for the first time throughout the West Bank and Gaza, as a symbol of what the people wanted. For the first time they felt able to express their aspirations openly. One might wonder how the people could find or make so many flags so quickly, but we were told of a feature on Israeli Television concerning a Jewish firm which was working overtime to meet the demand.

However the Military Order still exists. Reuters reported that at Christmas 1993, the authorities ordered the removal of a Palestinian flag from a pole outside the City Hall in Manger Square in Bethlehem, because it could not be flown from a public building. It had been erected on 21 December to the rage of Israelis. On the night of 22 it was removed to the rage of Palestinians. Next day Fatah unfurled two flags on the roof of the City Hall. Mayor Elias Freij threatened to cancel the Christmas celebrations and sought advice from PLO headquarters, saying the removal of the flag had sapped confidence in the Peace Agreement. Fatah brought more flags into the Square and eventually in the afternoon a flag was placed on the pole again without any opposition from the authorities.

It should be noted that legal protection may not protect the national flag or prevent other flags being flown. It is interestingly that in America where the flag is given such respect, it is also regularly damaged and burned as a protest. Cases have been brought to court, but the courts have ruled that there is a higher principle than protection of the flag. This is freedom of speech which is enshrined in the Constitution, and so the charges have failed.

Symbols as a Means of Protest

Not following the conventions in relation to flags and anthems constitutes disrespect, and can be a cause of offence to those for whom these symbols are important. This comes from the idea of showing disrespect for a leader or a nation by the inappropriate use of the flag. In battle, seizing an opponent's flag as a trophy of war showed one's power. Damaging flags and burning them is a way to express disapproval of a nation or regime, especially when there is no way to make a more direct protest. It has been a common practice in Iran and other Moslem states to burn the flags of Western states, the United States in particular, during protests against their policy. Within the United States itself, opponents of the Vietnam war often burned the national flag, but the Stars and Stripes is not the only flag which is burnt. On the 27 March 1993, during tension between British and French fishermen, some French fishermen boarded a British fisheries protection vessel moored in Cherbourg and burnt the white ensign. Speaking on radio the next day, the Member of Westminster Parliament, Teddy Taylor, said that 'kidnapping our sailors and burning our flag is the most appalling insult you could imagine.'

Sometimes it is difficult to know the precise implications of the way a flag is being used. Native American Indians traditionally wore their war trophies as a sign of status. To-day they may incorporate the United States and Canadian flags in their traditional regalia. What does this mean? Are they showing their acceptance that they are part of those states? Are they wearing them as a trophy of past wars? Are they treating them casually and disrespectfully by sowing them on their clothing? Or are they simply using them as colourful adornment? There may well be no single message.

Conventions can be broken with the express intention of offending or annoying others. The greater the annoyance and the greater the reaction, the greater the satisfaction. This quality is well caught in a Scottish description of the theft or 'liberation' of the Scottish Stone of Scone from Westminster Abbey in London. 'The British authorities took the incident very seriously indeed – which simply added to the fun for the Scots.' (SNP, 1993) The Stone of Scone has a symbolism which shares some of the features of national flags and anthems.

Flags can be used to challenge another group, to assert dominance or to seek a confrontation, as we noted already in some of the ways the Confederate battle flag is used in the Southern United States. A recent incident demonstrates one way this can be done, and shows how a situation can quickly escalate. At the end of the 1993 school year, in one school in Birmingham, Alabama, the football team had T-shirts made on the theme of the controversy over the Confederate flag, a blue cross with white borders on a red background, and made a connection to the black hero, Malcolm X who was topical because of the recent film of his life story. The T-shirt said on the front 'We have our X, you have yours' On the back was a picture of the confederate flag, and underneath in a Southern drawl 'It's a Southern Thang [Thing]' The message was that no one should interfere with our flag. The school was predominantly white with only about one hundred and fifty black pupils out of two thousand, and the football team strutted around the school asserting themselves.

Next day one of the whites was caught by some black students. He was manhandled and the shirt was torn off him. The staff immediately took action and the white student was expelled for two days, although he was about to leave anyway. The leader of the black group who removed the shirt was not punished. The situation was very tense and about forty-five riot police were called in to keep the two groups apart. The whites were resentful at the assault on their friend and at the reaction of the school authorities. They were all ordered to remove the shirts, which in any case violated the school rules. This is an interesting rule because students are not allowed to dress alike or wear the same colours. This is an attempt to tackle the problem of gangs because similar clothes are a sign of gang affiliations. There may be a lesson in this for other cultures. One individual wearing particular colours is an expression of individual freedom. Worn as a group, they are more likely to be designed to challenge or intimidate others.

We have already referred to a less explosive incident in another American school where a pupil was sent home from a school in South Carolina because he refused to stop wearing a T-shirt with a picture of the New South flag on it. A group of 25 black students had worn the T-shirts to school and white students objected. They were told to remove the shirts, but one refused and was sent home. As a result the school decided to ban the display of any symbol that depicts heritage or race, including the Confederate battle flag and the Malcolm X logo.

This is one example where alternative flags and anthems may cause offence, and attempts to prevent their use can provide opportunities for farther protests. In the 1920s, the British authorities in India wanted to prohibit the display of the new Congress flag which they saw as subversive, and this gave Gandhi the opportunity to make a strong non-violent statement, demonstrating the strength of the Congress Party, and mocking the British attempt to stop them. The new flag was carried by thousands of people in relays across the country for two months. We will refer later to similar examples from Northern Ireland.

It would be wrong to suggest that the only reason that conventions are broken is to cause offence. There does not need to be any intention to dishonour the flag and a careless or ignorant action can be enough to offend those who identify with the flag. People may forget, or the symbols may not matter to them. The conventions are often broken without any intention to upset anyone else. The situation is somewhat different with anthems. Normally flags are flown continuously while anthems are only played on specific occasions. One is expected to follow the conventions for showing respect for the flag at certain times, such as when it is being raised or lowered, but most of the time one can continue with one's normal business without any formal recognition of its presence. With the anthem the conventions should be followed by everyone present, and that means the physical act of standing to attention. It is very obvious to observers if someone does not stand up and they will often make inferences about how the person feels about the anthem and what it represents. With flags there are three choices: to respect the flag, to do something disrespectful or to do nothing. With anthems there are only two choices: to act respectfully or to act disrespectfully. People sometimes try to find a middle way. They stand up but in a half-hearted way. They keep their head bowed, or they do not join in singing. What they are trying to do is to avoid giving a strong message of opposition, but at the same time demonstrate that their support for the state is less than total.

Case Studies of The Use of Symbols

The next chapter will relate the general principles to the case study of Northern Ireland. First, however, we offer three short case studies which we feel illuminate the issues and choices which are available. The first is of a specific field of activity, sport, and the others are of two states, India and South Africa.

Sport
We often associate sport with flags and anthems. In fact the popular perception is that sport is one area where there is a great deal of controversy over flags. There are two main features of sport which encourage the use of national and other symbols. A good deal of sport is representative and competitive. Individual sportsmen and women often are part of a team.

Even in individual sports such as athletics, individuals often take part as team members. As in other situations where people identify with a group, symbols are used to identify the team and to show support for it. Supporters will indicate their loyalty and encourage the players by waving flags and singing songs.

Most sport is about winning, and progressing to more prestigious events, such as finals or international competition. Many sporting bodies use flags and anthems to add to the sense of ceremony at important occasions. At the opening ceremony of major games such as the Olympic and Commonwealth Games and World Championships, the teams parade under their national flag. Sometimes the head of state or other dignitary will be present and this is an additional reason why the national anthem is played and the national flag flown. Award ceremonies are a way to recognise achievements. Typically after the winners have received their awards, an anthem will be played for the winning team or individual and the appropriate flag flown. These rituals are comparatively modern, but are constructed from older traditions to give a sense of history.

Normally these displays do not cause problems, and the ruling bodies of sport try to avoid controversy. But the potential is there. In modern times there has been something of a contradiction in individual sports such as athletics between praise for the individual achievement and the national achievement in producing the winner. A sporting journal, *Barcelona '92* (p199) said of the Olympic ideal, 'by placing such emphasis on national, rather than individual participation, de Coubertin [the founder] was inviting trouble from the start. When the flag is at stake, sport becomes a proving ground for national prestige and a symbol of political will rather than international harmony.'

Many countries have used sporting success to make a political statement, asserting national strength and promoting national pride, and some, notably the Democratic German Republic, created a national project to achieve sporting success. The hosting of such games is also a symbol of national pride and achievement, the most notorious example being the 1936 Olympic Games, when Hitler refused to present a gold medal to Jesse Owens the black American athlete who had beaten Germany's pride.

It is therefore very difficult to divorce sport from national symbolism in some form or other. These ceremonies provide a very public opportunity to express alternative allegiances. One of the first such incidents involved an Irish sportsman, Peter O'Connor, who won the Olympic long jump in Athens in 1906 representing the United Kingdom of Great Britain and Ireland. He did not want the Union flag, the 'pirate's banner', as one report put it, at the medal ceremony. A passing Irish spectator provided a green flag which he happened to have with him, and it replaced the Union flag (Hayes-McCoy, 1979, p182). It is not recorded what anthem was played, if any.

It is hard to imagine an athlete being able to exercise that influence today, but they can still make a protest when the national flag is raised At the 1968 Olympics in Mexico the 200 metre gold and bronze medallists from the United States, Tommie Smith and John Carlos, stood bare-foot, heads bowed and giving the clenched fist black power salute during the playing of the national anthem. They were protesting against the treatment of black people in America, as did other American athletes at the Games. The picture of the protest has been a graphic symbol, but the protestors made it clear that 'it is not a picture to make money. It's not a picture to be famous. It's a picture for solidarity.' These protests are not easy. One of them said afterwards: 'You know how long that National Anthem is? It's two days long.' And they claim that they were ostracised by the United States athletic establishment.

Already there is concern that there may be problems at the 1996 Games in Atlanta, Georgia, because the Georgia state flag, with its reference to the Confederacy, may be a focus for protests by black civil rights groups. A Georgia State Senator from the Democratic Party has said (*Atlanta Journal*, 29 January 1994) that they will contact African nations and let them know about the issue. As *Barcelona '92* says 'As long as the band strikes up a national anthem every time a gold medallist steps up to the podium, as long as flags are brandished at opening ceremonies ... governments will continue to use the Olympic Games as a political football.'

But symbols can be used sensitively at sporting ceremonies to make a more positive statement. Before the Barcelona Olympics there was concern about possible tension between the regional Catalonia Government and the Central Government of Spain. Each could be offended if they were not given the place of honour. In the event, the Spanish and Catalonian and Barcelona flags were all respected, and both languages, Castilian Spanish and Catalan, were used at the opening and closing ceremonies. At the opening ceremony the King of Spain stood to attention as the Catalan national hymn was sung, followed by the playing of the Spanish national anthem. The Catalonian hymn, 'Els Segadors', or 'The Mowers', was written as a song of revolt sung during a seventeenth century Catalonian revolt against the King of Spain at that time, Philip V.

The subtleties of the arrangements may not have been evident to the observer from outside the country, but 'the Olympic games in Barcelona were a positive experience in treating ethnic conflicts, an experiment in sharing Spanish and Catalonian identities, and in offering the Spanish identity as the natural, encompassing extension of the Catalan identity' (Gutierrez, 1992, p12). Gutierrez puts this kind of event into context:

> On the one hand a positive noteworthy experience in nurturing a spirit of conviviality and reconciliation in a fancy international scenario, and as such an important part of the solution of a centuries old ethnic conflict. On the other hand a screen in which a smooth veneer of the real conflict appears, overshadowing its hard core, a bundle of unresolved conflicting political and daily issues. A single event can help, but cannot solve a protracted conflict.

India: an evolving pattern
The development of the Indian flag is interesting, because it went through a number of changes, beginning with a concept rather like the Irish flag, then

changing the colours slightly, and giving them a different meaning. These changes were publicly argued and are well documented in official papers (Smith, 1980, pp35–6). Its origins are in the flag of the Indian Congress Party which was white, green and red horizontal stripes with a spinning wheel in the centre. The original idea in about 1920 had been to use red and green stripes to represent the two largest religions in the sub-continent, Hinduism and Islam. The white was added at the suggestion of Gandhi to recognise the minority religious groups. Indian had become dependent on imported cloth, and the spinning wheel was used by Gandhi as a symbol of self-reliance to indicate the contribution everyone could make to the independence of the country by making their own cloth.

The flag became popular with Indians, but we have noted already that the British authorities thought that it was provocative. They challenged the right of Indian nationalist to display the flag and as a result gave the Indians a way in which they could challenge the authority of the British. Peaceful demonstrations were organised and the flag was carried in relay across India by thousands of people for two months.

There was some dissatisfaction with the flag. Some thought that separate stripes for the separate communities emphasised the differences in the country rather than symbolising the potential unity between them. Some members of the minority religious groups, especially the Sikhs, objected to a single stripe representing them all. In 1931 a committee was appointee to consider what should be done. It proposed fairly similar colours but with different meanings, representing core values and ideals. Red was replaced by saffron to represent courage and sacrifice, white for peace and truth, and green for faith and chivalry.

With one change, this flag was retained after Indian became independent in 1947, and a republic in 1950. The spinning wheel was replaced by the Wheel or 'Chakra' of Asoka, connecting the new state to the 9th century emperor who was seen as one of the great rulers of India, and to the roots of the religion. The 'Chakra' is the wheel of the Law of Dharma, and denotes motion and virtue and peaceful change.

Although the colours stayed the same, their significance was reinterpreted, demonstrating both the flexibility of colours as symbols but also their lack of definition. We will give a flavour of the language used to describe the flag, as it is not untypical of the rather grandiloquent and inspirational language used in other states, a language that the people and government of any country might find hard to live up to. The First President, Sabra R. Krishna, explained in the Constitutional Assembly that the green represents 'our relation to the soil, the plant life here on which all other life depends'. White is said to represent the 'path of light, truth and simplicity' and saffron 'the spirit of renunciation, humility and disinterestedness'. An even more florid explanation of the saffron is used by Anderson and Damle (1987): 'colour of holy sacrificial fire that gives the message of self immolation in the fire of idealism and the glorious orange hue of the rising sun which dispels darkness and sheds light all around'. This is very different from the common place language which would be used to explain flags in Britain and Ireland.

In spite of these detailed explanations some Indians are still uncertain about the meaning of their flag, assuming that it represents the main religious groups. Saffron is a colour associated with the Hindu religion, and at times of ethnic tension saffron flags are much in evidence. Green flags are also carried by Muslims, though in view of their minority status, not to the same extent.

South Africa: the meeting of different forces
The flag of the Union of South Africa prior to April 1994 was designed to reflect the constituent parts of the Union: the two British colonies of Natal and the Cape and the formerly independent Boer Republics of the Orange Free State and the South African Republic (the Transvaal). An official committee was set up to design the flag, but it could not agree whether the Union flag should be incorporated in the new flag. The committee had to be dissolved and a new commission was set up which decided on the design which is still used. The main element of the flag is an orange white and blue tricolour similar to the original Dutch flag which the settlers brought with them. In the middle of the central white stripe are small versions of the Union flag, and the two flags of the former Boer Republics. It was adopted by act of parliament in 1927 and first hoisted officially in 1928. Formally this flag was always flown with the Union flag until 1957 when the Flags Amendment Act scrapped all reference to the Union flag, and the flag was flown unaccompanied. The flag remained unchanged at independence.

'Die Stem van Suid Afrika' ('The Song of South Africa'), the sole national anthem until April 1994, was written by C.L. Langenhoven in 1918. It was thought that it was a possible national anthem though the music did not find favour. A new melody was written by the Reverend M.L. De Villiers in 1921 and it was first sung officially at the hoisting of the National flag in 1928. In 1938 it was sung together with 'God Save the King' at the opening of parliament. The origins of the anthem were closely bound up with the struggle to give greater official status to the Afrikaan language, and there was only an Afrikaan's version. As it became widely used it was felt an official English version was required for non-Afrikaan speakers. A committee recommended an English translation in 1952 and it was first sung in Cape Town in that year. In 1957 the Prime Minister announced the adoption of 'Die Stem' as the National Anthem, confirmed by an Act of Parliament in 1959.

Die Stem makes no reference to the black majority in South Africa, and opposition groups to the Apartheid Government adopted their own flags and anthems. The most widely used are the flag and anthem of the African National Congress (ANC). The flag is composed of black, green and gold horizontal stripes, representing the people, the soil and wealth of the gold fields. Their anthem is 'Nkosi Sikelela iAfrica' ('God Bless Africa') which normally has been sung in Xhosi. This hymn to Africa was written by a clergy man to be sung at funerals and other religious occasions. It became very popular and was adopted as the official song of the ANC, and is the basis of the national anthems of other African nations.

Right wing groups also adopted their own flags, which make their own political statement. The flag of the Afrikaner Weerstands Beweging (AWB or, in English, the Afrikaner Resistance Movement) has a close resemblance to the flag of Hitler's Nazi Party. The AWB deny this and say that the central symbol is made up of three sevens, the holy number of the Bible. This may be true but it is indisputable that the colours and shape are the same, and the 'three sevens' symbol in the middle is made up in a way which is similar to the Swastika. It therefore gives the impression of the Nazi Party and appears to convey the message to the observer that the AWB wants to oppress the Blacks of South Africa in the same way that the Nazi Party oppressed Jews.

With the changes in South African society, the future of the existing flags and anthems was in doubt. It appeared that the White Government was resigned to a new flag and anthem, and the ANC was willing to search for new symbols for the new nation, in order to achieve consensus and accommodation. The national anthem was important to whites as an acknowledge of the turmoil of the past and the hopeful future'. The national flag was also associated too closely with the Apartheid regime to be acceptable to the black population. The flag and anthem of the ANC were not so contentious, though the anthem was said by blacks 'to be a moving evocation of their struggle'. None of the symbols of other parties were likely to be considered.

One of the first times that a choice had to be made was at the Barcelona Olympics in 1992, when a sports team from South Africa was allowed to compete for the first time following the end of the sports boycott. The team chose to use the flag of the South African Olympic Association and as a theme Beethoven's 'Ode to Joy'. The theme had no obvious South African connotations, and the flag was not universally popular as the Olympic Association policies did not please all parties. But yet it demonstrated that the society could find an acceptable, if not ideal solution, when they were committed to overcoming the obstacles.

The solution which was adopted eventually and put into effect on 26 April 1994 was to have a new flag and, with regard to the anthem, to adopt the unusual practice of having two anthems, 'Die Stem' and 'Nkosi Sikelela iAfrica' . The plan for the flag was to select one from the entries in a competition, but it was decided that none of them were suitable. It was then put in the hands of a flag designer who came up with the present geometrical pattern. It is made up of wedges of black, yellow and green, moving out from the hoist of the flag into bands of red, white and blue towards the tail. The three colours towards the base are in fact the colours of the African National Congress. The outer colours towards the margins are almost the colours of the old flag, with red instead of orange. However the colours are apparently of no special significance. They are in fact the colours of the Olympic flag.

The intention to use both anthems is genuine. They have been translated into all the main languages of the peoples of South Africa. When the new arrangements were used for the first time at an international football match, the President, Nelson Mandela was present. He spoke to the crowd during the half time interval, and used the opportunity to upbraid them for not knowing the words of Die Stem. He told them to go home and learn it.

CHAPTER 2

British and Irish Symbols and Their Significance

All round my hat /heart I wear a blue/green ribbon
All round my hat /heart until death comes to me,
And if anyone should ask me why I am wearing it,
I wear it for my true love I ne'er more shall see.
Traditional (colours vary depending on the version)

In this chapter we want to give an overview of the flags which are important to different sections of the community in Northern Ireland, and their reactions to them. This is a more complicated exercise than it sounds. First, there are so many symbols. Second, each community is not only concerned with its own symbols, but they also have a variety of reactions to the symbols of other sections of the community. And thirdly there are many shades of reaction. To deal with this we have separated out artificially four different aspects of the reaction to symbols and will consider them in turn:

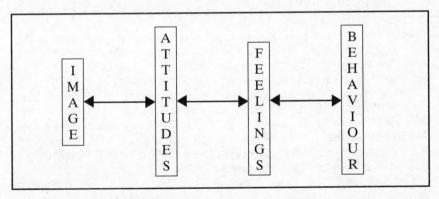

Figure 2.1   A model of reactions to group and national symbols

In looking at a symbol, we see the **image**; secondly we have an **attitude** towards that symbol based in part on what it represents, thirdly we have **feelings** which are evoked by the symbol and what we understand it to mean, and fourthly we may **act** in ways which are influenced but not solely determined by those feelings. Of course this is not a linear process as each

33

element interacts with the others, but for present purposes we will look at each of these in turn across the cultural and political spectrum. The images, attitudes and feelings will be described in turn in this chapter, together with some observations on differences in Catholic and Protestant perspectives. The way these perspectives are expressed in the community and the way conflicts are managed will then be the subject of subsequent chapters.

It is also evident that there are many shades of opinion within each community. It would be impossible to discuss all the nuances of each individual's views and attitudes. Instead we have identified the main strains in unionism and nationalism and we treat them as ideal types in order to describe the main trends and orientations. In this we follow Jennifer Todd who has identified two strains of unionism: Ulster loyalism and Ulster Britishness (Todd, 1987) and three elements in nationalism: Catholic communalism, Irish nationalism and social justice (Todd, 1990). Obviously there is great individual variation within these broad groupings.

Symbols of the United Kingdom, England, Wales and Scotland

The most obvious symbol of the United Kingdom is the Union Jack or, more correctly, the Union flag. It is based on the crosses of the patron saints of England, Scotland and Ireland. The Cross of Saint George was adopted by England in the thirteenth century. There was no obvious reason to connect Saint George with England and it is generally assumed that he was adopted by English knights taking part in the Crusades. The Scots adopted Saint Andrew on the strength of the story that a monk carrying relics of the saint was shipwrecked off the coast of Scotland. Barraclough (1971, p21) thinks it is possible that Andrew was chosen as the patron saint over native saints as a 'compromise candidate.'

The crosses of the Scottish and English patron saints were combined in 1707 at the time of the Union of Scotland with England and Wales. There was some sensitivity about how it should be done so that one cross should not seem to have precedence over the other. Scots felt that the most common design seemed to give more prominence to the cross of Saint George. With the Union of Ireland and Great Britain, it seemed appropriate to incorporate some feature to represent Ireland, and an obvious solution was to add the cross of the Irish patron saint, Patrick, to the existing two crosses, although we will see later that this was not a symbol widely used in Ireland (Barraclough, 1971 and Osmond, 1988).

The additional cross made it even more difficult to give equal status to each national symbol than in 1707. For a long time it was not clear how the verbal description should be given visual expression, and a number of versions existed, some making the bars of the Cross of Saint Patrick wider than the underlying Cross of Saint Andrew. The common version used in modern times makes the Saint Andrew's Cross much broader.

The Cross of Saint George is still the flag of England, flown regularly and especially on Saint George's Day. In Wales the national flag is the dragon of Wales on a green and white background. The Cross of Saint Andrew continues to be the flag of Scotland, together with the lion of Scotland on a yellow background.

The only other flag which needs a passing reference is the Royal Standard which is the Royal Arms of the Queen. It is only used when the Queen is present and so most people have seldom seen it flying. However it is of interest in the present context, because it is another example of the consequences of trying to combine harmoniously the representative symbols of different groups. This can cause resentment among the people who feel their symbol has been diminished, but the other group or groups may not even understand the depth of feeling.

The Royal Standard is quartered, and has gone through many forms, but he present version has been virtually unchanged since it was adopted by George III in 1800. It comprises the emblems of England, Ireland and Scotland. In the case of Ireland this is the harp on a blue background, and it is perhaps rather ironic that this is also the Irish President's Standard. Since there are four quarters and only three emblems, the three lions symbol of England is included twice which in heraldic terms implies seniority. This has caused some resentment in Scotland. Prior to 1800 the French arms occupied one quarter and so England and Scotland were treated equally. It has been suggested that there should be a Scottish Royal Standard which would include the lion of Scotland in two quarters. However it is the wish of the Queen that there should be only one Royal Standard, representing the Unity of the United Kingdom (Allison and Riddell, 1991). It may not have the same importance for the Queen as for Scottish nationalists.

Another solution would be to place the Welsh dragon in the fourth quarter (Barraclough, 1971). Wales is neither represented in the Union flag or the Royal Standard, because, it is argued, it was already united with England before the union with Scotland. More nationalistic Welsh people find these issues irrelevant and their aim is to see Wales as a region of Europe together with the other constituent parts of the United Kingdom. There has been some discussion of the idea of creating a flag which incorporates the Welsh dragon and the twelve stars of the European flag.

We also need to mention one other emblem associated with the British state and the British forces: the poppy, which is used as a symbol of those killed, serving Britain in war. It originated at the end of the First World War and is an important element in the annual remembrance ceremonies in November each year.

Emblems of Ireland

A number of flags and emblems have been associated with Ireland over the centuries: the colour green, the harp and the shamrock are the most obvious. In comparison the Tricolour is of more recent origin. Belinda Loftus (1994) has studied their development as national symbols, and this section owes a great deal to her work. She also suggests that we should include the land itself and the distinctive Celtic strapwork patterns familiar to us from the Book of Kells. The history of these symbols reveals clearly the complexity of the process by which they took on a symbolic function, sometimes different for each section of the community. At one point a symbol may have been banned and at other times it was promoted and used by the British administration.

The harp is a good example. The harp has been long played in Ireland but it did not become a national symbol until comparatively recently. In the Middle Ages it was banned within the Pale, the area around Dublin controlled by the British. It was not an instrument which was associated with the ordinary people. It was played for the old Gaelic aristocracy and as such could be considered a threat to the Dublin administration. Paradoxically it began to be promoted as a national emblem when the English king Henry VIII used it on Irish coinage, surmounted by the crown.

Subsequently the English began to use it in many ways and James I included it in the Royal Arms, where it has remained, apart from one interruption, which led to a rather unusual scene recorded in his diary by Samuel Pepys. He was sent to meet the new monarch in Holland and bring him back to England. On the journey over they were informed that the Harp must be taken out of all their flags, 'it being very offensive to the King', presumably because it had been given greater prominence in the arms used during the Protectorate which followed the execution of his father. Pepys describes the rather amusing scene of last minute preparations on the day before they reached Holland. '13th (Lord's day.) To the quarter deck, upon which the tailors and painters were at work, cutting out some pieces of yellow cloth in the fashion of a crown and C.R., and put it upon a fine sheet, and that into the flag instead of the State's arms.' (Pepys, 1953, vol 1, p52)

Apart from Charles II's disapproval, the harp was adopted across the political spectrum, and it was used also by forces opposed to the English, including the Catholic Confederacy and Owen Roe O'Neill. Of course in English usage the harp was often surmounted by the crown, and it was normally placed on a blue background or field, which was the background colour of Saint Patrick's Cross in English heraldry. The harp on a blue field is now the President's Standard. O'Neill placed it on a green background, and much later this green harp flag became the accepted symbol of Ireland and at one stage might have become the flag of the independent state.

Belinda Loftus (1994) traces the origin of the identification of Ireland with green in the literary tradition going back to the eighth century, and she explains it as a direct reference to the green land. Its association with nationalism and opposition to English rule dates from the eighteenth century. The United Irishmen wore green uniforms and carried green flags, and Loftus (1994) quotes from *The Press* on 25 November 1797 that simply wearing a green ribbon 'would subject a man to imprisonment, transportation, the rope or the bayonet, and expose women to the brutal insults of the common soldiery.' This is of course the background to the song 'The Wearing of the Green'.

The shamrock is sometimes thought to be the origin of the association of Ireland with green, but in fact the shamrock first appears in the seventeenth century, in the story of St Patrick using the shamrock as a symbol of the

Holy Trinity. It quickly became the custom to wear shamrocks and green ribbons on Saint Patrick's Day, and it continues to be presented to members of Irish regiments, in both the Irish and British armies. It has also been used as a decorative motive, in crafts such as china, glassware and embroidery, and more formally by the British administration in heraldic shields and coins. In this respect it is equivalent to the English rose and Scottish thistle.

In 1801 at the time of the Act of Union a new flag was devised for the new kingdom of Great Britain and Ireland. As we have seen it was based on the design which had been created in 1707 for the Union flag of England and Scotland. The cross of Saint Patrick was a similar motif to the crosses of Saint Andrew and Saint George, but it had not previously been a popular symbol of Ireland. As John Osmond (1988, p174–5) says:

> It is commonly believed that the Union Jack also includes the Irish Cross of St Patrick, but this is not the case. The red saltire [diagonal cross] is, in fact, the arms of the Fitzgeralds, descendants of the Geraldine family, Welsh Marcher Lords sent by Henry II to conquer Ireland. Not having been a martyr, St Patrick was not heraldically entitled to a cross and, in any event, the symbol had never been used by the Irish people.

Barraclough (1971) makes the same point, but according to an account referred to by Loftus (1994), in 1628 Irish troops stationed in England honoured the saint's day by wearing his heraldic emblem of the red cross. Hayes-McCoy (1979) agrees that there is evidence that the cross was worn on Saint Patrick's Day, but suggests it was a symbol of Ireland and the association with Patrick may be later, perhaps at the time of the foundation of the Order of Saint Patrick in 1783, when the Order adopted the cross as its badge.

The shamrock, harp and green have continued to be used as symbols of many different types of Irishness. For some they are symbols of Irish nationalism, for some they are romantic images, no more revolutionary than a leprechaun. They are also establishment emblems and, in association with the crown, all three are incorporated in the uniform of Irish regiments in the British army and of the Royal Ulster Constabulary.

In comparison with these emblems, the national flag, the Tricolour of green, white and orange stripes, has a comparatively recent origin in ribbons worn by some of those involved in the 1798 rebellion. The French revolution popularised the idea of a tricolour flag throughout Europe and probably influenced the creation of the Irish Tricolour. The conventional explanation of the colours is that white in the centre signifies the everlasting peace between the Orange (or Protestant) community and the Green (or Catholic) community. A number of authorities including the Irish Government (*Department of Foreign Affairs, Fact Sheet 2/91*) refer to an occasion in 1848 when Francis Meagher carried it on his return from France as a gift from the French and as an emblem of the Young Ireland movement. Meagher is quoted as saying romantically 'The white in the centre signifies a lasting truce between the 'Orange' and the 'Green' and I trust that beneath its folds the hands of the Irish Protestant and the Irish Catholic may be clasped in heroic brotherhood.'

Whether this is in fact the reason for the combination of colours is not certain. It is in fact not clear if orange was the original colour in the flag. It could have been saffron, a traditional Irish colour which was banned in the sixteenth century. It could be gold or yellow, which might be taken to have some connection with the papal flag of white and yellow, though that is hardly likely to have been in the minds of United Irishmen. White also has a variety of associations. It was the colour of the Jacobites and was the symbol of the Catholic Defenders in the late eighteenth century . It appears in an Orange song about a skirmish in 1791 at Lisnagead, County Down: 'We had not marched a mile or so when the white flag we espied/ With a branch of podereens[1] on which they much relied' (Zimmermann, 1967, p306). The combination of green white and orange was used by different groups probably for different reasons, so there is unlikely to be one explanation of the choice of colours. But whatever its origins, most nationalists in the twentieth century would incline to the explanation that the flag expresses the aspiration towards co-operation and friendship between the main traditions in Ireland.

It has already been noted that the Harp on a green background could well have become the flag of the independent state, and at the beginning of the twentieth century the Tricolour was not widely known. In the end the Green Harp flag's 'supercession by the Tricolour was, to put it mildly, emphatic.' (Hayes-McCoy, 1979, p9) The Tricolour became the national flag, but there is no explanation of how that change came about. At the beginning of the twentieth century, the Tricolour became associated with republicanism because it was adopted by the Irish Republican Brotherhood, who advocated complete Irish independence from Britain. The Green Harp flag was identified with the more moderate demands for home rule. They were both flown on the General Post Office and other occupied buildings during the 1916 Rising. The legacy of the Rising was the growth of support for militant republicanism, which was represented by the Tricolour, while the older symbols were rejected because of their identification with British rule. 'The sacred word Nation had been 'corrupted' because British hirelings had profaned our symbols – the shamrock, the harp and the green flag – to destroy their old time significance', as it was expressed in a pamphlet by Fr. Gaynor, quoted by Hayes-McCoy (1979, p223). So in little more than a year a transition had taken place, and the Tricolour had become accepted as the symbol of Ireland, 'not as the flag of an Irish Union in the vision of Meagher [and others] but as the flag of an Irish Republic, the flag of an actual revolt.' (Hayes-McCoy, 1979, p220).

The speed of the acceptance of the Tricolour is remarkable in view of the emphasis we have placed on the social process through which national symbols become established and are associated with history and tradition. It is an indication of the impact of the Easter Rising and the response by the British administration. Although the Tricolour became the flag of the new state through practice, it was not formally and legally designated as such until the Constitution of 1937, (Article 7).

Another flag which was also present at the Easter Rising was the Starry Plough, a green flag bearing a representation of a plough, superimposed on which were the stars of the plough constellation. It had come into existence at the beginning of the twentieth century, as the flag of the Irish Citizens' Army, formed by members of the Irish Transport and General Workers Union. There is some doubt about who designed it. Hayes-McCoy is satisfied that it was probably conceived by AE (George Russell) and designed by William H. Megaw, though Sean O'Casey, the playwright and member of the Irish Citizens' Army, in his autobiography (1963, p612) states that AE declined to take the credit and that it was sketched by a Galway Art teacher. The thinking behind the design is not recorded, but it was clearly a symbol not of nationalism but of the socialist movement. It incorporated the typical socialist theme of the worker's tools and was an early example of the use of stars in socialist flags. In O'Casey's play, *The Plough and the Stars* (1974 ed. p94), one character, the Covey, protests at its use in the Easter Rising:

> They're bringin' nice disgrace on that banner now . . . Because it's a Labour flag, an' was never meant for politics . . . What does th' design of th' field plough, bearin' on it th' stars of th' heavenly plough, mean, if it's not communism? It's a flag that should only be used when we're building th' barricades to fight for a Worker's Republic.

The plough's cutting edge was actually a sword, a reference to the Biblical pacifist image, 'They shall beat their swords into plough shares' O'Casey's (1963, p613) own appreciation of its message was 'the plough will always remain to furrow the earth, the stars will always be there to unveil the beauty of the night, and a newer people, living a newer life, will sing like the sons of the morning.' Loftus (1994) describes it as 'a typically Celtic revival fusion of rural and celestial themes.'

The flag fell into disuse until the 1930s when it was revived by the labour movement, but there were two important changes. The plough was dropped and only the stars remained. The field was changed from green to blue. No one could actually remember what the flag had been like, and the consensus was that it had a blue ground. O'Casey referred to it as blue in his autobiography in 1945. It has been used in more recent times by Republican groups which wanted to express their socialist principles.

In 1981, a flag with no previous Irish connotations appeared in nationalist areas. Those who wanted to show their feelings at the deaths resulting from the republican hunger strikes put out black flags. As they became wide spread in republican areas, and as feelings towards the British Government intensified with each new death, they expressed not just grief but anger, and began to take on a rather menacing and threatening meaning for non-republicans. One Protestant clergy man explained this by saying that 'they represented an event which was a threat.'

It would appear that the Irish Republican Army has no flag, which is remarkable when one notes their use of colour parties and other military display. The Sunburst is the flag of the republican youth movement, the Fianna. It was originally blue, but like the Starry Plough it has changed over the years. It is now yellow, with a gold segment of the sun from which rays and stars are bursting out. On occasions individual brigades have designed their own standard, but they have never been widely used. IRA colour parties will normally carry the Tricolour and the flags of the four provinces and perhaps the Starry Plough.

There are other symbols with Irish or republican connections. It is important to mention the Fainné, a small ring which is worn in the lapel and indicates that one is an Irish speaker. The language, as with minority languages elsewhere, is seen by some as an expression of national identity. For some this does not have any political or constitutional implications. Others associate it with the desire for the unification of Ireland, and some, including Sinn Fein, believe that speaking the language contributes to the campaign to bring about a united Ireland.

Another significant badge is the Easter Lily, which occupies a somewhat similar position to the poppy in the United Kingdom, as a symbol of remembrance of those killed in war. The lily was introduced by the republican women's organisation, Cumman na mBan in 1926 to commemorate the Easter Rising of 1916 (Loftus (1994) and is still worn at Easter by those who wish to remember those who have died in the fight for Irish independence.

Lastly the colours and badges of football clubs such as Glasgow Celtic are often worn by younger people, partly to express support for the team and partly as identity symbols.

Emblems of the Catholic tradition

Flags are sometimes used in the Catholic community as part of religious celebrations. There is a custom of decorating churches, and sometimes homes and streets for visits by the bishop, ordinations, holy days, especially on Saint Patrick's Day, and parish festivals. The Vatican flag (the papal flag) and the Vatican colours of yellow (gold) and white are most common. Catholics do not connect these displays with the nationalist tradition, and the Vatican flag is explicitly seen as less political than the Tricolour or Saint Patrick's flag. This is a distinction which is not apparent to Protestants. A wide variety of colours are used in bunting, and they do not seem to have any special significance. Sometimes they simply use the colours to hand. One loyalist said that when it comes to bunting 'nationalists [Catholics] don't care what colour it is. It only matters to hard line republicans.' A nationalist said 'our crowd was never too particular about colours.' In 1993, for example, St Columb's Well in Derry was decorated for Saint Columb's Day in red, white, blue and green. There are of course many other emblems, badges and symbols which denote aspects of the Catholic community, such as the Sacred Heart of Jesus, but there is no need to discuss them in detail here.

Emblems of Ulster and Unionism

As with Ireland as a whole, there are a number of symbols which are associated with Ulster or Northern Ireland, and in addition most unionist and loyalist organisations have their own flags and symbols, many of recent origin. The most ancient symbol is the red hand, whose origins go back long before the present divisions in the community to the story of the struggle between two chieftains for possession of Ulster. It was decided that the land would be given to the chief who first touched it, and so as they approached land, one of them cut off his hand and threw it on the beach, thereby gaining possession. This symbol was adopted by the O'Neills and, when they became Earls of Ulster, they incorporated it in their arms: a red cross on a yellow background, in the middle of which was a red hand in a small white shield. This was also the arms of the Province of Ulster and is still the provincial flag.

In 1924/5 the Government of Northern Ireland, which had just been established, was granted a coat of arms based on the O'Neill arms. Two significant differences were in the central red hand symbol. The small shield on which the red hand was mounted, was replaced by a six-pointed star, surmounted by a crown. The reason for the addition of the crown was a clear indication of loyalty to the British monarch, but the meaning of the six-pointed star is less clear. It has been suggested that it was an old Ulster symbol, or that it was related to the Jewish star of David, but we know of no authority for either of these explanations. It seems reasonable to accept that it was chosen to denote the six counties of Northern Ireland.

The yellow field of the O'Neill crest was changed to white, making it look like the Cross of Saint George. An O'Neill flag is still incorporated in the coat of arms as one of the small flags above the shield. It is unclear why this happened. There is no explanation of why the background colour was changed. It was not necessary from a heraldic point of view since the other changes were sufficient to distinguish it from the O'Neill arms. It is rather intriguing that some copies of the coat of arms were drawn with the O'Neill red cross on a yellow background. As late as 1947 this version appeared on a map of Northern Ireland.

The reason for the change is not known, but it is not unlikely that the Northern Ireland Government decided to change the field to provide a closer association with the flag of England. The Cross of Saint George has had a presence in Northern Ireland for a long time as it is incorporated in the coat of arms of the city of London and it was therefore used by the Irish Society which was granted large parts of County Coleraine in the seventeenth century, changing its name to Londonderry. Their emblem is still found in a variety of institutions from school crests to the coat of arms of Derry City Council.

In 1925 a flag of Northern Ireland was introduced. This was a blue ensign, or a blue flag with a Union flag in one corner. It also incorporated the O'Neill shield surrounded by six stars. At the same time a naval ensign was introduced for boats belonging to the Government of Northern Ireland, and a Governor's flag which included a union flag, a shield of Saint Patrick's Cross and a red hand in a six-pointed star, but none of these flags ever became well known.

In 1963 a new Northern Ireland flag was designed by W.R. Gordon, based on the coat of arms. Its appearance was reported in the *Belfast Telegraph* of 2 July 1953:

> For the first time, the Northern Ireland Government banner was flown as a flag over Parliament Buildings today in honour of the Queen's visit. The banner consists of the Red Hand of Ulster on a white background sur- mounted by a crown. During the coronation celebrations, the Minister of Home Affairs announced that while the Union flag was the only standard officially recognised, those who wish to have a distinctive Ulster symbol might use the banner.

It is worthy of note that the Minister stressed that the flag was not to take the place of the Union flag, but it seems that the Government was inviting the public to adopt this 'distinctive Ulster symbol'. It is also interesting that the description of the flag leaves out a number of important features which are incorporated in the present version. There is no mention of the red cross or the six-pointed star. It may be that this was simply a case of inaccurate reporting. This flag became popular, especially after the dissolution of Stormont in 1972, though in recent times the crown is not always included. As with other flags which have been used by the unionist community, a small Union flag is also sometimes incorporated in the top corner.

There are many flags which are unequivocally associated with the union- ist community. The Crimson Flag, which actually looks more like maroon, is a flag associated with the Siege of Derry as it is recorded that it flew over the cathedral during the siege (Stewart, 1977, p66) . It is the predominant colour of the regalia of the Apprentice Boys of Derry, and is flown in the city and on the Cathedral during their celebrations. The exact origins of the flag of the Orange Order are not known, but it too has connections with the Williamite Wars of 1688–90. It is based on a flag carried at the Battle of the Boyne, and is also associated with King William of the House of Orange. It is orange with a purple star in the middle., which is also an emblem from the battle. It sometimes includes a Cross of St George in the top corner.

Protestant paramilitary groups have given great importance to military colours. It is not surprising that the symbol of the formation of Ulster Resistance, when it had no members or organisation, was the parading of the new colours first at the Ulster Hall and then in different parts of Northern Ireland. The paramilitary groups use their flags to provide a sense of legitimacy. The Ulster Defence Association has a pale blue flags with the UDA shield: the red hand of Ulster on a white background, surmounted by a crown and underneath the words 'Quis Separabit' or 'Who will make us separate'. Each regimental flag replaces the shield with the regimental insignia. Just before the mass rally at the Belfast City Hall in November 1966 as part of the 'Ulster Says No Campaign', the UDA regimental flags appeared from the crowd and were paraded onto the platform. This was a moment pregnant with meaning because many Unionists who were about to appear on the platform would not want to be associated with the UDA. And the crowd greeted the flags with the same applause they were soon to give the Unionist leadership.

The Ulster Volunteer Force flag is based on the flag of the original UVF of 1912, and the flag of the 36 Ulster Division which had UVF members as its core. It is crimson or maroon in colour and bears the cap badge of the UVF, with the motto 'For God and Ulster'.

One moderate unionist said that in this way the UVF was 'trying to add historical and military weight to the organisation.' In the same way, the adoption by the UDA of a Latin inscription and traditional heraldic scroll-work around its shield gives an air of historical legitimacy. A very different example of unionists adopting a style with other associations, can be found in the campaign against the Anglo Irish Agreement. This campaign in the mid-1980s coincided with the growth of the Solidarity Movement in Poland, and for a short time stylistic features reminiscent of their campaign appeared in unionist posters and emblems. Red was a dominant colour, the shapes of characters were similar to the distinctive Solidarity lettering, and barbed war was used as a symbol of the struggle against oppression. Solidarity was challenging the totalitarian state. Unionists felt that they were also challenging an unresponsive state and it is probably no coincidence that they portrayed themselves in the same tradition It may be somewhat ironic that one of Solidarity's main inspirations was Catholicism.

Other flags, associated with specific organisations and institutions are familiar in the unionist and loyalist community, but they are mainly used by the relevant organisation. The flag of the Vanguard Party for example was popular for a time in the 1970s, but it disappeared with the decline of the party.

There are many badges and pins and other insignia which are worn by unionists as expressions of their identity. Most of them are based on some of the insignia already mentioned, but some favour the badges and colours of football teams which are identified with their community, particularly Linfield and Glasgow Rangers.

National Anthems in Ireland and the United Kingdom

After the multitude of visual signs and symbols which exist, the situation with national anthems is much simpler. Each state has an official anthem, though there are some other songs which have a special status as patriotic songs. The United Kingdom national anthem is a hymn addressed to the monarch. It does in fact appear in many hymnbooks. It has already been referred to in Chapter 1 as being the first song or tune to be identified as a national anthem. Because of its age, the origins of the British anthem are obscure. Hammond (1993) suggests it may have begun as a sixteenth century galliard tune which he notes regretfully 'has since shed any implications of frivolity'.

Allison and Riddell (1991, p349) note that there is a manuscript copy of the words and music in Antwerp, which says the anthem was composed on the discovery of the Gunpowder Plot in 1605, and attributes the words and music to Dr John Bull, an early sixteenth century organist. There is a record of similar words being sung to the French King Louis XIV in 1686 – 'Grand

Dieu sauvez le roi' – but these words are scarcely unique. Whether or not
the anthem had its origins in the Gunpowder Plot crisis, it surfaces again
during another crisis, after the English defeat at the battle of Prestonpans
during the Jacobite Rising of 1745 (Sadie, 1980). It had in fact been published the year before in a version by Thomas Arne, but the threat from the
Young Pretender, Bonnie Prince Charlie, gave it a heightened significance.
The fourth verse is clearly anti-Scottish, with references to Marshall Wade
crushing the rebellious Scots. To restore morale, it was played at the Theatre Royal, Drury Lane, and the idea was taken up the following night at
Covent Garden, and was played in both theatres for several subsequent
performances. This is probably also the origin of the custom of playing the
anthem at theatrical performances.

It has already been noted that the words are a hymn in honour of the
monarch, but it also includes more divisive and war-like imagery, as in the
anti-Scots verse and the well-known lines from the third verse:

Scatter her enemies,
And make them fall.
Confound their politics
Frustrate their knavish tricks.

In the context of the Gunpowder Plot and the Jacobite Rising, such sentiments would come easily to the Establishment, who found the Monarch a
stabilising influence and felt threatened by forces they saw as subversive and
destabilising. However they seem less appropriate in modern times and are
something of an embarrassment. They are not in fact sung any longer.

There is one practice which we will mention here. It is not a song but it has
somewhat similar connotations to the anthem. It is the Loyal Toast to the
Queen, which is proposed at the end of a meal before other toasts. It was
once common at all kinds of events, even wedding receptions, but is now
restricted to more formal occasions.

In an earlier section it was already mentioned that there are a number of
other songs which have a similar patriotic tone and might well have been the
national anthem. Some have argued that Land of Hope and Glory would
make a better anthem if only because the tune is much better, but there is no
desire for change within the country.

Similarly in Scotland there are a number of patriotic tunes, but no recognised Scottish anthem. 'Scotland the Brave' comes nearest to being an
anthem, but the recent song 'Flower of Scotland' has become very popular
with spectators at sporting events, (see p49). Wales and the Isle of Man do
have anthems. The Welsh Anthem, 'Land of Our Fathers' is very old and
only ever sung in Welsh. It was described by one Welsh nationalist as
'bloodthirsty and nationalistic.'

There is a long tradition of patriotic songs in Ireland, with themes about
the oppression of the Irish and their attempts to gain independence from
Britain. Many of these have some of the qualities of a national anthem. We
can think of 'The Wearing of the Green', 'A Nation Once Again' or 'God

Save Ireland', which for a short time after independence was used as an anthem. However in 1926 the comparatively recent 'Soldier's Song' was adopted. It is the first verse of a poem written in 1907 by Peadar Kearney who also wrote the music with Patrick Heeney, and was one of the songs sung by the participants in the Easter Rising to keep up their spirits.

It is not know why it was chosen as national anthem, though there are reasons why the other songs referred to would not have been suitable. Some had appropriate tunes and their titles refer to the broad themes and high ideals and aspirations, typical of anthems. But as with most Irish patriotic songs, both Orange and Green, the words refer to very specific events, which would be too narrow for an anthem. They are also inappropriate because they are placed firmly in the historical context of the period before independence.

Hammond's (1993) assessment of 'The Soldier's Song' is that the words do have a specific Irish significance, and that 'there is what I would say was a very characteristically Irish turn of phrase in the final musical sentence – but it has always seemed to me to be more akin to music hall Irish and therefore out of place in a tune designed to raise the level of national pride.'

There is no song which is recognised as a Northern Ireland or Ulster anthem, which is not surprising since the residents do not have a shared sense of national identity. Loyalists and unionists have Orange songs such as 'The Sash', which is itself about a unionist emblem. To some degree they fill the gap. They offer a sense of a political identity and express the political divisions in stark terms. They do not offer a sense of national identity, but we shall see that for many in the unionist community citizenship and political identity are more important and the unionist community as a whole does not have a strongly developed sense of a separate national identity.

Meaning and Use of National Symbols

In the earlier parts of this chapter which describes the variety of symbols which matter to the people of Northern Ireland, we have made some passing references to what is their significance. Now we need to look more closely at what the symbols mean, because there are complex shades of opinion which are difficult to distinguish. The views of the smaller ethnic groups, including travellers, South Asians and Chinese, are not included. Their views and any concerns they have are important, but in this study we have concentrated on the nationalist and unionist communities.

We will begin with a cautionary tale which reminds us that we can read too much political significance into symbols. A Maintained (Catholic) primary school in inner city Belfast was embarking on its first joint venture with a controlled (Protestant) school, a visit to America. The hosts from America visited Belfast and a religious service was organised during the visit. The parents and children were coming and some of the children were to read the lessons or carry out other special roles. The principal was understandably nervous. He reminded the children that they had to be on their best behaviour next day, and stressed that they were to tell their parents that they had to wear their best clothes, and be neat and tidy. He was horrified next day to find that the boy who was to read the lesson arrived wearing a Glasgow Celtic shirt. But he had done what he was told. In a deprived family it was his only good shirt and a prized possession.

British Symbols and the English

Before considering attitudes to national symbols in Northern Ireland, it is necessary to consider for a moment attitudes in Great Britain. There are marked contrasts between feelings in England compared to Wales and Scotland, so they are considered separately. There are a number of unusual features and apparent paradoxes in attitudes in England which can confuse both Ulster unionists and Irish nationalists. At one level English attitudes to symbols seems completely casual to the point of negligence, but in some circumstances they become extremely patriotic.

There is also very little censure when people ignore the national anthem. It is played much less often than in the past. During the war, it was encouraged in cinemas, at dances and as part of other social events because it boosted morale, but since then its use has become less and less common at, for example, theatres (Allison and Riddell, 1991, p349). It would appear that the Royal Family do not object to this trend, because often it is not played even when members of the Royal Family are present. The management of the theatre or concert hall has to inform the Royal Household of its plans for such a visit, and this would show if the anthem was to be omitted. If the members of the Royal party wished that it should be played, the management would be informed and the anthem would be played. It is thought that the members of the Royal family do not wish to disrupt the proceedings and prefer to enter the theatre quietly and become part of the audience. The anthem is more likely to be played at a special event like a Royal Command Performance.

The Union flag has no legal protection as exists in most other countries, either protecting the right to fly the flag or prohibiting misuse of the flag by subversive or militant groups. As recently as 1985 in the Government White Paper, *Review of Public Order Law* (Cmd 9510, paragraph 6.4) the Government reviewed the arguments for prohibiting misuse of the flag and decided it was not desirable to introduce any legislation. There is no limitation in how the Union flag motive can be used in advertising and it can be made into bags, T-shirts or household goods. In contrast the Lord Chamberlain's office would refuse permission for the Royal Standard to be used in any way.

But the general demeanour towards national symbols has to be contrasted with the behaviour of the audience at the last night of the Proms, with its abundance of patriotic imagery, songs and emblems. It is hard to know how seriously the audience and performers enter into the jingoistic mood, and it seems bizarre in the context of serious music. It is also important to reflect on the sudden surge of patriotic feelings which surfaces from time to time, as happened during the war over the Falkland or Malvina Islands. Large photographs of the Union flag were much in evidence in the popular press.

One explanation of this is that the feeling of English identity is not normally expressed through symbols like the anthem and the flag, as in America for example. Both English and American interviewees told us that the flag is the key symbol of the American state and its territory, as is clear from the pledge of allegiance, but Englishness is not expressed so clearly in a sense of territory. The key symbol is the monarch as figurehead. Osmond (1988, p174) supports this view when he says that the 'the agencies of Statehood – most notably monarchy, Parliament, police and armed forces – are a primary reference point for English identity in a way that territory is not'. He also argues (p 19), perhaps less soundly, that 'the emblems of the Crown [provide] a civil and moral authority that is not available to comparable countries.'

Secondly the status of the Union flag has always been a little unusual. The original Union flag came into existence before the concept of the national flag had been developed fully, and in fact the role the union flag played in Great Britain helped in the development of the idea of national flags. Originally it was a flag for the monarch, and it could be argued that this is still the situation.

According to *The Royal Encyclopaedia:*

It is not so clear who is entitled to use it. The older heraldic view is that it is properly a royal flag; indeed in the form of a shield and ensigned by the royal crown it is one of the royal badges. When the present design was made official in 1801, in the reign of George III, it was ordered to be flown in all His Majesty's forts, castles, etc. and not by His Majesty's subjects. Thus it is flown over Windsor Castle except when The Queen is in residence, but not over Buckingham Palace which is unfortified. According to this view, it is an emblem of 'Her Majesty's Service' and in particular it is the flag of the Army, which unlike the Royal Navy and the Royal Air Force does not have its own ensign. It could therefore be said that it should not be used by ordinary citizens whose flag on land is that of St George, St Andrew or St Patrick's, depending on their birth or ancestry, and is at sea the Red Ensign.

Nevertheless many people do fly the Union flag. Its use is a long established custom which is never likely to be interfered with. Indeed, it has been stated in both Houses of Parliament during this century that there is no objection to British subjects using the Union flag ashore. (Allison and Riddell, 1991, p550)

In line with this concept of the Union flag, it was mainly used in Ireland on military establishments, as was Saint George's Cross before the Union flag came into existence in 1707. But the general public may not appreciate the subtleties of these distinctions. Osmond (1988, p174) asks 'what kind of sensibilities do the English have in relation to their 'national flag', and answers 'when England plays Scotland at football matches the English supporters wave not the flag of St George but the Union Jack.' We shall now look at what flag the Scottish supporters wave to encourage their team.

British symbols in Scotland and Wales
While there are many people in both Scotland and Wales who identify closely with the United Kingdom and the British state, there is a strong nationalistic tendency which is resentful of what they see as English cultural and political domination of the United Kingdom. They feel that their interests are ignored and the Scottish and Welsh cultures threatened. It is interesting to contrast how that feeling is expressed in attitudes towards national symbols in these two countries and in Northern Ireland. George Boyce (1991) has said 'The questions of legitimacy and nationalism in Wales or Scotland appear to be but feeble echoes of the intense conflict in the north of Ireland.' Anti-English feeling is expressed more freely in Scotland and Wales because there is little hostility between those with different views on the subject and there is unlikely to be a serious confrontation between those who favour and those who oppose British symbols. There is also no opposition to Welsh or Scottish symbols within the country. A third factor, which partly explains the other two, is the absence of the fear of a neighbouring country which is felt by a large number of the Protestant community in Northern Ireland.

In Scotland 'the Union Flag is thoroughly disliked in (and also far beyond) SNP circles' says Kevin Pringle, Research Officer of the Scottish National Party (SNP) (personal communication). He goes on to make the interesting point that 'speaking personally, I find the Union Flag more acceptable at, for example, a war memorial than when it is flying from Scottish public buildings such as Edinburgh Castle.' This fits with the military connotations of the Union flag, though from that point of view Edinburgh Castle may be a rather unfortunate example to choose as it is still a military establishment.

The two Scottish flags, the St Andrew's Cross and the Lion Rampant of Scotland, are both accepted by Scots, but until recent times the Lion Rampant was the dominant image. This is resented by Scots nationalists because the Lion Rampant is first and foremost the symbol of the royal household in Scotland. In the words of Mr Pringle, 'the SNP favour the continuation of the monarchy in an independent Scotland. However, this commitment does not extend to the use of a monarchical symbol in our logo.' The emphasis given to the Lion Rampant is seen as part of a deliberate attempt by the British establishment to make Scotland 'North British'. However in recent years the Saint Andrew's Cross has grown in popularity, as seen at football and rugby matches where both flags are common.

Turning to the anthems Mr Pringle says

One interesting instance of Scottish society becoming much more distinctively 'Scottish' over the last few years is the music played at Scottish International football and rugby matches. 'God Save the Queen' always used to be played, and it was always drowned out by boos and whistles at the football matches (rugby crowds are rather different)! A number of years ago, 'Scotland the Brave' and sometimes 'Flower of Scotland' began to be played at football Internationals. Rather more recently – and to great acclaim – 'Flower of Scotland' has been played at rugby Internationals too.'

The President of the Scottish Rugby Football Union, the Princess Royal, has no problem in joining in the singing when she attends.

One final example can be taken from the world of pipe bands. When the Northern Ireland Branch of the Royal Scottish Pipe Band Association organised the World Pipe Band Championships they used 'The Queen' and the Union flag alongside the Association flag. In Scotland the Association play 'Scotland the Brave' and fly the Cross of Saint Andrews.

Irish symbols can also be relevant in Scotland. Stephen Bruce (1992) notes that few Scots are likely to get involved in Irish affairs, but nevertheless there are Scots who identify with unionists and others with nationalists. At football matches between Glasgow Rangers and Glasgow Celtic the Union flag and the Tricolour can both be seen. Mr Pringle points out that this has no 'contemporary political significance'.

The flag is of much less significance in Wales, but the anthem is a more important issue. The Welsh are very aware that they are not represented in the Union flag, and for many the flag represents Englishness. Around the period of the Investiture of the Prince of Wales the feeling against the Union flag was more evident. At the one hundred and fiftieth anniversary of the Merthyr riots the Union flag was burnt ritually. The Welsh Party, Plaid Cymru, tends to dismiss the importance of flags and emblems, because they are irrelevant to the real issues and could become a substitute for real policy.

The anthem may generate more controversy because it involves words and therefore it is connected to the language issue, which is so important to many Welsh people. In the late 60s and 70s people would remain seated while 'The Queen' was played, especially in Welsh speaking areas. Now the question seldom arises because, as in England, the anthem is much less likely to be played at events. It is still played during graduation ceremonies at the University of Wales at Aberystwyth, together with the Welsh anthem. Some students stand for the Welsh anthem, but sit down when the United Kingdom anthem is played. The Welsh and Scottish experience is relevant to unionists and nationalists in Northern Ireland, because the Scots and the Welsh are able to use symbols to express positive or negative attitudes without provoking or intimidating those who disagree with them. The trends in England are also of interest as a comparison to the way symbols are used in Northern Ireland. But the English perspective is also important because it provides an insight into the way the national symbols are identified more with the state institutions rather than the nation as a people.

Unionists and British Symbols
Both unionists and nationalists treat the symbols as representing the institutions of the state, not the people or the territory, although they may not articulate this distinction, or perhaps even recognise it consciously. For unionists it is the institutions of the United Kingdom which are important.

They do not particularly identify with the territory or the people. But the national anthem and the Union flag represent the state institutions which exercise sovereignty over Northern Ireland, and thereby provides a sense of security in the face of the risk of the unification of Ireland. One Protestant who was critical of the British Government's role in Northern Ireland could still respect 'The Queen' to some degree, because he stressed it was not a national anthem but an anthem to the monarch. British symbols also provide a sense of identity, which many, but not all, unionists do not find within their own community in Northern Ireland. This is partly a reflection of Britain's imperial past, which gives the state and its citizens a larger part on the stage of history. It is also partly to do with Britain's contribution to thought and ideas. One loyalist said that 'The Queen' expresses his highest ideals for society, referring not to the first verse but to later verses.

An influential member of the Unionist community described the feelings that the Queen and the Union flag aroused in him: 'It expresses my Britishness which I feel is under threat . . . Pride is involved – pride for the nation of Ulster in the Nation of Britain – what they are and what they have given. The use of the national flag and anthem also often bring forth pictures of members of the security forces . . . being buried for their country.' He also described the national anthem as a symbol of national pride. Interestingly he commented that he thought the feelings of nationalists were very similar, but in relation to the symbols of the Irish state. Another unionist connected Britishness and the symbols of the monarchy in a different way: 'If the monarchy finally collapsed Ulster Loyalists would find themselves another symbol of Britishness.'

It is perhaps useful to note in passing that this analysis offers an explanation of the nature of the Britishness which is important to unionists. Unionists are often told that Britishness is not a real identity; there is no British nation; Britishness is an expression of citizenship. But this argument misses the point of what unionists want from their Britishness: citizenship in the sense of identification with the institutions of the state. They are not necessarily looking for a sense of nationality, or if they are they may be looking elsewhere.

For unionists these feelings are evoked as easily by the colours, red, white and blue as by the actual flag. Casual observers may have been surprised to find the Yugoslavian flag of blue white and red stripes appearing on the streets of Belfast in 1993. Was it a sign of solidarity with the Serbs in the Balkan conflict? Closer inspection revealed that there was red writing and symbols on the white stripe. It says 'Ulster, No Surrender', flanked by two line drawing of King William of Orange. It may simply indicate that the colours are as important as the actual flag. But perhaps some enterprising Belfast textile merchant had found an alternative market for some flags destined for the Serbian market but blocked by the Balkan conflict and the sanctions on the former Yugoslavia. Orange and blue for the orange order are also favourite colours of unionists.

Unionists do not understand British attitudes to national institutions and national symbols, and they feel hurt and insecure when English people do not take them seriously. For an Ulster unionist, if the Union flag is not flown, or if the national anthem is not played, it is a sign that the link with Britain is being weakened, and if the English do not seem to care, that means that they are abandoning the Unionists. Unionists do not understand that this simply reflects how the English behave within England, and that they expect unionists to adopt similar attitudes in Northern Ireland. This would be the case regardless of whether the government and people of Great Britain want to maintain the link with Northern Ireland.

Unionists deal with their dissatisfaction in different ways. Some have made greater efforts to promote British symbols and to keep England involved. They will continue to sing the national anthem in spite of their perception that the United Kingdom is willing to abandon them. 'It is not for them to take it away from us – we can keep it if we want.' Some are very critical of government policy, but are not prepared to reject the British connection on that account. One politician said 'I don't believe because the Government does something despicable, it means I have to eschew every- thing to do with the State.' At times others have wanted to express there resentment of British policy but are not willing to reject normal conventions completely. So they stand for the anthem, but they refuse to sing or they bow their head. Others have begun to identify more strongly with local symbols and to rely on their community's resources.

Ulster loyalists have a strong identification with the Scottish Cross of Saint Andrew. It is often carried in band parades and is a common sight on loyalist murals. There are a number of possible explanations for this. It could represent a community who could express their aspirations without the internal conflict found in Northern Ireland, but this was not accepted by loyalists we spoke to. They gave the much simpler explanation, that there are close relations between Ulster people and Scots and it is a sign of that fraternal relationship. We were also told that Ulster people, who had gone to Scotland, have taken their culture with them and retained it. It is interest- ing that they seldom use the Rampant Lion flag which is the more 'royal' Scottish flag. To a lesser extent there are similar feelings about Canada and its flag.

Nationalist attitudes to British symbols
When nationalists see the British flag or hear the national anthem they also do not think of them as representing the people or territory of the United Kingdom. Like unionists, they are more aware of them as symbols of the state. One small example is provided by some work carried out by a youth worker. She shows the Union flag to young Catholics and the Tricol- our to Protestants and asks them to list the words that they associate with the other tradition's flag. In most groups of Catholics the Union flag re- minds them of the Crown, the Queen and the army, which are the institu- tions of the state.

Unlike unionists, nationalists do not have the same benign view of that state. For them it is an imposed order within Ireland. In its most hostile form, it is seen as an imperialist system, and they would identify with the most critical analyses of the British Empire which were to be found in Africa and other colonies during the period of decolonisation. This was expressed symbolically when we were reminded that in Africa the Union flag was known as 'The Butchers Apron'. One republican said that 'all the intricacies of the struggle between Irish identity and the British Empire can be telescoped down into two flags.'

Not all nationalists would share that level of hostility towards the British state. They are willing to respect the symbols, though they tend to feel they are overused and unnecessary on many occasions. One nationalist made the distinction that it is all right to play the anthem at a Government function but it is out of place at a social function. In particular, it should not be used to make party political points, which he described as 'an abuse of the anthem.'

Nationalists are also less sensitive about colours than Protestants, though we were told that 'anything that there is red in' is associated with Britain, possibly because it is a reminder of her military traditions. Even though many nationalists tolerate British symbols, at another level the symbols have no meaning for them. From this point of view national symbols express and encourage feelings of national identity. For them that identity is Irish and it is expressed through the Irish flag and anthem. We have seen that the British symbols are more connected with citizenship than nationality, and in any case, nationalists do not feel either a British or English identity. Therefore the Union flag and 'The Queen' are at best irrelevant to nationalists and could not compensate for the symbols with which they do identify and which give them a sense of national pride. We will now look at the meaning of these Irish symbols for people in Northern Ireland.

Attitudes to Irish Symbols in the Republic of Ireland
We did not have the opportunity to investigate attitudes to Irish symbols in the Republic of Ireland, but nevertheless it may be useful to summarise the information and our tentative impression for completeness. The general impression is that Irish people are very proud of their flag and anthem as symbols of their independence which still seems comparatively recent, though in fact it was gained over seventy years ago.

We have noted that the Republic of Ireland is one of the few states which has a flag code. There are more flags on buildings in Dublin than are evident in Belfast or London, but some people would like the practice to be more universal. They are flown in a formal way from a permanent flag pole, and they are all clean and in good condition. Flags attached to lamp posts as territorial markers are rare, and confined to the border area. The tricolour design is also used rarely in merchandising or clothing, but pictures of the flag are widely used as a symbol of Ireland in tourism, on leaflets and postcards for example.

The national anthem is not widely played apart from formal occasions. It is not necessarily played even when the President is present. In chapter 3 we will note the public and political pressure which was put on the Irish Rugby Football Union to play the anthem in 1930s. The situation is very different now. Nevertheless people invariable stand proudly for the anthem and there is strong resistance to any suggestion that the anthem should be changed, as we shall see later in this chapter.

Nationalist attitudes to Irish symbols

Nationalists have a sense of Irishness, whether or not they want the early reunification of Ireland. Some do not feel reunification is possible in the present circumstances, but that does not lessen the wish to identify with the Irish people. An important way of expressing that identification is through the Tricolour and 'The Soldier's Song'. For some it is so natural to identify with them that it is almost impossible to explain it. For example, in Ireland as a whole, the Gaelic Athletic Association takes it completely for granted that it should fly the flag and play the national anthem. For some the feeling is very similar to that of émigrés from any country. The knowledge that they are not going back to their mother country increases the commitment to its symbols and its achievements. It does not indicate any political commitment to the nation.

On the other hand many nationalists do aspire to a united Ireland, and would work for that goal. They can share some of the émigré sense of attachment to the symbols of the motherland. One republican said that seeing a Tricolour as he drove around the countryside gave him a warm glow inside. The more important aspect of the identification with the flag and anthem is as an exile or colonial subject. The symbols speak of what could yet happen. The exile may be able to return home. The colonial subject may see the country become free. This is the perspective of the republican movement: 'The anthem is used to reinforce national identity. How else do you express opposition to foreign sovereignty? It may be a necessary part of the assertion of identity.' The symbols can actually help to bring about the change because they remind people of their aspirations, they tell them that the struggle is not finished, and encourage them to work to bring it about. In other circumstances, if they were confident that identity was not under threat, the symbols would not have the same importance.

The republican movement has a slightly ambivalent attitude to the national symbols, and we will return to this point later. They recognise they can have a powerful role in mobilising support. But at the same time they were described as the 'most banal expressions of nationalism.' Volunteers in the IRA were educated to respect 'The Soldier's Song' and the Tricolour. In the 1970s they trained to stand smartly to attention when the anthem was played. However this meant that they were easily recognised at social functions as they were standing much more erect than everyone else. As a result they were told that for security reasons they should respect the anthem but not in a very military fashion. In a similar vein, Loftus (1994) notes that 'the Provisional IRA ceased marching in formation by organisations and areas from the mid 1970s because this gave the security forces too much information.'

Saint Patrick's flag is not much used by nationalists. Even on Saint Patrick's Day the Papal flag is much more common. One person said that many Catholics would not recognise Saint Patrick's Cross. If they saw it they would associate it with the Union flag, and they would connect the red with Britain.

Attitudes of Revolutionary Groups to Irish Symbols

Some people are very critical of state structures in Ireland both north and south, and would want to bring about a totally new system of government on an all-Ireland basis. They reject symbols of British involvement and unionist separateness but they are unhappy about the symbols of the Irish state. Some republicans feel like this, but they would still encourage the use of the Tricolour and 'The Soldier's Song' because they recognise that they are powerful symbols in their campaign for a united Ireland. At a minor level republicans take exception to the phrase 'Sinne Fianna Faíl' which means 'we are soldiers of Ireland', and seems to identify the anthem with the political party, Fianna Faíl. Therefore they changed the phrase to 'Sinne Laochra Faíl' or 'we are heroes of Ireland', and to the initiated who listens to the words closely it is possible to tell if the singer has republican sympathies.

Not very many people would take the argument to its logical conclusion and object to Irish symbols. But occasionally it happens. Purdie (1990, p131) refers to one incident in West Belfast in 1968 when a memorial parade for James Connolly's centenary was delayed because the Young Socialists would not march behind a Tricolour – 'A bourgeoisie flag'. It had been decided to carry it in the first place because republicans refused to march without it. Some years later an English woman visiting Donegal did not stand for 'The Soldiers Song' at the end of a social night because she did not realise what it was when it was played. She was accused of being some kind of revolutionary from the north.

Unionist attitudes to Irish Symbols

Unionists are very aware of the connotations of the Irish flag and anthem as symbols of exile. And they are very aware of the part those symbols can play in maintaining the will to bring about a united Ireland. They have greater difficulty in appreciating the 'émigré' identification with them without necessarily wanting to change the constitutional position. Of course they are aware that the émigré could become an exile and that the symbols of nationhood could help to bring that about. The symbols of the Irish state are seen as irredentist and threatening and unionists would prefer that they are controlled. They do not understand how the English, with their superficially relaxed view of national symbols, do not appreciate the threat.

One unionist said 'The Tricolour is a symbol of violence – a symbol of the "armed struggle" and though it might have been created artificially and idealistically to suggest a truce between Orange and Green, it represents only evil for me.' Another unionist said 'because there is a dispute about nationality, there is in some areas a strong animus against it.' A third argued that Ireland does not respect existing national boundaries, peoples and their rights to self-determination, supporting his argument by reference to the

Anglo-Irish Agreement and articles two and three of the Irish Constitution. In these circumstances he finds it difficult to treat the Irish symbols like those of any other country.

Others do accept that the Tricolour and 'The Soldier's Song' are the symbols of a neighbouring country, a fellow member of the European community, and therefore should be treated with due respect. One unionist quoted earlier also said 'I would stand for the National Anthem of any state I was in at the time – that is a mark of respect despite a belief that in Ireland the Tricolour and "The Soldier's Song" are symbols of violence.' Another unionist said the Tricolour is simply the flag of another European country and should be treated with appropriate respect. While a third said he shows it the same respect as he would expect to be shown to his flag. He said he did not give it a thought when the anthem was played in the Republic of Ireland, but he can get annoyed by the Irish flag and anthem in Northern Ireland because in this context it stands for the IRA. Like the Irish language and other Irish symbols they are used to divide the community when they should help to unite it.

The Tricolour is associated in some Protestant minds with religion as much as with the Irish state. We mentioned earlier in this chapter the project where young people are asked to look at the flag of the other tradition and list the words they associate with it. In most cases Protestants do not immediately associate the Tricolour with the Irish state, but with religion: the Pope, 'Taigs' or Catholics. They are very sensitive about the colours in any context. Even talking about the clothes some people will say 'We don't want those Fenian colours here.' They find 'The Soldier's Song' equally offensive.

Finally some Protestants take a positive view of the use of Irish symbols. One Churchman said 'Flags express community identity. I am delighted to see our neighbours flying the Tricolour. It is a peaceful indication of identity.' However we did not find widespread evidence of this level of acceptance.

Unionist Attitudes to Ulster Symbols
The Ulster provincial flag, the O'Neill flag, means little to unionists, and some may not even be aware of it as distinct from the flag of Northern Ireland, with which they do identify. Their use of the latter flag has become more marked since the beginning of the present Troubles, and especially since the signing of the Anglo-Irish Agreement. One loyalist said that he had always felt that the Northern Ireland flag was alien and not part of the local tradition, because it was based on the Cross of Saint George.

However most unionists would feel some affinity with both the Union flag and the Northern Ireland flag, though they would have a preference for one over the other, depending on political orientation. Those who doubt the commitment of the United Kingdom Government to the link with Northern Ireland will feel closer to the Northern Ireland flag. One unionist wondered if flying the Northern Ireland flag in preference to the Union flag indicated a negative attitude to the flag, or was it simply a 'sign of a positive attitude to

Ulster and the Ulster identity.' Another unionist politician considered that the Northern Ireland flag had been hi-jacked by the UDA, and he preferred the Union flag himself.

There is a danger in assuming too much about a person's political views from the precise choice of flag which he chooses to display. We might interpret the inclusion or exclusion of a crown or a Union flag as indicative of his or her view of the link with the British state. Most unionists would accept a range of flags, and in reality their choice is often determined by what is available in the shops. So the prevalence of a particular flag may say more about the political inclinations of the flag maker or shop owner than about the people using the flags.

Nationalist Attitudes to Ulster Symbols

There is a clear difference between the way that unionists react to Irish symbols and the way that nationalists react to symbols of Ulster and Northern Ireland. Protestants invariably see Saint Patrick's Cross, the harp and shamrock as non political symbols, but the Tricolour and 'The Soldier's Song' always have strong political connotations of an irredentist state. They do not appreciate distinctions in the motivation and the way they are used. Nationalists react to the British symbols in a fairly similar way, but their response to Ulster symbols is more influenced by the way they are being used. Perhaps this is because they see them as a subset within Irish symbols as a whole.

At the same time they do not have a close affinity with many Ulster symbols. In the same way that unionists feel that the Catholic and nationalist community has monopolised Irish identity and made it fit their own concept, nationalists feel Ulster symbols have been monopolised by unionists. Ulster has been made synonymous with Northern Ireland which is only six of the nine counties of the traditional province, and so the name itself and the Red Hand are seen as Protestant and unionist symbols.

The Ulster O'Neill flag does not have those connotations, and is therefore used by nationalists as a provincial symbol without political connotations. It is therefore acceptable to use it in this way in both the largely nationalist Gaelic sports and the mainly unionist rugby football, and indeed in many other sports.

Nationalists are not familiar with the distinctions between the other flags used by unionists. They are most aware of the Northern Ireland flag, and consider that the way it is used is contentious and provocative. They think that unionists use all flags too often, and that they are often making sectarian and political points. They point to parades which they see as attempts by unionists to assert their dominance and to prove their right to go where they like and do what they like. In their eyes it is also used deliberately to offend and provoke. At the same time they did not express any hostility to the flag as such.

One person from the political centre wondered if moderate nationalists were coming to associate the Northern Ireland flags with militant loyalism and therefore the Union flag was becoming more acceptable. Republicans would take a different view. One republican said the Northern Ireland flag was much more acceptable than the Union flag. The Union flag was a symbol of domination representing the state to which he was opposed. He did not see the Protestant community as the 'real enemy' in the same sense, and in any case the flag seemed to him very much like the O'Neill flag of Ulster. It was even more acceptable when loyalists leave out the crown. It was our impression that unionists are not aware of this nationalist attitude towards the Northern Ireland flag, but there are few other examples of even this degree of tolerance of each other's symbols. This raises the question: 'Should we be looking for new symbols?'

New Symbols?

In March 1993, the Green Party's member of Dail Éireann, Trevor Sargent suggested the Irish national anthem should be 'toned down and replaced by one which is less patriotic.' In a written Dail question Sargent asked whether the words were 'appropriate to a society which ought to promote non-violence, tolerance and co-operation.' He is not the first person to make this suggestion in recent years. Hayes-McCoy (1979, p231) was mildly critical of the flag on aesthetic and political grounds: 'The flag of other countries attest symbolically the facts of history . . . but the Irish tricolour still represents no more than an ideal. It represents the ideal of a united Ireland. That it does so in a manner which seems to assert that the Union has been accomplished is resented in Northern Ireland.'

Some years ago Fine Gael suggested it was time for a change. The UDA, in an *Irish Times* interview on 3 April 1993, describe it as 'full of war-like images and glorified death and destruction', which may seem rather ironic, given some of the activities of loyalist paramilitaries. The Minister for Finance, in his reply to Mr Sargent, seemed to accept the point to some degree when it said 'The words of the anthem can be seen as a reflection of a particular time in this State's history arising our of our quest for independence', but he went on to say that 'Insofar as I am aware, the question of a change in the anthem is not an issue which is of general concern at the present time.'

There has been a lot of opposition to such suggestions, including letters to the papers and personal letters to Mr Sargent. In our interviews nationalists expressed strong opposition to the idea, in one case with real passion. He said it was a very dangerous thing to interfere with a people's history and to appear to be denying that it had happened. Another nationalist said that he did not like the 'belligerence' of the words. However, he added that since it is sung in Irish most people are not fully aware of its sentiments, and therefore there was no reason to change it.

The appropriateness of the symbols of the Northern Ireland Government have also been questioned over the years. It 'surfaced obliquely' at the inter-party talks in 1992, when one nationalist explained that he feels very alienated at Stormont because the building is 'replete' with symbols of its unionist past. Austin Currie, a former SDLP member of the power-sharing Executive of 1974, made a similar point in a television documentary some years ago. There are many features associated with England and the monarchy, but a visitor to Stormont would not be aware that there was a Catholic community in Northern Ireland. There are portraits of former unionist politicians, but none of nationalists who served in Stormont in the past.

The comment at the inter-party talks led to some informal discussion about the public symbols which would represent any future Administration which is established. The Northern Ireland Assembly of 1973–4 faced the same question and it was decided to make everything simple and to avoid symbols as much as possible. If it is intended that all traditions could identify with a new system of government, would new symbols be required to represent that inclusiveness? The old Northern Ireland Parliament had a Mace. Would that be necessary for a new body? What form should its public ceremonies take? Even the crest on the letterhead would have an impact on the recipient. Nationalists considered these things are important because they are connected to the whole issue of allegiance. They accept that there will be a demand for ceremony and symbols, but it is important to select them carefully. The form that the symbols take is an indication of what the people are being asked to pledge their allegiance to. However unionists dismissed it as a matter of no importance.

Generally unionists and nationalists are equally wary about changing symbols, especially those to which they are committed. Each sees the need for their opponents to change their 'offensive' symbols. At the same time they claim that they see no need to change their own symbols, and any suggestion that they are divisive is motivated by the desire to stir up trouble.

Practically, one unionist was doubtful if either side would drop all the old flags and emblems and embrace newly created neutral ones. We return again to the idea that flags and anthems are history and tradition, and giving them up means giving up history. Other nations have been able to change their symbols without denying their history, but the resistance in Ireland is stronger, possibly because both communities feel that their heritage is threatened.

There is also an opinion that considerations of changes in symbols should be left until there has been some resolution of the substantive issues about future relationships and systems of government. John Hume, the leader of the SDLP, said recently on the BBC Radio Election Talkback programme that the first necessity was to reach agreement on how we are governed: 'Then we will give loyalty and allegiance to the institutions and symbols of the state.'

It was argued that there are enough issues to worry about without introducing the question of symbols. Disagreement about what form they should take would be an unnecessary complication which could impede progress on other more fundamental issues. It was also suggested by a nationalist that symbols are ephemeral things which gain their importance from the institutions they represent, so the institutions must be created first. On the other hand symbols can be quite powerful. He was also concerned that symbols could become established without clarifying what they represented and this would limit the scope for negotiating the structure of new institutions and predetermine the outcome. For example there are different views on whether Northern Ireland, made up as at present of the six north-eastern counties of Ireland, should be the basis for future negotiations. If a flag or anthem which clearly represents that geographical entity, gained widespread cross-community acceptance, it would then be more difficult to argue for a solution on a completely different geographical basis.

Given these reservations, it may not be possible or advisable to replace the existing national symbols. But some people feel it should be possible to find additional symbols with which the whole community can identify, and which can be used on appropriate occasions to acknowledge that different traditions are present. In time they may become a shared heritage which helps to break down barriers and bring people together. One unionist thought that at an all-Ireland level there should be 'a common song for common activities.'

Co-operation North commissioned Dave Lyle of McCann Erikson, the advertising agency, to write what was called 'A New Song For Ireland' (See appendix 2) which was tried out at two rugby matches, an international in Dublin and the rugby Schools Cup Final in Belfast in 1991. The words were handed out to the spectators who were asked to sing it before the match. The well-known 'Londonderry Air' or 'Derry Air' was chosen as the tune, which made it easier to sing unrehearsed. There was no attempt to replace the existing national anthem, and 'The Soldier's Song' was also played as usual at the international. The song is about reconciliation and peace and does not attempt to evoke or create a sense of shared national identity.

There are existing songs which are used by groups who need a song which is not divisive. Paddy Devlin (1981, p125) drew attention to an incident during the Outdoor Relief Strike of 1932.

> with their supporters, numbering around 60,000 of both religions, [the strikers] marched from the Labour Exchange in Frederick Street to the traditional 'free-speech' forum at the Custom House steps where four platforms of speakers addressed the vast crowds. It was a torch-light parade, led by bands which, to avoid giving religious offence, played the neutral tune, 'Yes, we have no Bananas' over and over again.

'And so it was that 'Yes We Have No Bananas' – the only neutral tune available – became Belfast's anthem of progress', as Paul Bew comments in his introduction to Devlin's book (1981, pvii).

Neither this song, or any other suggestions attempt to create or respond to a shared sense of identity. They either ignore the conflict entirely and perhaps refer to the shared territory, or they are intended to promote reconciliation. In the next chapter, we will discuss in more detail how sports deal with the issue. The Women's Institute song (see Appendix 2), written by a member, Molly Frizzell, is interesting since it describes the countryside which is shared by all sections of the community. It refers specifically to each of the six counties of Northern Ireland, as there is a separate organisation, the Countrywomen's Association, in the Republic of Ireland. This means that the song draws attention to the constitutional issue, but nevertheless it is one of the few songs which takes the countryside as a unifying theme.

In the 1980s the Ulster Independence Committee wrote and distributed a song (Appendix 2), which is intended to be an anthem to replace the existing anthems. The movement wants to promote Ulster nationalism comparable to Scottish and Welsh nationalism. Like the concept of independence itself, the song was designed as an alternative to identification with the rest of Ireland or the rest of the United Kingdom. It does not have specifically Ulster references apart from the phrases 'Sons of Ulster' and 'land of Ulster'. Its imagery and language are in fact Biblical and reminiscent of the Old Testament, which is more likely to appeal to Ulster Presbyterians. Perhaps its most interesting phrase is the last line 'be a nation once again', which seems to be a reference to the Irish patriotic song of that name, and may be intended to appeal to nationalists. It has not been widely adopted.

There has been less interest in producing new flags, but in the 1980s the Ulster Independence Committee also designed and promoted an Independent Ulster flag. They attempted to avoid symbols which were associated with either state and with what they see as the 'old defunct government of Northern Ireland', and which might be offensive to either community in Northern Ireland. It is based on the red saltire Cross of Saint Patrick, but it is placed on a blue rather than a white field. Although Saint Patrick's Cross is normally associated with the whole of Ireland, they think it is appropriate because they argued that he was mainly associated with places in Ulster, including Slemish, Downpatrick and Armagh. They also date it to the fourteenth century and therefore it is older than the other Irish symbols. In the centre is a red hand on a six-pointed star, as in the flag of Northern Ireland, but the star is gold or yellow and there is no crown. They claim that the red hand and the six-pointed star have Biblical as well as Ulster roots. They say that they have kept away from the colours red white and blue, but in fact red ad blue are the flag's main colours.

The flag has been taken up by some people outside the Ulster Independence Committee and it is seen occasionally on flag poles and wall murals. It appeals to a small number of loyalists, most obviously those who were prepared to consider independence as a political option for Northern Ireland. One person said the flag meant more to him than the Northern Ireland flag because it was made up of traditional Ulster symbols. The majority of unionists do not see it that way at all. They claim that the Independent Ulster flag has no historical legitimacy, having been created by a small group of people in recent times, and it represents a political position which many of them consider misguided and dangerous, in that it puts at risk the link with the rest of the United Kingdom.

Most nationalists are not even aware of the existence of the flag and anthem. The Ulster Independence Committee did not want their movement and their flag to be seen as a negative unionist reaction to the political changes which have been taking place, but it grew out of the unionist community and is associated almost entirely with some elements in the unionist community. There is almost no support at all in the nationalist community for the concept of an independent Ulster, certainly not on a six-counties basis as is suggested by the six-pointed star. This last point is a reminder of the difficulty of obtaining support for symbols before there is support for the entity and institutions which the symbols are intended to represent.

The Impact of British and Irish Symbols

In the last section we have described in broad terms how the different sections of society perceive the most common symbols. While there is to a large degree a shared understanding of what the symbols represent within each community, there are wide variations in the impact of those symbols and in the intensity of feelings in response to them. We need to understand something of these variations before we can consider how the symbols are actually used in everyday situations and at special ceremonies.

In chapter one we suggested some of the factors which are important in determining responses to symbols. Characteristics of the individual can be significant. For example, age may be important. In more peaceful times older people may value national symbols more highly, but at times of conflict young people will be more engaged. People with right wing views identify more closely with national and group symbols. We also noted some of the situations which may intensify feelings about symbols: where identity is insecure or threatened, or where different identity groups are in conflict.

It might be assumed that there is a simple range of responses from indifference to symbols at one end rising in intensity to strong commitment at the other. But our responses are much more complex, not least because of the range of factors which are significant. They include our feelings about flags in general, about patriotism and group identity, the strength of our sense of identity, the importance of the Northern Ireland conflict and our commitment to one particular outcome. All these factors can operate independently of each other and influence us in different directions. For example some people will have a strong sense of identity, but may not be committed to any particular outcome to the conflict. And strong commitment to one set of symbols does not imply a strong reaction to opposing symbols.

Nevertheless, we were able to identify a number of different patterns of response, which are found to some degree within both the unionist and nationalist communities. Clearly, we have had to simplify and leave out some variations. They do not represent a linear progression from low level of feeling to high intensity of feeling. Opposite ends of the continuum have some things in common, and therefore we find it helpful to place the different responses in an arc (figure 2.2). In some ways the biggest contrasts are between responses at opposite sides of the arc. We find this a useful way to conceptualise the different responses because they can be related to specific types of behaviour as we have done in figure 2.3. But there are, of

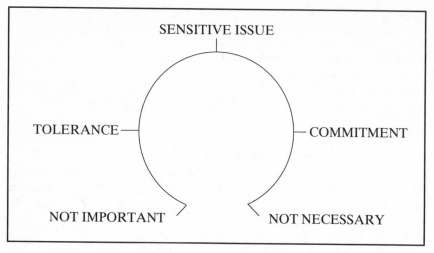

Figure 2.2   Feelings about group and national symbols

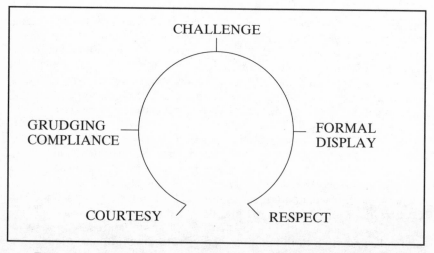

Figure 2.3   Behavioural responses to group and national symbols

course important variations within each group which will become apparent when we examine each situation in detail.

Neutral
Many people treat all symbols with respect, but for a variety of reasons. For some they are not important. They are neither interested in symbols or in the conflict and therefore what other people do with their symbols is a matter of indifference. They do not use any symbols themselves and some

ignore them when used by others. This is sometimes taken as an intended insult by others. However, most people who are indifferent about symbols do not wish to offend others and will act with courtesy to symbols, without feeling it is an act of any importance.

Flexible /adapters
Some people are not too worried about the display of symbols, but at the same time they do have a strong sense of their identity in relation to the Northern Ireland conflict. Their identity is sufficiently secure that it is not necessary to express it through symbols which they find superficial and not capable of articulating fully their sense of themselves. One unionist said he did not need to 'flaunt' them: 'I don't have to hit someone over the head with the flag to show I have a deep affinity with the British way of life.' People like this on both sides do not feel threatened by the symbols of political opponents. They are willing to restrict the use of symbols in their own tradition if it caused offence, because they recognise that symbols are sometimes used provocatively. However they will not be happy if they think that the symbols of their community are being treated unfavourably.

Abstainers
There is another category of people who will not display their symbols if it is going to cause conflict. While symbols are important and they like them, it is not necessary to display them. Their respect may be a feature of their personality, and it may have been encouraged by participation in a uni-formed organisation perhaps as a young person. They will have learnt to respect their own national symbols, and appropriate codes of behaviour, but they will also have learnt to respect other people's symbols, and they will be unhappy if they are insulted. They do not want to create confrontation over symbols and, to avoid this happening, they will waive the right to display their own symbols. This would be particularly true of leaders in uniformed youth organisations who would also be concerned about their responsibility for the young people in their care.

Celebrators
Others also value symbols highly but are much more committed to using them. They think people should be proud of their symbols and use them to express there allegiances and identity. They value diversity and think the display of symbols of different traditions is a demonstration of diversity. They do not like them to be used in aggressive or provocative ways and normally prefer them to be restricted to formal ceremonial and other special occasions. They are not a very large group in Northern Ireland, though common in other countries.

Grudging acceptors
A different kind of response was to tolerate the symbols of the other community but in a rather grudging way. It was not something over which to cause offence. One example of this kind of response is mainly found in the unionist community, and another in the nationalist community. Among

unionists there are those who have a strong commitment to their own symbols, and want them treated with respect, because they are an important expression of their identity. They may be hostile to the symbols of the other community, and will avoid them whenever possible. But because they want their own symbols treated with respect, they are prepared to accept the symbols of the other community in formal situations 'as the flag of another country'. On the other hand in the nationalist community there were those who are relaxed about symbols and do not thing they were very important. They do not use their own symbols much but they will be offended if they were insulted in some way. They do not like the way unionists used symbols so much but they are prepared to respect them if they are used appropriately and moderately. In both cases the acceptance of the other symbol is far from positive.

Confronters

There were two types of people who are very sensitive to the way symbols are used and will use their own flags and anthems at every opportunities and resist the attempts by the other community to use their symbols. Firstly there are those who feel that their identity is challenged or threatened or that they are powerless, and therefore they want to demonstrate their power and express their identity in some way, of which the display of symbols is one. The same result is achieved by opposing the display of the symbols of another group, but if they are unsuccessful they will be left feeling more uncertain and insecure. Of course if a group cannot express its identity either because of the opposition of another group or the state, they will have an even stronger need to find some way to assert themselves.

Others took a more pragmatic approach to symbols, and used them as a weapon in their struggle against their opponents. They might not feel very strongly about them, but they knew it was a way to challenge the other community and to assert their aspirations. They were more purposeful in their approach, calculating what advantage might be gained by challenging their opponents. Both groups go beyond self expression in their use of their own symbols and their objection to other symbols. They can use symbols to define and demarcate boundaries, or to assert control and dominance, or to intimidate or to provoke.

These distinctions are important in understanding the dynamics of specific situations. The interactions of these approaches has an important impact on the development of conflicts about the use of symbols, and this is a recurring theme in the situations described in the following chapters. Some types of behaviour are more influential than others, even when they are adopted by only a small number of people. Confronters for example can be quite aggressive and forceful and their behaviour can set the tone for the management of a dispute even when the majority would want to deal with it in a different less contentious way.

Interpreting Behaviour

It can be difficult to distinguish the different approaches from each other. It would be convenient if behaviour could be placed on a continuum from least offensive to most offensive. But it is not always easy to interpret different types of behaviour and recognise the underlying dynamics of the situation. Even those involved may not be clear about their own and others' motivations. It is not surprising because people are often acting in a dual way. In particular celebration and confrontation are often influences on behaviour which are operating at the same time. As a consequence it is not easy to set objective standards of acceptable and unacceptable behaviour. We therefore need to consider what we can learn from common behaviour patterns: how do people display their symbols, how do they react to other symbols and how do they react when their own symbols are not respected.

If a person's demeanour towards the flag and anthem are joyful and light-hearted, it is fairly clear that the dominant feeling is celebratory and an expression of oneself. A nationalist said that where there is a genuine mark of celebration, he might not join in, but he can accept it and be happy that it gives pleasure to others. A very formal and solemn demeanour signifies a dominant feeling of respect and deference to the person or state which is being honoured, and this approach is also generally accepted, though it may be associated with hostility to other groups and their symbols.

Other behaviours were criticised, often because they seem to be actually using the symbols in a disrespectful way. A number of people, unionists, nationalists, and also people from other countries, thought national symbols should be used sparingly and kept for special occasions. It was said that it belittles the national anthem to play it too often. Party political use was described by one nationalist as an abuse of the anthem. Questions were also raised about the number of flags people needed, and a display of many flags may give a different message from a more restrained form of self-expression,

Slovenly behaviour or ignoring protocol were also criticised. One unionist, who prefers formal display, said that it is embarrassing when unruly or drunk people sing the national anthem. He also said 'It is a disgrace to fly a tattered Union jack as a territorial marker at the marching season or whenever else.' Another person from the centre of politics said that people who fly tattered flags or paint kerbstones 'are in fact denigrating exactly what they are trying to display their loyalty to.'

These practices may not only be dishonouring the national symbols, but may be designed to annoy and provoke opponents. The word 'flaunting' was used in this context, without being defined in terms of specific behaviour. One unionist noted that flags have become an *excuse* for disputes and quarrels, and then observed 'to use the flag in a provocative manner is to dishonour it – it must be used with dignity.' Many practices were accused of being provocative, but few would admit that they were using symbols in this way. It is convenient to accuse opponents of trying to score points because it discredits their actions and means that you do not have to take their claims seriously. A person from the political centre made the interesting, but unsubstantiated, claim that 'nationalists are generally more politicised and shrewd than unionists and they can often protest to score points.' He went on to argue that concessions made to this kind of demand leads to farther demands.

We also need to consider responses to symbols. We have seen that most people will respect national symbols even when they do not like them, but there are alternative behaviours which can be associated with motivations which range from making a personal statement to insulting the other group through its symbols. A typical confrontational response is to act in a rowdy and insulting way with the aim of annoying or provoking opponents. For example, football supporters will often whistle and try to drown out the national anthem of the opposing team, though in the context of a large crowd it may signify nothing more than unruly high spirits.

An alternative response is to make a public protest in a dignified and formal way, perhaps by refusing to stand or by making some sign of protest. Small examples we have already noted are standing with head bowed during the anthem. This is normally an act of self expression by someone for whom symbols are important, but who is critical of the symbol and the state it represents. The protest is not intended to be provocative, but in many cases it is not meant to be ignored either. A third option is to quietly avoid the situation, by arriving late or slipping away early. This is the action of someone who does not feel comfortable with the symbol but at the same time they are not wanting to make a public sign of disapproval. They are rather like the reverse of those people who abstain from flying their flag if it is going to cause conflict. By not being present they avoid being compromised.

It is more difficult to interpret these strategies, particularly avoiding the situation, because other pressures may influence behaviour. We were told one story of a group of supporters of Linfield Football Club who would be natural confronters. They went to see their team play at Waterford in a European competition. The night before the match they spent in a bar, and enjoyed the company of the locals in spite of different religious, political and football allegiances. Towards the end of the evening one of the locals said to them that the bar would soon be closing and they would be singing 'The Soldier's Song'. He was warning them so that they could decide what to do. They left rather than stand up and offend their own feelings, or sit down and offend the company. A few minutes later they all met up again outside to find what else Waterford had to offer. Both groups worked together to avoid a confrontation and spoil the party.

The biggest pressure to conform comes from the public disapproval of others present which can even take the form of physical violence. This brings us to the question of reactions to insults. The most common response was given by one unionist, who accepts grudgingly Irish symbols: 'When people do not stand up [for 'The Queen'] I feel a mixture of sadness and anger at their lack of courtesy. But this anger would not become personal violence.' However confronters would take much more direct action. It is revealing and perhaps paradoxical that they themselves will ignore the anthem and believe that it is more important to turn their attention on the individual who is not willing to join in the ritual. People who were brave or foolhardy enough to remain seated in such company during the national anthem have been manhandled and forced to stand up. One person to whom this happened in the middle of a strongly loyalist crowd at the Irish Cup final said he stood up because otherwise he knew he would have received a worse beating. Even those who would normally be confrontational will avoid such situation, but if they are caught unawares they will usually conform. Those who do not accept others' rights to express their identity by sitting are themselves acting in a confrontational way.

This brief analysis demonstrates that we can infer something about people's motivation from the way they behave, but it is difficult to be precise, and often they have mixed motives. We have been able to distinguish behaviour which is a personal form of self expression with no intended implications for others, secondly behaviour which is making a statement to others but is not meant to provoke a response, and thirdly behaviour which is clearly intended to annoy and provoke a reaction from opponents.

This leads us to consider the concept of offence and provocation. In terms of fairness and good order there is a desire to draw a line between acceptable and unacceptable behaviour. One suggestion is that behaviour which offends and annoys should not be allowed. We will return to this issue when we discuss specific situations, but at this point there are a number of general points which need to be noted. Unionists were particularly unhappy with this suggestion. One said 'not accepting normal conventions of respect for symbols is a political statement' in the same way as displaying symbols can be a political statement. Another thought that 'there are a lot of Catholics who are waiting to be offended to make a point out of it.' He also made an interesting if rather elliptical point: 'the fact that you are annoyed or offended is as unforgivable as annoying or offending.' In other words if something is harmless it is wrong to take offence, and that reaction may in itself be offensive.

The right not to be offended is a difficult concept to defend, as everyone is likely to be offended by something, and sometimes causing offence is justified because we need to be shocked out of our complacent about some social problem such as homelessness or AIDS. We often disapprove of other people's behaviour, and may be offended by it. But this in itself is not sufficient justification for curtailing the behaviour. Pornography and questions of good taste are other areas where this debate arises. Card (1987, p51) quotes Lord Monson making this point in the House of Lords debates on the English Public Order Act: 'People can be distressed by what other people consider to be quite trivial matters. A person of puritanical disposition might be distressed by someone wearing a rude T-shirt.' There needs to be additional grounds before behaviour should be curtailed by law. One unionist acknowledged that 'very often we can understand what offends us but not what offends other people. I accept that some nationalists might be offended by us, but cannot know or feel when those occasions might be.'

We therefore need a more objective test of what constitutes unacceptable behaviour. We are satisfied that the distinction can be based on the principle of not imposing on the free will of others and not inciting others to do so. In simple terms this means unacceptable behaviour would include imposing symbols on others; invading with symbols the personal and communal space of others; making people conform with specific practices; assuming and expecting consent and approval of specific practices; limiting people's freedom of movement or expression because of the way specific practices take place; or causing loss or damage to people who do not conform to specific practices. It is evident that this is a behavioural test, and does not attempt to place limits on attitudes in themselves, no matter how reprehensible they may seem.

In the following chapters we shall look at the impact of these different behaviours and approaches as they operate in social situations, and attempt to assess how far they have been or need to be regulated. But in order to understand what is happening we need to consider the political context, and in particular the difference in unionists and nationalist perceptions of the issues.

Symmetry and Asymmetry in Unionist and Nationalist Attitudes

As we examine attitudes towards flags and anthems, it becomes apparent that the issues are significantly different for unionists and nationalists in a number of ways. It is important to take account of these differences as they help to explain how symbols are used and why people react to them the way they do. It is particularly important to put these attitudes into the political context of Northern Ireland. Otherwise it is difficult to understand the intensity of some of the reactions.

Power and Sovereignty

A central aspect of conflict is about power, and national symbols themselves make a statement about power. The ability of a group to express itself through its symbols is a test of the power balance between the groups. This explains a group's reluctance to accept the presence of the other group's symbols or to forego opportunities to use its own symbols. Opposing groups will be aware of this and will understand what the other group is trying to do.

Equally important in the Northern Ireland situation, is the question of sovereignty, and national symbols also give important messages about sovereignty. They are a reminder of where sovereignty lies by their use in formal ceremonies, and they give a legitimacy to the exercise of sovereignty because of the shared international conventions about the way symbols should be treated. For example, if the national anthem of a state is played at a public event and all those present show respect for it, that seems to express an acceptance of the authority of the state. On the other hand as one unionist politician put it, 'attacking the flag is an attack on sovereignty. As the conflict is about ownership of [the land], flags are contentious. They are not unimportant symbols.' Speaking of the Tricolour he said that the reason people fly it and the reason it is resented is because it is 'a flag of sovereignty.'

Unionists feel that it is in their interests that British sovereignty is retained and the conflict is focused on the issue of sovereignty. Therefore it is important for them that displays of sovereignty, including playing 'The Queen' and flying the flag, are maintained. They argue that the question of sovereignty is above party politics, and on that account the flag, as the emblem of the state, represents the people as a whole and is also above politics. They want the British national symbols to be treated more favourably than the symbols of other states, as is common practice with the national flag in most parts of the world. They expect the British government to assert its own sovereignty, and when the British Government fails to do this they feel insecure and betrayed. They want strong measures to be taken against any attempt to challenge the exercise of British sovereignty.

Nationalists do not want to give greater legitimacy to the exercise of sovereignty by the British government, even if they do not actively oppose it. They would therefore prefer not to focus on the display of British symbols as the expression of British sovereignty, but as the expression of unionist triumphalism. They would prefer to locate the conflict in the issue of power between the two communities. One expression of this is the effort over the years to equalise the right of each community to display its symbols, and to put equal restrictions on each community to limit the use of its symbols. The goal is to make all symbols equal, so that none have special legitimacy, nor can they confer special legitimacy on those who use them. It was argued that the unionists' use of symbols has created the nationalist response. One nationalist said that unionists have grabbed the symbols of the state and it is not surprising that their political opponents have used the symbols of 'a foreign power'. Republicans would of course go farther and argue that the British state and British symbols are illegitimate and therefore the Irish state, with its attendant symbols, should be the only legitimate authority throughout Ireland.

We can see from this analysis that unionists and nationalists are in fact interpreting the nature of the issues in quite different ways. At the same time that they are disagreeing over practical problems and demands, they are also trying to establishing their own version of the nature of the issues. Sometimes each side seems to be unaware that the argument is proceeding on both levels, so that there is no point of contact. Sometimes it seems to suit one or other side to blur the distinctions because it seems to give them an advantage to do so. However, if there is to be a resolution of this and the more fundamental problems on a basis which is acceptable to all sides, it will be necessary to acknowledge and deal with the different interpretations of the issues.

Privilege and Equality

Nationalists and unionists have very different perceptions about the need for change. Unionists' symbols held a privileged position in the past. They were the symbols of the dominant group. As we have seen neutral symbols like the red hand became identified with the state and the unionist community. Some of them had legal protection, while the symbols of other traditions were likely to be removed and the people responsible were prosecuted. Any change will inevitably lead to a reduction in the privileges of

unionists. Some changes will occur anyway, simply because of developments in social patterns, but in the circumstances of Northern Ireland,
unionists will see any change as an attack on their community. Loyalists told
us that opposition to national symbols is political and therefore concessions
are appeasement. But they also recognised that there is 'a drift away' from
flags and anthem.

We have seen that the national anthem is now seldom played at social
functions in England, simply because it seems out of place to many people
as society becomes more informal. In Northern Ireland unionists resist such
changes because they appear to undermine the union with Great Britain.

Changes also occur in the nature of symbols. Fashions in graphic design
change at frequent intervals, to give the appearance of freshness and progressiveness in the organisations and products associated with them. The
modern trend is for more angular and simplified symbols, and the traditional emblems do not lend themselves easily to this style. It is interesting
that neither the Northern or Southern campaigns to buy local products
(Product of Northern Ireland or PONI and Guaranteed Irish) have used
logos derived from traditional symbols.

The red hand of Ulster was removed from the logo of the bus company by
the Government of Northern Ireland at the end of the 1960s before the
present conflict intensified. The independent television company, Ulster
Television or UTV, has recently changed its corporate image. It has decided
to emphasise the initials UTV and particularly the initial 'U', instead of the
full name. Does this mean that they are diminishing the connection with
Ulster? The Northern Ireland Tourist Board has recently replaced its rather
traditional logo of the shamrock and red hand for a more modern geometrical design. In the process the red hand has been lost. The new logo is a green
hexagon representing the Giants Causeway and the land, and a white
simplified shamrock shape. There is an acknowledgement of the red hand in
that one leaf of the shamrock is red. Does the removal of the red hand
suggest that the Northern Ireland Tourist Board is losing its connection to
Northern Ireland, and is preparing to merger with Bord Failte, the tourist
agency in the Republic of Ireland?

It is important to understand that many loyalists believe the answer to
these questions must be yes. They connect this with the limitations which
have been put on their flags in the work place and in public parades and it
should not be surprising that they feel that their whole culture is under real
attack. Loyalists say that there are two sides to the conflict but only one is
being asked to remove its symbols and accept the symbols of their opponents. The result, they say, is feelings of fear, isolation, hopeless, bewilder-
ment, confusion and a sense of loss like a death which you cannot bury.
They quote a phrase used by ATQ Stewart 'a deadly silence which speaks',
and warn the end result could be violence. Not all unionists would share
many of these sentiments.

At the same time nationalists have experienced the changes very differently. They are pleased to find limitations placed on unionist displays, partly
because they feel that some curtailment was justified, but many nationalists

take a certain pleasure in seeing unionists having to make concessions. Many feel there is still some way to go, especially in the area of street parades. Nationalists have also seen a relaxation in the restrictions on Irish symbols though discretion and the demands of public order mean that they can not be displayed in every situation.

This is not to say that the situation with regard to flags and anthems should have remained as it was. But it is important to understand the profound impact of the new situation, different in each community. It is also important that those who are resistant to change should recognise the important part played by the unstoppable shifts in social norms and customs, which are quite separate from the conflict between unionists and nationalists. It is one reason why nationalists can be more relaxed about national symbols while it is an intense issue for unionists. But there is probably more to it than that.

Intensity of Feeling

We were often told that flags and anthems were much more important to unionists than nationalists. One loyalist said that you could see this from the flag pole holders outside homes in Protestant areas, and it is possible to chart population shifts by identifying the Catholic neighbourhood where flag pole holders are common. The houses were once occupied by Protestant. Another loyalist said that this difference was noticeable during the 1981 hunger strike, because he thought nationalists had been very inefficient at putting out flags through lack of practice. Loyalists are much more competent at this job.

Even in the days when republicans were fighting to achieve Irish independence, they seemed rather casual in their approach to flags, according to one report (Caulfield, 1963, p23). It would appear that after James Connolly, Patrick Pearse and the others had taken over the General Post Office they found they had no flag with them. Sean T. O'Kelly, later to become President of Ireland, was hanging about waiting for instructions:

'Are you busy, Sean?' shouted James Connolly.
'No, not at all,' replied O'Kelly hopefully.
'Well, will you go to Liberty Hall and bring me back a couple of flags?'
'Glad to,' said O'Kelly, and after being instructed where to find them, trotted off.
He returned shortly, carrying the traditional green flag of Ireland and the Sinn Féin Tricolour of green, white and orange.'

The green flag carried a harp and was presumably the same one that Connolly had flown over Liberty Hall a few days before on Palm Sunday, when his followers paraded, and presumably he saw it as the national flag. It is interesting though fruitless to speculate that if O'Kelly had not found the Tricolour and brought it back to fly over the GPO, it might not have become the national flag. Hayes-McCoy (1979, p209) quotes other sources which tell a similar story, including a report Kelly later gave to the *Irish Press* (12.7.1961) that Connolly said they had forgotten 'something very important'. This comment suggests that they did take the flags seriously, but none the less they still forgot them.

The Tricolour has never been common in workplaces even where the work force was overwhelmingly nationalist. Loftus (1994) comments on the poor display at Easter parades in West Belfast and elsewhere. Flags are a recurring motif in loyalist murals. There are very few which do not incorporate some emblem. Republican murals often have no flags in them at all. A republican suggested that this was because flags can only convey a very simplistic message, and republicans want to communicate more complex messages about their analysis of the situation. In the same way as we might try to judge a person's politics from the flag he possesses, it is tempting to try to interpret the politics behind loyalist wall murals, by studying the flags which have been included and those which have been left out, or placed in a subsidiary position, somewhat in the manner of old Kremlin watchers who assessed the status of Communist party leaders from the order in which they stood on Lenin's tomb in Red Square during the May Day parade. Certainly the painter has probably made a more conscious choice than the person buying a flag in a shop. A tour of wall murals, or a perusal of Bill Rolston's (1992) book on the subject, can allow the observer to judge how successful each group has been in achieving its aim, but there is no doubt that, for what ever reason, flags are more common in loyalist murals.

Another explanation, from a republican, is that symbols are associated with fascist and right wing nationalist groups and they want to be more balanced in the way they used them. This view is similar to a comment of Belinda Loftus (1994): 'republicans repeatedly emphasise that ... military regalia is something alien to Irish nationalists, who see it as part of elitist British tradition. This claim is readily endorsed by the nature of the Easter parades. Apart from the colour party, the guard of honour and the generally not very numerous bands, nearly all those attending display a single emblem. This is generally a paper Easter lily.' nevertheless the republican movement uses symbols because they know that they are helpful in motivating support.

One loyalist suggested that the restriction on flying the Tricolour until the 1980s meant that nationalists had little opportunity to fly it or develop customs and practices associated with it. The opposite might well have been the case. Once it was possible to fly it more openly, it might have been used with great enthusiasm. Loftus (1994) appears to lean towards the view that nationalists did not feel free to make public displays: 'the numerical dominance of the Protestants in [Northern Ireland], and the political stances taken by its members, have made it difficult for nationalists to construct such public political imagery as their loyalist counterparts, and has encouraged them to develop private or oblique emblems situated in the privacy of the home.' On the other hand she goes on to say that 'this imbalance in access to the public arena must not be over-emphasised. Since the 1870s the nationalists in Northern Ireland have held fairly regular parades of varying sizes, albeit sometimes with great difficulty.'

Whatever the reason, the more relaxed stance of nationalists compared to the greater intensity of unionist feeling influences how successfully each community is able to handle disputes when they arise. However it does not follow that nationalists do not care about the things which the symbols represent. We would argue that they do care very deeply about identity, but in general they express it in a different way which creates another asymmetry between the communities.

Expressing identity
For many unionists the sense of self is very closely bound up with self expression. For many nationalists the sense of identity exists whether it is expressed or not. In any case there are many ways that Irish identity can be expressed, including identification with the wider Irish community, the language, the culture, the Church in Ireland, and so on. Loftus (1994) suggests that

> much of the traditional nationalist imagery in Northern Ireland is displayed not in the public thoroughfare but within the privacy of the home or the prison cell. There can be found the framed copies of the proclamation of the Irish Republic at Easter 1916, the political posters, badges and greetings cards, the hand-crafted emblems made by republican internees, the paintings, calendar photographs and postcards of wild Irish scenery, the illustrated books celebrating Ireland's national identity, and the highly emblematic covers used to enclose records of republican songs and traditional Irish music.

If this analysis is correct it would suggests that flags and anthems are less important to nationalists than unionists, and this creates another asymmetry. But we would suggest that this is not a completely satisfactory explanation. We would suggest that flags and emblems are important for each community, but this is expressed in different ways. Nationalists do not appear very concerned about using their own symbols, but they are sensitive to anything which denies that they are legitimate, as happened in the past with the restriction on flying the Tricolour in Northern Ireland. Many nationalists are also unhappy with any action which would seem to undermine their symbols, as was evident in the strength of the reactions to proposals to change the words of the Irish national anthem. The other side of the coin is their resentment at any action which seems to impose British and unionist symbols.

In contrast it is important for unionists to be able to display their symbols in public, and have them accepted by everyone. Consequently treating both communities equally will not necessarily satisfy everyone and unionists in particular are likely to feel dissatisfied.

Rolston (1992) helps to explain the unionist attitude when he says that they have a civic culture, and share the triumphalism of civic displays in other communities. In his turn, Bell (1990, 20) provides an important insight into unionist perspectives:

In reality the Loyalist sense of identity achieves its positive valency (that is, being more than simply non-Irishness) in being actively paraded. That identity *is* dependent on the rehearsed myths, ritualized practices, and confrontations of the marching season. Indeed these symbolic practices in which the young play such a significant part today – the bonfires, the painting of kerbs, the erection of flags, arches and bunting, the marching bands and the parades themselves – are the specific means by which an exclusive Protestant identity is represented and renewed in the loyalist mind. Here primarily an embodied ideology is at work. It is the sound of the Lambeg drum rather than the resonance of political ideology which brings tears to the eyes of a Loyalist.

The sound of the anthem and the sight of the flag will have the same effect. Unionist identity needs to be expressed in order to exist fully.

Common perspectives

In conclusion, each community relates to the issues in quite different ways. But we were very struck how in other ways nationalist and unionist feelings about flags and anthems mirror each other.

Even when people say that symbols are not important, from both sides we heard comments that indicated an emotional response to national symbols – expressions like a 'wee surge of pride' or a 'tingle in the spine.' Both nationalists and unionists associated flags with identity. They also agree that there are important issues about sovereignty and control involved in disputes about flags and anthems, which is why the disputes are not ignored.

Comments were made on both sides of the sectarian divide which put limits on how far people should go in asserting their claims in relation to national symbols. A unionist talking about the removal of flags from the work place said that he would encourage employers to turn a blind eye, but he would not want them to fall foul of the law. A republican, talking about flag days, said that he would encourage the manager of a local government office not to fly the flag, but said he would understand if he said he did not like the flag but would lose his job if he did not fly it. The republican added in parenthesis that this would not stop him trying to remove it himself.

The political representatives of both communities are reluctant to change the symbols they like, but ask for change in symbols they do not like. Nationalists think the symbols of Northern Ireland are not acceptable, and if new institutions were established in Northern Ireland it would be necessary to identify new symbols with which the whole community could identify. Unionists think this is an irrelevant issue. However unionists recognise the importance of new symbols for Ireland if some degree of rapprochement between the North and South of Ireland is to be achieved, and nationalists were very resistant to such changes. Both are concerned that a minority and its symbols are in danger of becoming submerged by the majority community, but only when they were talking of a situation in which they themselves might be the minority: Northern Ireland for nationalists and Ireland for unionists. One might assume the same arguments would apply in both cases.

Each community found it hard to understand that their symbols caused problems for the other community, but were very clear that they did not feel comfortable with their opponents symbols. One loyalist said it was like trying on another person's coat. It does not fit. But the other side of that image is also true. The loyalist's coat may be uncomfortable on a nationalist.

It was very striking that each side could not see that they were often complaining about behaviour by the other community which was similar to how they themselves behaved or wanted to behave. Both claimed that there needed to be a sense of proportion in the way flags and anthems were used, but only thought the other community were excessive in their practices. For example nationalists argued that it was excessive to sing 'The Queen' at a golf club dinner, but that it was acceptable for 'The Soldier's Song' to be played at a Gaelic football match.

Each community accused the other of playing politics with symbols and could not appreciate that their behaviour might be a genuine expression of identity. Attempts to limit the use of British symbols was 'a well orchestrated campaign by nationalists.' For nationalists Orange parades are 'triumphalist', while for unionists the symbols at Gaelic games are 'a threat'. This is an example of a key process in the maintenance of conflict: the ability to understand one's own behaviour as self expression and opponents' behaviour as a false use of symbols for political purposes. It is a recurring feature in all the dimensions of the Northern Ireland situation and of many other inter-community conflicts. It allows us to ignore the legitimate aspirations and claims of our opponents and to be complacent about the darker hegemonic tendencies in ourselves.

To avoid this pattern we need to understand more clearly all motivations and inter-actions which are present in disputes and controversies. Having provided a context and framework within which issues involving flags and emblems can be understand, we will now look at how symbols are actually handled by social institutions and by individuals in their everyday life in the community.

Notes

1 Rosary beads, from the Irish *paidrín*.

CHAPTER 3

Special Occasions and Social Institutions

They left before the anthem,
out of seats and up the aisles
the lights still down, in glow
Johnston Kirkpatrick: 'Catholics'

It may be arbitrary to divide the situations we shall discuss into those which concern the institutions of society and those which occur in everyday life in the community, as one merges into the other. However the circumstances in each case are often different. Social institutions are important because they set the standards which influence social norms. This is true in relation to flags and more importantly in a general sense. 'Social interests . . . have to be nurtured through collective associations and shared sentiment before they can be mobilised in the formal political arena.' (Sugden and Bairner, 1992, p44). Groups with political interests are very aware of this truth, regardless of which side of the argument they are on, and the practices of institutions are of great interest to them.

Social institutions normally use flags and anthems in formal and ceremonial situations, while in the community at large the situation is much more fluid. This chapter is also an appropriate place to discuss the use of flags and anthems on special occasions in general since these functions are organised by social institutions who also make the decision that they should be designated as special. Debate about whether an occasion warrants flags and anthems often hides an underlying disagreement between those who accept and those who reject the symbols in question. If we want to incorporate the symbols we will say that the occasion is special. If we are against the symbols we may say the specific situation is not sufficiently special to warrant flags or anthems.

A number of questions recur as we consider the practices of different institutions. On what basis do they decide when they will use flags and anthems? Is it possible to identify how and by whom decisions are made and practice evolves? Often influential individuals in institutions may apply one set of standards for the organisation and another for their private life. We want to understand the reasons for this discrepancy and its consequences.

Flags are flown and the anthem is played when royalty is present in the United Kingdom and when the President is present in Ireland. Flags are also flown on designated flag days and we will comment briefly on this practice in the next sub-section. But the situations which we will give most attention too are sport, entertainment, the church and political organisations and some other specific issues.

Flag Days

Flag Days and Government buildings
In most countries flags are flown on a set of special days. In Northern Ireland these are the same days as in Great Britain, with a few significant exceptions. The protocol which governs the selection of flag days, as with other aspects of the protocol on flags and anthems, originates with the monarch. The Lord Chamberlain's Office within the Royal Household advises the Department of National Heritage which then informs other departments and public bodies of the days and the procedures to follow.

The Northern Ireland Office in turn passes on this information to relevant bodies in Northern Ireland. It will be noted that all the days are associated with the Royal family, apart from the Patron Saint's Day in each country, Commonwealth Day and Remembrance Day. This is in line with the identification of the flag with the monarch, which we have discussed already. It means a lot to unionists, who support the monarchy and the British state. But the practice has little meaning for those who have no interest in the monarchy, and it annoys them by reminding them of a flag, a monarch and a state they do not like, or to which they are hostile, and which they feel has been imposed upon them. One example was mentioned of unionists not following the wishes of the monarch. When the last pope died, the Queen expressed the wish that flags should be flown at half mast, but at least one unionist council refused to comply. It was suggested by a supporter of the Alliance Party that they were acting inconsistently.

It should also be noted that the Northern Ireland list has included some additional days. It is flown on the main religious festivals and New Year's Day which does not seem particularly contentious. It is also flown on the Twelfth of July which is an important day for the unionist community, but is something with which the nationalist community cannot identify, and therefore appears to be a sectional decision in their eyes.

Properties which are owned and used by Government bodies follow the list of days laid down, and there is a copy of the guidelines in most buildings. In the past some properties carried flags throughout the year, but this practice has stopped. In some cases it was thought flying the flag at all times appeared to identify the department too closely with one section of the community. It is interesting therefore to note that we discovered some police stations which fly the flag at times other than designated flag days. They seem to be exclusively in nationalist areas, though the practice seemed to be declining even during the short period of our observation. Is there some connection between the location of these police station in nationalist areas and the decision to fly the flag more often than elsewhere? Could it be intended to make some kind of statement to the local community? One station had a very tall and prominent flag pole compared to stations in unionist and city centre areas.

Flags, Local Authorities and Other Public Bodies
Other organisations including public boards and local authorities make their own regulations about flying flags. One large institution, with property in a number of locations, has only a flag pole at its main building. Its representative said 'it would be a waste of money to install more.' The universities use the flag sparingly. Queen's University flies its own flag apart from Remembrance Day when it flies a Union flag. The University of Ulster flies the Union flag at the Coleraine campus on five days in the year.

In our survey two health and social services boards replied, saying they flew flags on the designated days. One only puts flags on its hospitals. It is not clear why only hospitals follow this practice, but it could date back to the practice of the Northern Ireland Hospitals Authority.

Shortly after it was formed one education and library board formally adopted the practice of the former County Education Committee that the flag should be flown at all controlled schools[1] and institutions of further education on all days when the school is in operation. The instruction also advised 'should a school not possess a flag or the necessary equipment for flying one, the Principal should so inform the Schools Branch [at Board headquarters]. The Branch will make good the deficiency.' Problems could have arisen for controlled schools in a contentious location, but we are not aware that any trouble has ever occurred. The Board still follows this practice, but it has not been adopted by any other board.

Eight local authorities responded to the questionnaire. One respondent was not absolutely clear on this point but seemed to indicate that no flags are flown. One council flies the Union flag at all times from its four main buildings. Five councils display the national flag on flag days, three at headquarters and two also on other buildings. One of the latter also flies it all the year round at headquarters on the grounds of problems of access to get it down. These councils have a range of political complexion from strongly unionist to balanced. None were clearly nationalist.

Apart from the survey, council practices can be observed. At least two councils have erected flag poles in central locations in the Council area and the Union flag is flown at all times. We do not know if they are taken down at dusk as protocol would demand. One council is strongly unionist but in the other the balance shifted to nationalists at the 1993 election, but interestingly the practice has not changed.

There is a trend for councils to create their own flags and emblems. This is part of the practice of developing a corporate image, which we discussed in the last chapter, and as we saw then it can have the effect of reducing the use of the national flag, even though this may not be the primary intention. One council in the survey flies the council flag, apart from the days when the Union flag is flown, and another council flies it at all times.

Derry City Council made interesting but unsuccessful attempts to resolve conflict over the flag. The nationalist majority wanted to adopted a new flag instead of the Union flag, but the unionist councillors opposed this. One suggested alternative was the Crimson flag of the city. This has strong unionist associations as it was the flag flown by the inhabitants during the siege in 1688–9 (Stewart 1977, p66). Nevertheless it was acceptable to the nationalist councillors because it was not considered as colonial as the Union flag. But for some unionists the removal of the Union flag was the fundamental issue, because it suggested that the link with Great Britain was being weakened. They would not consider any alternative, including a unionist symbol. The problem was never resolved because a committee recommended that the crimson flag should be used, but it was referred back at committee. The council still flies no flags on council property.

The councils in the survey also gave information about other practices. Four councils play the national anthem at formal occasions, but this appears to be very infrequent. They gave examples which included a Royal visit and the Freedom of the Borough ceremony. One of them also observes the Loyal Toast at all civic functions.

Sports

We have seen in chapter 1 that throughout the world sport is often drawn into politics and the use of flags and anthems provides many opportunities for groups to use sport for political purposes. In Ireland too, sport is often thought to be a potential arena for controversy. Some sports are, of course, played by only one section of the community, and in others individual clubs are segregated along sectarian lines (Sugden, 1993), and so there is often no internal dispute about flags and anthems among members. Nevertheless many sporting bodies try to avoid the use of symbols which may possibly causing offence.

Different considerations apply, depending on whether the sport is organised on an all-Ireland or a Northern Ireland basis. In the former case club and county competitions may take place throughout Ireland and there is often a system of matches between the four provinces. For these purposes the Ulster team represents the traditional nine provinces. If a flag is required at this level, there is no obvious alternative to the provincial flag, and there is no obvious anthem. At international level when the team represents the whole island, some sports use 'The Soldier's Song' as an anthem and fly the tricolour, but there are a number of alternative flags which teams may use if they feel it will make people feel more included. Most popular seems to be Saint Patrick's Cross or a flag comprising the emblems of the four provinces. There is no obvious alternative song.

When the sport is organised on a purely Northern Ireland basis the Ulster flag or the Union flag is sometimes used, and both may be used together. The Ulster provincial flag might appear to be another option, though more correctly it represents the whole nine-county province. Where an anthem is required, 'The Queen' is sometimes played, but in competitions involving Scotland, England and Wales, the Union flag and 'The Queen' are not distinctive to Northern Ireland. The most widely used alternative song is 'The Derry or Londonderry Air'.

The Empire Games (later the Commonwealth Games) team were the first group to adopt the Derry or Londonderry Air. Although it was chosen from the first Games in 1938, Northern Ireland did not win a gold medal until 1954, when it was played for the first time at Vancouver to mark Thelma Hopkin's success in the high jump. It was chosen as a tune which was identifiable with the country, and the version used is by the 55th Old Boy's Silver Band.

The tune has only been changed once, for the 1962 Games. They won no medals and had no opportunity to try out the replacement tune. The Londonderry Air may be lucky. But the Commonwealth Games Committee are often asked about changing the tune. Unionists have asked why they do not play 'The Queen'. But the Committee stress that it is a victory tune, and is not an alternative national anthem. In the past 'The Queen' was shared by many of the countries and they all, including England, chose an alternative. Others have commented that, as a love song, the words are not appropriate, but it is chosen as a tune not a song. As a victory tune the words are not relevant and they are not normally sung, apart from the celebrated occasion in Auckland 1990 after Wayne McCullough had won a gold medal. For the only time in the entire Games the sound equipment broke down. However, the person responsible for playing the appropriate tune stepped into the breach. By coincidence he was a native of Northern Ireland, and knew the words. Although it is not intended that the words should be sung, on many occasions spectators and competitors will sing along.

Many individual sporting bodies in Northern Ireland have since adopted the tune. In fact they often take the Commonwealth Games Committee's tape because they forget to organise one for themselves. The Ulster Games Federation recently took another approach when they had a tune written specially for them by Phil Coulter.

There are thus a wide variety of possibilities, and a wide variety of practice. Thirteen sporting bodies returned the survey questionnaire, giving information on their practice on flags and anthems. One other organisation did not complete the questionnaire, but they responded by letter, giving their policy, and they gave enough information to be included here. One organisation was a non-competitive sport and their responses are not included in the following statistics, which deal with formal competitive events. Of the twelve organisations which supplied information, seven are organised on an all-Ireland basis, four on a Northern Ireland basis, and one is a branch of a British organisation.

Of the twelve bodies which described their practice, three flew no flags. Very few used the official national flags. The member clubs of one organisation flew the national flag at their grounds together with the flags of the competing teams. Two sports use the flags of the competing nations, but did not make it clear what those flags are. In the case of one sport which has separate organisations for each part of Ireland, the Northern body flies the flags of competing teams at internationals, but they have an arrangement with its opposite organisation in the Republic of Ireland that at matches between them only the home flag is flown.

A number of organisations use flags associated with the provincial emblems. Two have chosen the Provinces flag, while a third uses their own flag which incorporates the shields of the four provinces, with the shamrock added. One flies the four provincial flags and its own association flag at inter-provincial competitions. The competitors also wear the provincial emblem on their sweaters. Finally one has created a flag which may be unique, a Saint Patrick's Cross, with a shamrock added in the middle, and it is flown alongside the association flag.

This small sample supports the view that most sports avoid the national flags, while some choose flags which have Irish references but are deemed to be more unifying and less controversial. They are even less likely to use national anthems. Eight use no songs at all. In the case of one sport the European Union has laid down the policy that national anthems should not be used. One plays the anthem of the winning team. Another played the national anthem when they had an association dinner, but this function no longer happened. Of the two which use alternative songs in international competition, one has the novel practice of selecting a different song for each tournament. The competitors then sing these songs as they enter the arena at the opening ceremony. The other takes part in regular competitions with England, Scotland and Wales, and they use the songs which are usually associated with the four countries.

Individual sportsmen and women seldom find the issue of flags a problem. The manager of the 1987 Rugby World Cup side could not remember what tune was the team's theme. There are what look like apparent anomalies from the outside, but they are taken for granted by those who know the sport. Northerners play in and sometimes captain the Irish rugby side. Wayne McCullough, from a loyalist area of Belfast carried the Irish Tricolour at the opening ceremony for the 1988 Olympic Games. Mary Peter, although born in England, has come to personify the best in Northern Ireland athletics, and perhaps Northern Irish sport in general. She is very proud to have represented her country and to bring fame to Northern Ireland, but wonders if her English heritage makes her more tolerant of other flags and anthems.

National symbols are used most widely in the main spectator sports, association football, rugby and Gaelic games. The organisers regularly use national flags and anthems in a ceremonial way, perhaps because the high level of popular interest makes their major events truly national occasions. The presence of large numbers of supporters has other important implications. To support their team they carry flags, often national flags inscribed with slogans. Some sportsmen and women do not like this practice as strictly speaking writing on a flag is one way of defacing it. Opposition to opponents may be played out by waving the flags and colours, and singing team songs or patriotic anthems. With the tradition of male voice choirs in the valleys, the Welsh rugby supporters are thought to intimidate opponents by the power and quality of their singing of hymns and songs such as 'Land of our

Fathers'. The sporting authorities cannot control closely the flags which the supporters chose to carry and the songs they sing, unless they are breaking the law (and even then in a crowd of thousands there may be little they can do which will not exacerbate the situation). In a sport which attracts few spectators they can choose to fly the Saint Patrick's Cross for example, and no spectator is likely to bring a flag. In a sport with a mass following, such as rugby, the authorities might decide not to fly the Tricolour, but it seems highly unlikely that the supporters will stop bringing Tricolours to the games.

Gaelic games
Of all sports, Gaelic games put the greatest emphasis on national symbols, and since they have never recognised the partition of Ireland, these symbols are the Tricolour and 'The Soldier's Song' in all parts of Ireland. The rule book of the Gaelic Athletic Association (GAA), the governing body of Gaelic games, is quite specific in saying that the flag should be flown and the anthem played at all matches. Often Tricolours will be prominently mounted on the road near the ground and create a rather festive air. It is preferred that a band should be present to play the anthem, but it is accepted that sometimes a recording may be inevitable. It is very seldom that these rules will not be followed, and then, it would only be at the most minor matches. The corollary of this high level of respect for the national flag is discouragement of its use as a banner of team support. In any case the flag is shared by all the teams. At county matches the county colours are evident, and as teams progress in the provincial and national tournaments their colours are widely displayed throughout the county.

People involved in Gaelic games take the use of symbols so much for granted that they find it hard to explain why the flag and anthem play such an important part in their activities. They say 'Gaelic games are part of the national culture' and 'they support Irish custom.' which restates the outlook of the GAA without explaining it. The GAA is more than a sporting body, and is also committed to nation building and the preservation of Irish culture, and 'it is in this regard that it must be seen as a powerful player in the politics of Northern Ireland (Sugden and Bairner, 1993, p35). The Association rule book (1991) makes this quite explicit:

> The Association is a National Organisation which has as its basic aims, the strengthening of the National Identity in a 32 county Ireland, through the preservation and promotion of Gaelic Games and pastimes. The Association further seeks to achieve its objectives through the active support of Irish Culture, with a constant emphasis on the importance of the preservation of the Irish language and its greater use in the life of the Nation; and in the development of a community spirit, to foster an awareness and love of the national ideals in the people of Ireland.

Most followers of Gaelic sports would at some level support these aims, and take pride in the national flag and anthem, not just in a sporting context.

The incoming President of the Association, incidentally an Anglican from County Dublin, thinks that the flag should be flown all the year round on public buildings in the Republic, because 'it is an identity badge.' As the policy reflects the views of supporters, it has never been a source of controversy within the sport. Indeed disturbances of any kind are rare at Gaelic matches. On the contrary, it would provoke controversy if it was proposed to remove these and other nationalist aspects of the organisation. Nevertheless the Association has been sensitive to the situation in Northern Ireland and in some places the Tricolour has not been flown if it is likely to cause controversy. This is not 'appeasement' but a way to avoid 'confrontation'.

Unionists are not aware of such self-imposed limitations, and are offended by GAA practices as they understand them. They feel that sports should respect the symbols of the state as it exists. They make a connection between these practices and other GAA rules, such as the ban on participation in the sport by members of the security forces, and think that they reveal long-standing hostility to Northern Protestants. Even though the ban has been changed, the Association still operates 'within the spirit of the ban.' (Sugden and Bairner, 1993, p29). Unionists cannot accept that the GAA gets statutory funding in spite of these practices, while at the same time the Government seems to be trying to limit the use of unionist symbols.

Rugby
Rugby football provides an interesting insight into the issues. It highlights the public nature of institutions and the distinction between individual and institutional positions. The policies of the governing body are watched with interest. As recently as the beginning of 1993, there was some media controversy over the sport's policy on anthems. The governing body's approach provides an interesting model, because it has adopted clear guidelines which are designed to avoid controversy. It applies them consistently, yet it can look inconsistent in the light of other factors.

Rugby has long been used as a model of co-operation between all parts of Ireland. It has been organised on an all-Ireland basis since the Irish Rugby Football Union (IRFU) was founded in 1847. Teams from different parts of the island have played together since before partition and an all-Ireland club competition has been established in recent years. The inter-provincial championship has been a major feature of the annual calendar, and international teams represent the whole island, attracting support from North and South. There are well known unionists who are keen rugby supporters and travel freely throughout the island with their clubs and are regular spectators at internationals in Dublin. Sugden and Bairner (1993) have reviewed the histories of rugby in Ireland (Diffley, 1973 and Van Esbeck, 1974 and 1986) and conclude 'It is undeniable that the IRFU has been assiduous in its efforts to avoid political controversy.' (p58) To this end it resolved after the partition of Ireland that it would not fly national flags at its matches. In 1925 an IRFU flag was designed which would be flown instead. The way in which this policy changed is instructive of the tensions between individual preferences, the accommodation of different opinions within an organisation, and the national role of sporting institutions.

The compromise of flying no flags did not meet with everyone's approval. It was raised a number of times and in January 1932 the Connaught branch proposed that the Tricolour should be flown at international matches at the Union's ground at Lansdowne Road, Dublin. The Union affirmed its existing policy. It became a matter of debate in the press. Finally it developed into a political issue with the intervention of the Minister of External Affairs in the Dublin Government requesting a meeting with the president of the IRFU to discuss the matter. As a result in February 1932, only one month after it had confirmed its policy, the Union deciding unanimously to fly the national flag alongside the IRFU flag at all international matches at Lansdowne Road. As a corollary, the Union flag would fly at international matches at the IRFU's ground at Ravenhill in Belfast.

This has continued to be the basis of IRFU policy, that the national anthem and the national flag of the host country should be used. Informally, supporters often wave the Tricolour. The policy means that the national symbols of the Republic of Ireland are used at matches in Dublin. The IRFU explains that it does this as a mark of respect to the state where the match is being played. Often the President of the Republic attends matches and this provides another reason for playing the anthem. It is not played for the team as representative of the state. From that point of view the words are not significant and for this reason, players are instructed that while the anthem is being played they should face the box of the president of the IRFU and not the flag. As it happens this means that they are also facing the national President. The anthems of other countries are not played and this allows the IRFU to be consistent when it plays overseas and asks that no anthem is played for the Irish team.

The policy at away matches is that no flags or anthems are used for the team apart from the IRFU flag. The only exception seems to have been at the 1987 World Cup in Australia and New Zealand when 'The Londonderry/Derry Air' was the team's theme song. The next World Cup in 1991 was played in the British Isles and the IRFU was able to implement its normal policy. Host countries sometimes find it difficult to appreciate the thinking behind the policy. They want to honour the team and assume the way to do that is by playing the national anthem, not understanding the sensitivities involved. When the Irish team toured America the hosts had to be told tactfully that the tourists did not want the Irish national anthem played. Sometimes the hosts had been practising the tune and were a little disappointed and hurt, but agreed. 'The Soldier's Song' was only played once, at the final dinner. There is often an amusing side to these situations. In New York the team were assured that everything was organised for their visits and the Police Band would play the Irish anthem at the match. Again the tourists' position was explained. Next morning the organiser returned looking very pleased. He had found that the band would be able to play as an alternative 'A Nation Once Again', a song which might have been more controversial.

A national anthem or patriotic song can motivate a team. We have mentioned the impact of 'Land of Our Fathers' at matches involving the Welsh team. The Irish team has to manage without that. More generally, one IRFU officer said 'it would be nice if there was a song we all feel comfortable with', but he could not think of any existing Irish song which would be good for encouraging the team. There are no rousing Irish songs. They are all too mournful. Sammy Wilson, who, as we shall see presently, has been criticising the IRFU policy, agrees. He said the 'Londonderry Air' is melancholic and therefore 'epitomises us'.

Northern players and spectators, unionists and otherwise, have appeared to have had no problems with respecting the symbols of the Republic. We were told that the Northern Branch of the IRFU have never received direct complaints about the anthem issue, though there are occasional anonymous phone calls. Sugden and Bairner argue that the rugby fraternity are hiding their differences and 'the reality, however, is much less encouraging and one suspects that rugby's friends protest a little too much when their sport's capacity to unify is questioned.' (p54) There is no doubt that among followers of rugby there are very diverse views on political and constitutional matters. Sugden and Bairner (1993, p61) argue that rugby in Ireland operates in a rather Protestant Anglo-Irish milieu, and therefore 'the anomaly is less that northern Protestants play rugby for Ireland than that southern Catholics are willing to represent their nation'. However Sugden and Bairner may underestimate the pride of the rugby fraternity in a shared sense of an identity which transcends political borders. There is a strong social element to the organisation of the game, and in particular at home internationals. Clubs from the north travel to Dublin for the week-end, play a match against a Dublin club and stay and socialise with them. None of this helps to diffuse political issues, but it is an important demonstration that a transcendent identity is possible, and it helps to explain the acceptance of Irish symbols by Northern supporters.

The Democratic Unionist Party press officer, Sammy Wilson, raised the issue on Radio Telefis Eireann at the end of January, 1993, following a string of failures by the Irish team on the rugby field. He says he would have no problem respecting 'The Soldier's Song' in the right context. For example he accepts that it is legitimate to play it for the Republic of Ireland soccer team. But he objected to the anthem being used at rugby internationals, because the Irish rugby team represented a geographical area which was not identical with the area of the state of Ireland. He said (*Belfast Telegraph*, 27.1.1993) 'many fans in Northern Ireland feel outside the whole thing [and] should not have to go through the indignity of standing while 'The Soldiers Song' is playing.' He argued that either the flag and anthem should be dropped or else the team should be split into Republic and Northern Ireland teams.

He feels that the question of the anthem is only a symptom of a wider issue. Where two countries try to work together, the identity of the smaller does not get recognised and becomes submerged. He argues this has damaged team spirit and he claims that the success of the Ulster provincial team over the rest of Ireland in recent years can be attributed to a sense of common team spirit 'players performed better for Ulster than for Ireland, because they had a closer emotional identification with the province. Players from the north are having an emotional crisis, they identify with Ulster and when they play for Ireland they do not have the same kind of tie.' (*Belfast Telegraph*, 27.1.1993) He is satisfied that where there are separate teams for Northern Ireland and the Republic of Ireland each team should play its own national anthem. But when there is a joint team, an alternative theme should be found with which they can all identify.

Mr Wilson's comments did not receive much public backing either from the media or from followers of rugby, though he said he had privately received letters of support. The public relations officer of the Ulster Branch of the Irish Rugby Football Union, Ken Reid, responded by saying (*Belfast Telegraph*, 30.1.1993) 'It seems that Mr Wilson is insulting every Ulster player when he states that they are having 'an emotional crisis'. Nothing is further from the truth. Every rugby player would love the opportunity to play for his country. Many Ulstermen have enjoyed that honour. None has besmirched it.' The *Belfast Telegraph* (28.1.1993) in its own editorial commented that 'if only our rugby ills could be cured by singing a different song, composers would be commissioned immediately.'

Mr Wilson mentioned a number of decisions which he claimed were evidence that different standards were being applied to British and Irish symbols. One unionist rugby supporter was very dismissive of Sammy Wilson's general allegation, but he said he would be 'horrified' if it was true that different standards were being applied. He thought Northerners should be courteous to the Irish symbols, but they had the right to expect similar courtesy and they should not be subservient. It is interesting to look at the specific claims made by Mr Wilson because in each case the rules appear to have been implemented consistently but the outcomes might seem inconsistent, because the surrounding environment has changed.

He raised the question of international matches at Ravenhill, and claimed that players from the Republic of Ireland refused to leave the dressing room until after 'The Queen' was played and as a result it was dropped. The incident he is referring to was in 1954, when, according to Diffley (1973) 'the southern players held a meeting on the morning of the match and decided that they were not prepared to stand to attention before the game for the British national anthem unless the Irish anthem was also played and the Irish tricolour flown.' According to Sugden and Bairner (1993) the problem was resolved 'by a compromise arrived at by a southern IRFU committee member and the players involved who agreed to go ahead with the game, and the preceding formalities, in exchange for a promise that they would never again be expected to play international matches in Belfast.' It would appear from this account that the players were not opposing the British symbols, but were asking that the Irish symbols should be given the same courtesies.

Another version of the incident is that only a couple of players were involved and that the other players made light of it and cajoled them to get on with the game. It is also said that the players were told they would never be selected for Ireland again if they did not come out for the anthem. Which is the more accurate account? It is true that no full Irish international matches have been played at Ravenhill since that time, apart from a 1991 World Cup match between two visiting teams when their anthems were played at their request. The decision not to play future games was already being considered at the time, because the demand for larger and better stadiums with higher gate receipts meant that Ravenhill was not adequate. The players may have been told in 1954 that they should get on with the game and forget about the anthem because the issue would not arise again anyway, which is somewhat different from the idea of a compromise in the Sugden and Bairner account. Since all international matches are now played in Dublin this means that 'The Soldier's Song' and Tricolour are always used. The policy is still applied consistently, but there is never an opportunity to see what would happen if a match was now played at Ravenhill.

Mr Wilson also raised questions about the arrangements for the British Isles touring team's 1993 tour to New Zealand. The team is officially organised by the Touring Committee of the Committee of Home Unions, made up of the English, Welsh, Scottish and Irish Rugby Unions. The team is officially called the British Isles Rugby Union Tourists (BIRUT), and is informally called the Lions or British Lions. Mr Wilson believes that in deference to an Irish request it has been decided that the team should only be called the Lions, leaving out the word 'British' and that for the first time 'The Queen' will not be played at matches. He argues that if the Irish feel unrepresented by 'The Queen' in an all-British Isles team they should be sensitive to the feelings of Northerners in an all-Ireland context. The probable explanation of what has happened is a useful insight into how changes can be misperceived.

BIRUT has a policy of no anthem or flags, apart from its own flag. Normally the home team will play its anthem, which in most cases was *The Queen* as most of them were former British colonies and are members of the Commonwealth. In recent years New Zealand and Australia have decided to have their own anthems, and so for that reason 'The Queen', the old New Zealand anthem, is no longer played.

Turning to the name, British Isles Rugby Union Tourists is the only official title, and there is no policy on the informal titles. Anyone can call the team what they like. It was suggested that 'British Lions' has always been more common in Northern Ireland than elsewhere in the British Isles. It is certainly true that the colloquial names of other rugby touring sides does not include the name of the county: 'the Wallabies', not 'the Australian Wallabies', 'the Springboks', not 'the South African Springboks' and so on.

The BIRUT flag, consisting of emblems of the four participating countries on a red background, is flown in a position of prominence at the ground. But it is not used by fans. They are usually only a small part of the crowd as the matches are all played away from home, and only some of them carry flags. Those who do, carry the national flag of their choice. The majority are Union flags, but the flags of Scotland and Wales and the Tricolour of Ireland can also be seen.

Following Sammy Wilson's complaints and the initial reactions, it appears that the matter has been allowed to rest, perhaps because the Ireland team has subsequently been more successful. But it is more likely that it may have been only a concern for a small number of people. Nevertheless it is described in full because it demonstrates the kind of issues which can arise.

Association football

Association football has experienced the most direct conflict over political identity. Many express their political allegiances through the team they support, not only at international level but at club level. At club level many fans carry national flags even in internal competitions. Supporters in other countries do the same and it is not clear what message this is meant to convey. In Northern Ireland, Linfield is very clearly associated with Protestants and unionists and many supporters carry Union flags. In the past Belfast Celtic was the equivalent club for Catholics and nationalist, though in the end it withdrew from the league over sectarian issues. Cliftonville would today be the team with the strongest Catholic support.

Violence associated with football supporters is a real concern for the sport's governing bodies throughout the world, and in Ireland they are very sensitive to the danger of sectarianism provoking violence. This has not led to any concerted attempt to remove flags from the supporters. The concern is even more marked at international level although the Republic of Ireland and the Northern Ireland teams have played against each other without any serious incidents of crowd trouble. In 1978 at the first match between the teams since the beginning of the troubles, a number of supporters of Northern Ireland travelled to the match in Dublin. Supporters were not allowed to take flags into the ground. Although there has been no trouble, restrictions have been placed on the sale of tickets to the fans of the away team at more recent matches. Since there are supporters of only one team, flags are again allowed. At the match in 1993 in Dublin there was a liberal display of Tricolours. It was interesting to note that one group of Northern supporters had managed to get tickets, but they were supporting the Republic of Ireland. Like the other supporters clubs they had a large Tricolour and on it they had sown the letters 'Cliftonville Supporters Club'.

The normal ceremonial arrangements have also been modified for these games. The governing bodies of football in Northern Ireland and the Republic of Ireland have policies that the flags of both participating countries are flown at internationals and both national anthems are played. The Ireland Football Association (IFA) the governing body in Northern Ireland, display both the Union flag and the Northern Ireland flag at home matches and away from home they accept either flag as the host county decides. In matches between the two parts of Ireland, it has been agreed that only the flag and anthem of the home country are used, so as 'not to create bother and annoy'. It is quite possible that supporters would whistle or jeer while the anthem is played but it is not certain if actual violence would be the result.

Sugden and Bairner (1993, p77) make an interesting point that the Northern Ireland football team is itself a political symbol of the separate identity of Northern Ireland: 'It was a living proof that Northern Ireland was and is a separate political entity, whatever politicians in Dublin and London might claim and nationalists in the Province might aspire to.'

As with other sports those involved do not seem to find symbols so much of a problem. Desie Gorman a Catholic footballer from Dundalk plays for Linfield in spite of the pervasive symbols and expression of anti-Irish and anti-Catholic feeling from the spectators. Roy Coyle, a Protestant from east Belfast manages Derry City Football Club, the only team from Northern Ireland which plays in the League of Ireland. He has never had any problems 'because it is a sport more than anything else'. Nor did his friends in Belfast mind his move to Derry City because 'they know my love for football and wished me all the best'. He reports that spectators from other teams will wave the Irish Tricolour but this does not concern him. It is only their right, and a traditional thing. He agrees that 'a certain element' would come to football to cause trouble, but they are not a big problem in Ireland. Some people, mainly from the Protestant community, feel that Derry City joined the League of Ireland to make a political statement, but the Club is at pains to point out that this is not the case. They were turned down for re-entry to the Irish League which is made up of teams from Northern Ireland, and it was only then that they applied to join the League of Ireland. In fact at that time the chairman and the majority of the Board were all Protestants.

Boxing

Boxing is another sports organised on an all-Ireland structure, which may explain some of the unusual situations, but there appear to be more examples than in other sports, and it is also interesting as its strength comes from working class communities and the Irish Army. Wayne McCullough has already been referred to as the carrier of the Tricolour at the opening ceremony of the 1988 Olympic Games, and the only competitor at the 1990 Commonwealth Games to have a live version of the Londonderry Air played for him, albeit without rehearsal. When he won a silver medal at the 1992 Olympic Games, boxing in the Irish team, Robin Wilson was in loyalist west Belfast to gauge reactions.

It might have been thought that the 1988 tricolour affair would have wrought a political explosion on the Shankill. But Wayne's sister April said there was no trouble locally afterwards – only 'a couple of rumours' ... More robust anti-nationalist sentiments might have been anticipated in the Highfield Rangers Supporters Club around the corner from the McCullough home. But a committee member, Billy Harrison, said: 'That's a lot of crap. I never heard it mentioned'

Mrs Pickering was unfazed by the fact that McCullough wore an Irish jersey in Barcelona. 'I don't care what flag they carry. It's an achievement on its own to get to the Olympics. Sport is sport and that's final.' (*Fortnight*, September 1992)

Barry McGuigan is another of the many boxer who has worn the Republic of Ireland's colours (in the 1976 Olympics in Moscow) and the Northern Ireland vest (winning a Gold in the Commonwealth Games in 1978). In relation to the Moscow Olympics he said that 'he dreamed of standing on the rostrum, listening to the National Anthem, the medal round my neck (McGuigan, 1991, p23).

McGuigan was particularly well placed to straddle the border, coming from Clones in Cavan, one of the Ulster counties in the Republic of Ireland. Although he is from the Republic of Ireland, when he became a professional boxer, he was based in Belfast and became a symbol of Northern Ireland:

> I know that I didn't make peace, but I knew there was peace when I fought, that these boys were holding each others hands and saying 'Come on, cheer this young kid on. He's fighting for us!' I was representing them and they wanted me to prove that not everything that came out of Northern Ireland is bad. (McGuigan, 1991, p278).

From his own account it seems that he and his manager, Barney Eastwood, were aware of the possible impact of his choice of colours.

> I never set out to become a symbol. I deliberately tried not to offend anyone, and I think Barney's attitude was that he didn't want to offend them by me wearing green or fighting under a Tricolour. He was probably more concerned about it that I was. I was already going with Sandra [later to become his wife] who was a Protestant, so I had no interest in being aggressively Catholic. When Barney suggested that I wear neutral colours, I said 'Grand'. (McGuigan, 1991, p277)

It may be that keen sportsmen and women gain the main satisfaction from participating and winning. There commitment to their sport and in some cases their success give them a new perspective outside politics. It is other people who want to use sport to make political points, and supporters, who may have less opportunities for self-fulfilment, find a way to express their political identity by following their team.

Entertainment

Very few places of entertainment responded to the questionnaire, but those that did made it clear that flags and anthems are no longer an issue. One touring theatrical company said that in thirteen years of touring in all parts of Ireland, the question had never arisen at any venue they had used. This does not mean that a flag was never flown as it is possible it had not been noticed, but it would be hard not to know if an anthem was played. But it was not always like this.

The anthem was played, usually at the end of events. Television closed down with the national anthem accompanied by a piece of film of the Royal standard floating in the breeze or the Queen at the Trooping the Colours, or similar ceremonial occasion. It is said that some people stood to attention in their own homes, as shown in a well known scene from the television comedy *Till Death Us Do Part*. We are not aware of homes where this actually happened in real life. It is still played by some, but not all stations.

In the cinema a piece of film was also shown, and people often recall with amusement the times at the cinema when patrons rushed out during the credits to avoid the anthem. If they stayed they would then have to decide whether to stand to attention . The issue was not necessarily about making a political statement, but might simply be a question of catching the last bus. It was noticeable that this never caused a problem in England in the 60s and 70s because most people were happy to walk out casually during the anthem and it was not a cause of social opprobrium.

The decline of the anthem as a feature of public performance is not related to changing political attitudes. One theatre said it had been abandoned as a divisive issue, but the other responses did not refer to politic factors. In fact it was clear from one questionnaire that the cinema would still fly the Union flag if a royal visitor was in the town and that they would be totally opposed to playing any anthem other than 'The Queen'. On the other hand a theatre company which said the question had no relevance to it, is well know for taking strong political stances against the present constitutional arrangements.

The change seems more to do with a general change in cultural customs, and this is true in Britain as well as in Northern Ireland. Respect for protocol is much less than in the past and informality is preferred. We have seen that even when royalty are present at a performance, the anthem is often not played. Sometimes the anthem is played at the beginning or end of a season of performances, when there may be a gala night.

But there are also logistical reasons why the anthem is no longer played. One cinema said that it was difficult to get a piece of film for the national anthem, but also made the interesting point that the titles at the end of films are much longer, with credits for everything down to individual songs on the films soundtrack. By the time they were finished, no one would be left in the cinema. One television channel, UTV now runs twenty four hours a day so there is no appropriate time to play the anthem. It is still played at the end of BBC 1 with a strange swirling design rotating around the station logo, but it can be hard to find because there are sometimes special late night programmes. It does not appear to be played on BBC2. Radio Ulster merges with another station to continue all night, but it is played at the close of Radio 4 from London. It is doubtful if many people actually hear it as it does not happen until after the shipping forecast. Irish television still plays it, a rather lyrical fully orchestrated version, accompanied by romantic film of the Irish land. This is similar to the practice in some other countries (for example the Basque Country) and it emphasises that aspect of anthems which encourages a sense of identification with the land.

Before we leave radio it is interesting to note that the call sign of the BBC World Service is 'Lillibulero' the Irish anti-Jacobite song which seems capable of straddling divisions. The tune is traditional Irish, and the original words were also Irish. But the song comes from the seventeenth century Protestant planter community, many of whom were Gaelic speakers, and the sentiments are opposed to the Catholic Stuart King, James II. The chorus 'Lillibulero bullenala' appears to be meaningless, but it is said to be a corruption of the original Irish 'An lile ba léir é – ba linn an lá' or in English 'The lily was triumphant – we won the day.' The lily is taken to be a reference to the orange lily. Perhaps here is a song which all Irish people could identity with, though its roots are in conflict. Lilies of different kinds are symbols of both the unionist and nationalist traditions. Now this very Irish song has been adopted to identify one of the most important British institutions through out the world, the BBC World Service

In the present social environment it is perhaps difficult to remember the controversy which once surrounded playing the national anthem in theatres, but it may be useful to recall past events as they may help to give perspective to current disputes. National symbols raise three issues in entertainment. It is sometimes argued in political terms. But there are also commercial considerations if people are going to stay away depending on whether or not the anthem is played. There is also a debate about aesthetics and whether an anthem is appropriate in the context of performances which stir more sublime emotions. And lastly there is the issue of artistic freedom and the concern that playing an anthem in some way limits that freedom. All these considerations have to be weighed against personal preference and again what an institution should do is not necessarily what the individuals in that institution would do in their personal life. The tensions between these conflicting considerations are clearly seen in the way conventions developed in Northern Ireland in the 1960s.

Promotion of the arts was the responsibility of the Council for the Encouragement of Music and the Arts (CEMA), until it was replaced in January 1963 by the Arts Council of Northern Ireland. CEMA was wholly funded by the Government of Northern Ireland, and the president was a Cabinet Minister, Dame Dehra Parker, and when she resigned she left a memo for her successor saying that the Cabinet had directed that the national anthem must be played at all events supported by CEMA, and at events promoted directly by CEMA.

The new President was J. Ritchie McKee who had unionist sympathies, and the Council secretary was H.A.C. Donner, a seconded civil servant, and neither had any wish to dispute this directive. However shortly afterwards Jack Loudon took over as secretary, and he was aware that the national anthem affected audiences. People of nationalist sympathies were staying away. It was also thought to be 'aesthetically undesirable', in that it did not complement the quality of some of the music during a concert. Mr Loudan described it as a 'codology' and found ways to circumvent the directive. He would arrange to 'forget' to turn up the volume on the record player or it would not be played until the audience had all left. In orchestral concerts the conductor was encouraged to find unusual and interesting arrangements.

The issue only concerned a small proportion of the population, mainly the

SPECIAL OCCASIONS AND SOCIAL INSTITUTIONS

middle class, as many people were not interested in the arts. But for committed unionists and nationalists it was a real issue because it was a test of loyalty. Just because they were very cultured people did not mean that the presence or absence of the national anthem did not evoke strong emotional reactions which they could not explain or analyse.

The situation remained unchanged until Mr McKee died suddenly and he was replaced by Peter Montgomery, a liberal 'squire' from County Tyrone. He decided that the issue had to be dealt with. On the grounds which were already familiar, he argued that it was a nuisance and it was also unnecessary. No formal decision was taken, and the matter never came before the Council Board, but from then on the directive was ignored. Mr Montgomery probably found it easier to make the change at this time, because the Prime Minister, Lord Brookborough had retired to be replaced by Terence O'Neill who had been at school with Mr Montgomery.

The anthem continued to be played in some places such as the Arts Theatre. Occasionally people would write asking why the anthem was not being played, and CEMA and its successor the Arts Council of Northern Ireland, would write back and explain it was a matter for the institution concerned. Although the policy was changed without any controversy, there was still 'folk lore' about the issue and its ramifications

The piece of this lore which most often comes to mind concerns the Lyric Theatre. The Lyric Theatre came into existence in 1951, and by the 1960s had established itself as a significant force in the theatre in Belfast, even though it was an amateur company. It had a coherent artistic philosophy, and had a clearly identified political stance which was not pro-unionist. This was primarily due to its founder and director Mary O'Malley who was a forceful person, ready to challenge and 'knock' the establishment, and expose hypocrisy wherever it might be found. The Lyric was moving towards becoming a fully professional company with a purpose built theatre. About the same time the Arts Council had decided that there was a need for a new theatre and it decided to make the Lyric the focus of its support because of its track record and achievements.

Until now the company had not had to deal with issues of public funding, and the restrictions this might impose. However, it had already considered the desirability of playing the anthem when it became a Charitable Trust in 1960. An insight into thinking within the company is given by Mary O'Malley's son, Conor in his book on the Lyric, and it is worth quoting at length:

At the very first meeting of the Trustees, the question arose as to whether the British National Anthem should be played at Lyric performances. This was a sensitive issue in the context of a divided North as the Anthem and the Toast to the Queen were an integral part of many public functions. In the eyes of some, such gestures had become symbols of 'loyalty' but occasionally ways of circumventing these obligations were found . . . On one occasion when the Abbey Theatre Company was invited to the Belfast Opera House, some of the players were concerned at the fact that they would have to publicly stand on the stage while the Anthem was

being played at the end of each performance. Ernest Blythe [the adminis-
trator of the Abbey] was not unduly worried about this question as he
considered it was the prerogative of the local theatre management. Eventually, it was agreed to play the Anthem after the curtain went down, as
soon as the actors had left the stage. So, at the Lyric, the question of the
Anthem was treated cautiously. In a minute dated December 28th 1960,
the following motion was passed unanimously by the Trustees:

That the Lyric Players Theatre should continue its policy of having no
National Anthem at productions etc, on the premises but that it may be
played at the discretion of the Trustees, at any outside function inside
Northern Ireland and elsewhere.

This policy remained intact for nearly eight years but it was always a
source of contention outside the theatre's ranks and confirmed official
perceptions of the Lyric's disloyalty to the state. (O'Malley, 1988, p76)

This account and other statements from those concerned confirm that there
was no direct pressure put on the Company to play the anthem, but that the
Trustees were sensitive of the impact of their decision on public opinion,
and therefore public support. There is also no mention of the 'aesthetic
relevance' of the national anthem at a cultural event, which was a concern of
the Arts Council. It was certainly known in theatre going circles that the
Company had a conscious policy of not playing the anthem. It had not
simply been carelessly overlooked.

It was also widely known that the playing of the national anthem was
something about which Mrs O'Malley felt strongly. She would avoid the
anthem when it was played at other theatres, coming in afterwards if it was
played at the beginning or leaving early if it was played at the end. In 1953
when she was a councillor on Belfast City Council, a meeting of the Poets,
Editors and Novelists Association (PEN) took place in Belfast. The City
Council hosted an Official Dinner and as was the Council custom the Loyal
Toast was proposed. This was apparently contrary to the rules of PEN. Mrs
O'Malley and her fellow Labour councillors remained seated. Years later
when she was awarded an honorary degree at Queen's University she was
not on the platform during the anthem.

These stories were in part inaccurate and certainly did not give the whole
picture. The family stress that they were not intending to make public
protests, though they were of course public figures in the world of the
theatre. Conor O'Malley remembers numerous occasions when the family
stood chatting in the foyer of the Arts Theatre while the anthem was played
and then slipped into their seats quietly as if they had just arrived. Whatever
her personal political views, Mrs O'Malley was expressing her opposition to
playing any anthem in the theatre. In the mid-1960s she questioned the
playing of 'The Soldier's Song' at the Abbey Theatre in Dublin. As a result
the practice was discontinued, and it is no longer played, even when the
national President attends. She felt the theatre should not be identified with
the state, any state, in this way, as it implied a restriction on artistic freedom.
Conor O'Malley explains in this way: to have no anthem 'is not making a

political stand ... but it is hard not to be seen to be making a political statement. They purely wished to be free of any political test.'

The distinction is nicely captured in the arrangements at Lyric performances at the Grove Theatre. In the 1960s the Grove Theatre was converted from a cinema by the Arts Council to provide a venue where theatrical companies could mount productions. The Lyric at this time was still operating from its small studio theatre in Derryvolgie Avenue and seized this and other opportunities to present its productions on a big stage. It also used the King George VI Youth Centre with no qualms about the name, and interestingly, in spite of its royal name there was never any discussion about playing the anthem there. When arrangements were being made for the first Lyric production at the Grove, the manager brought up the question of the anthem. Mrs O'Malley said she did not want it, and the manager said he had to play it, not least because the theatre was in a unionist district. Mrs O'Malley said that was a matter for him. He could play it if he liked, but in that case it would be the Grove and not the Lyric who was playing it. The production was a musical, *The Heart's A Wonder*, so the theatre manager asked if the Lyric's small orchestra would play the anthem. The Lyric's musical director also asked if they should play it. Mrs O'Malley was clear that if it was played by the orchestra, it would mean that the Lyric was playing it, so while she accepted the management's right to play it, it should be done with a recording over the theatre's public address system. This was in fact done. The niceties of these distinctions were lost on the general public, who already had their own ideas of what Mrs O'Malley thought, and by the next morning the papers were receiving complaints about the squeaky recording which was a slight to the anthem. The matter was referred to the Arts Council who supported Mrs O'Malley's position.

There is a story that Mrs O'Malley insisted that 'The Soldier's Song' was played for her company when they performed at a festival in Sligo. In view of her stand on anthems, it would have been out of character to ask for the anthem to be played at Sligo, but it demonstrates the public perception that she wished to promote Irish national symbols. It also shows how political arguments quickly become intertwined with artistic arguments. In 1960 some friends of the Lyric on the Board of CEMA proposed that the theatre should be given a grant. The Board refused and the Chairman, Mr McKee said Mrs O'Malley 'was a subversive element in the community.' Some friends advised that he should be sued for slander, but it was a situation which she could not succeed, since a court case would have made her seem even more subversive in the eyes of Mr McKee. Six years later the Lyric did get a small grant to help with wages for some of the company.

At the point when the first major Arts Council grant was awarded in 1968, the Trustees wrote to the Arts Council for clarification of a number of points, one of which was the requirement that the theatre should play the national anthem. The Council wrote back diplomatically that this was a matter where the Council had no guidance to give. It was entirely a matter for the theatre trustees. The O'Malleys are clear that the responsibility for deciding lay with the theatre management and that the Arts Council should not be put under pressure to rule on the matter. In fact they did not think that the trustee's letter was asking for guidance on the Arts Council policy. Nevertheless there is a feeling that the theatre would have highlighted any evidence that the state was trying to exert influence or any indication that it had changed its policy on anthem because they felt strongly about the issue.

Conor O'Malley's account of the internal discussions within the Company in 1968 is again worth quoting:

> Once the building of a professional theatre became a certainty, the old problem of the Anthem emerged. It was one thing not to play it in a small studio theatre at the back of a private house, but quite another not to play it in a large public theatre, subsidised by public money. Several Trustees believed it was necessary to review the policy. A month before the new theatre opened, a series of meetings were held to discuss the issue. Pearse O'Malley suggested that the Anthem be accepted as part of 'the ceremonial involved on special official and public occasions'. Other Trustees preferred that the procedure used at Covent Garden (where the Anthem was played at the beginning and end of the Season) be adopted. Their view was that it was a necessary step to ensure 'maximum public support in building up an audience and in the Fund Raising Campaign'. It would also help to counteract, in their view, the Lyric's cultural 'image'. Mary and Pearse O'Malley opposed this as they felt it would 'affect the artistic independence of the New Lyric' and that 'all donations had been given unconditionally and a change of policy would do less than justice to Lyric supporters'. Following the passing of a motion by majority decision the Anthem was played on October 28 1968 (the first public performance – the theatre had been formally opened on October 26). Pearse and Mary O'Malley resigned their positions as Trustees and their executive functions as they felt the theatre had been compromised politically. The remaining Trustees were surprised by their drastic action, explaining that they would not have pressed the issue had they known this would happen. Dr O'Malley, accepted the explanation and returned to the Board. Mary O'Malley would not return as Trustee but agreed to act as Artistic Adviser temporarily as the theatre was in severe difficulties. The divided views of the Board remained unresolved. (O'Malley, 1990, pp77–8)

This account again indicates the pragmatic concern about the impact of the decision on the theatre-going public and whether it might affect box office receipts. The question of the anthems aesthetic relevance still is not mentioned, though it may have been in the minds of those involved. The issue of artistic independence now surfaces. For Pearse O'Malley there was also another issue: the need to distinguish individual preferences from the policy of an institution. He believed that when the Lyric was founded if they 'had not established that separateness it would not have happened. People would have felt imposed upon. People were allowed to embrace others without feeling their basic beliefs were being interfered with.' His view was that this separation could be achieved with a policy which recognised the expectations of the state, even if you did not agree with them, but did not allow them to dominate. His suggestion means that the anthem would be played occasionally, and those who objected could stay away for that one evening.

Only one year later the issue surfaced again. Four new trustees had been appointed, one of whom, Frank Benner, was elected chairman. They were concerned about the perception of the theatre as anti-government. He wanted to say in the programme that the anthem would be played, but this idea was dropped. They invited the Governor General of Northern Ireland to attend a performance, when the national anthem was played in recognition of his presence.

The chairman then enlisted a group of business men to help with fund-raising. They said that money could be raised from business sources, but the problem was that 'the Lyric is still politically suspect in some business circles' and 'this could be a very serious barrier to fund raising.' The group then submitted a statement for approval by all the Trustees, on the basis of which the group would support the theatre. It included a reference to the theatre's policy on the anthem. Dr O'Malley refused to sign it. Later, in a press release (reproduced by O'Malley, 1988, pp144–147) he said the statement was 'a 'semi-political' document, 'innocuous in itself', but he argued that it represented an attempt to control artistic policy and 'monetary freedom could not be bought at the expense of artistic freedom. 'He was on the point of resigning as he thought the artistic policy of the theatre could not survive. All the Trustees had to sign the statement before the business-men would get involved, so the four new members of the Board threatened to resign if Dr O'Malley would not sign the statement. As a result Dr O'Malley decided to stay, accepting the consequences that fund raising could be difficult if the businessmen's offer was not accepted on their terms. The new members resigned, the Board was reconstituted, the Arts Council continued their backing, and the theatre entered into its most successful phase with no farther controversy about the anthem or the underlying issue of political control.

Whether the anthem would have meant, or even been perceived to mean, political control was never tested. There was certainly no direct pressure from the Arts Council or government to play the anthem, and 'all donations had been given unconditionally'. Nevertheless, there was something of a perception that the Lyric had been the test case for not tying statutory funding to the condition that the anthem must be played. Was the controversy really about political control? The more general issue was whether it was better to change practice quietly, without formal decisions, as popular opinion changes, as has happened in other societies. That continues to be an issue in other areas of life in Northern Ireland, though no longer in the arts.

The Lyric erected a flag pole for the laying of the foundation stone of the theatre and flew a flag based on its own symbol. It was a harp and the head of Cuchulainn with the raven on his shoulder, the same image as is now being used in some loyalist symbolism. When the theatre was finally complete they had chosen not to incorporate a flag pole to avoid any question of when they should use it.

Flags are no longer an issue in the theatre though they were a theme in John Boyd's play Facing North which was first performed in 1978. Part of the plot concerned an incident over flags in the work place, and we will refer to it again in Chapter 6 where that subject is dealt with more fully.

Flags have never been such an issue in the arts. One incident arose which concerned the Ulster Museum. The Whitechapel Gallery in London had put together an exhibition of work by Conrad Atkinson, and the Ulster Museum was mounting it in Belfast. However the security staff and porters were disturbed when it arrived because some of the works included Irish flags. They exerted pressure to have it withdrawn. The Director of the Ulster Museum, Alan McCutcheon was also doubtful, on the grounds that he had not been informed of the nature of the exhibition. Taking out the offending pictures was not an option, as the organisers in London felt very strongly that the show had to be mounted in its entirety. Negotiations took place, involving the Chairman of the Arts Council, Stanley Worrell, and in the end the exhibition was moved to the Arts Council Gallery. This incident raised issues not just about flags and emblems but about artistic freedom, and about the control of gallery policy. Should the director of a gallery or the support staff decide if something is offensive?

Education and Youth Services

Work with young people provides some examples of how national symbols can have an integrative effect rather than increasing polarisation. But over-all, flags and anthems have a much smaller place in work with young people in Northern Ireland, and indeed in the United Kingdom as a whole, than in other parts of the world. We have noted that in the United States there is a flag in the corner of every class room and each day the students take the pledge of allegiance to the flag. For Americans encouraging a sense of civic pride and commitment to the nation is an accepted part of education. In contrast, in Chapter 1 we had the description of a confrontation in a school in Birmingham, Alabama.

There is unlikely to be confrontation over symbols inside schools in Northern Ireland, because most schools are segregated. Formally flags are not much in evidence. We have seen that the Union flag is flown outside all controlled schools in the North Eastern Board's area. In some other schools the flag is flown on public occasions. The national anthem is seldom sung, though a few schools would include it in their Prize Day programme or as part of the Remembrance Day service, if there is one. One head master said that it would be a denial of history if it was not played at the Remembrance Service. This school, like others, would encourage pupils to wear the poppy and the headmaster makes the Remembrance Service relevant to the school by focusing on former pupils who died.

Pupils in many schools are not permitted to wear badges apart from school badges and the Duke of Edinburgh Award badge. The Fainné might be considered provocative in some controlled schools, but it is not know if permission to wear it has ever been requested or refused. One headmaster said it would be allowed because it is a sign of academic achievement and not a political sign.

National symbols cause more concern during inter-school activities or on the way to or from school. We have already mentioned in Chapter 2 the story of the boy who wore his best Glasgow Celtic football shirt at an inter-schools service. Outside the school the pupils' uniforms and football scarves are sufficient to identify 'the other sort'.

In integrated schools the pupils come from the different traditions of course, and the schools are committed to 'equal expression of the two major traditions', in the words of the Statement of Principles of the Northern Ireland Council for Integrated Education. Its Practical Guidelines state that they should 'promote an atmosphere in which pupils will neither conceal nor flaunt their own cultural traditions.' Balancing concealing and flaunting may be a fine line. Two other guidelines say that they should 'promote the learning of shared culture, beliefs and traditions' but at the same time 'ensure that no symbol likely to be seen as offensive or divisive shall be displayed in the school premises or worn by pupils.' Flags should only be flown in a European context, or with an educational purpose in mind. The distinction is made between 'displaying' a flag which is acceptable and 'flying' it which is not.

They have a practical concerns about school uniforms as they may attract abuse from both the main traditions, so they favour uniforms which are not very striking. Many people involved in integrated education do not think symbols are very important. Badges and emblems are not allowed apart from the exceptions permitted in many other schools: Duke of Edinburgh Award and school badges. The Fainné and poppies would also be acceptable.

Many teachers avoid the subject of national symbols. There are no specific references to flags and anthems in the official curriculum, though there are opportunities to raise it. If teachers wanted to explain to their pupils about the meaning of flags and anthems it could be included in cultural studies or the Cultural Heritage theme of the core curriculum. Alternatively the topic could be incorporated into History at Key Stage 3: Core 3 'Ireland and British Politics in the late 19th and early 20th centuries', Key Stage 4: Core 1 'Northern Ireland and its Neighbours since 1930' or in a European context at Key Stage 4: Core 2 'Europe since 1919'. It could also be developed as a 'School Designed Unit' at Key Stages 2 or 3, either as a 'Study in Depth' or a 'Study of a Significant Aspect of the 20th Century'. Feedback from history field officers in the Education and Library Boards suggests that one of the most popular School Designed Units on 'A Significant Aspect of the 20th Century' is the First World War, which has obvious potential to focus on flags and emblems.

In fact the European Studies (Ireland and Great Britain) Project designed material entitled 'Attitudes to Conflict' which contained a unit on 'Symbolism and War' and examines, for examples, the use of the poppy and the Easter lily, types of war memorials and crosses on war graves. It does not deal with flags and anthems as such. This is expected to be published soon by the Northern Ireland Centre for Learning Resources.

Flags can be found in the set of teaching material called 'Law in Our Lives', which was launched by the Northern Ireland Curriculum Council in October 1993. It is hoped that they will be used as a personal and social education programme for young people over 16, or as part of business studies or home economics. One unit is on 'Law in the Workplace' and it uses as a case study a scenario which deals with flags in the workplace.

Although limited the curriculum does provide opportunities to learn about the history of symbols and what they really mean, and it may take some of the passion out of the reactions to flags. Knowing more about them can make them more common place and like the flags of other countries, rather than symbols of the conflict.

National symbols are more often used in youth work. Uniformed organisations encourage respect for any national flag, because it is 'the symbol of the honour, tradition and sometimes the history of the country or body it represents.' Flag training is only a small part of their activities but they carry their own organisation's flag and the national flag at parades and fly them at camps. Members learn the correct code for respecting the flag and they discourage the use of flags in a derogatory way. They are one of the influences which encourage us to become celebrators, taking pride and pleasure in flags when they are flown properly. When groups from different countries are together they have no problem flying each other's flag and respecting them. But they do not think it is appropriate to fly flags when they might cause offence and therefore they are willing to desist, especially if they feel it might lead to trouble for the young people in their care.

Unusually for uniformed organisations the Catholic Boys Scouts of Ireland seldom use national flags in either part of Ireland. At the present time troops in Northern Ireland are not encouraged to carry any national flag, or use a national anthem. In the same way the CBSI Scout promise does not refer to the national President in the way that the Boy Scout promise normally refers to the monarch or head of state. One reason they developed in this way was because the founders were wanting to set up a middle way between the Baden Powell Scouts which seemed too British for many citizen's of the new state and the Fianna, the republican scouts who seemed to extreme and militant. As a result they have developed with a stronger orientation to the Church rather than the nation, and they often carry the Papal flag at parade. They themselves say that their focus is the individual, and respect for other individuals.

Informal youth workers do not have this interest in the formal use of flags, but they will discuss the importance of flags and young people's feelings about them. Some workers find them a useful way of encouraging discussion of controversial issues. Sometimes young people, and adults, find it difficult to begin discussion, and a variety of symbols can provide the stimulus for a frank discussion. Items which have been used include rosary beads, orange drums and the national flags. This may be particularly effective when working with one tradition because the other group are in a sense represented by their symbols. But it is also used in mixed groups and sometimes a mixed group is asked to design new symbols with which they could all identify. In chapter 2 we mentioned the findings of the exercise where young people are asked to comment on each other's flags. They then respond to the comments and that leads into an open discussion of the different traditions.

The flags can be used to highlight the conflict and, in the process, provide a context for the experience of the different sections of society, and also make connections between them. A mixed performance project was invited to prepare a presentation to take to Canada. One talented song writer in the group wrote a direct hard-hitting song about the experiences of his nationalist community (Freedom Songs, see Appendix 2). The group recognised the quality of the song, but were uncertain how to relate it to the unionist experience, so the author and a Protestant girl were asked to go away and work on it.

They came up with a solution which satisfied the group. They punctuated the verses of the song with readings by the girl of letters by Protestants and Catholics. The letters were by people in prison, people who had to go to England looking for work, and a British soldier stationed in Derry. They brought out the similar but not identical experiences of both communities. However, they did not want to deny the conflict between the communities so when they staged the song the girl stood in front of the singer holding a Tricolour and a Union flag which she waved sometimes individually and sometimes together. The flags were used because they wanted to make people more aware of the song at an emotional level and to symbolise the part nationalism plays in the Northern Ireland conflict.

The result was a very effective and challenging performance which enhanced rather than detracted from the theme of the song. Some members of the audiences got a 'bit edgy' when they saw the flags, and in Canada some members of the audience thought they should have avoided the conflict, and concentrated on more traditional folk songs. But many others thought it was an important thing to do. The way they used the flags seemed to both demonstrate the conflict and bring the two traditions into juxtaposition. These creative uses of flags are examples of what can be done with imagination to stimulate new perspectives on the traditions which they symbolise.

When inter-community groups from Northern Ireland go overseas their hosts are confused about what to do about national symbols. Often they want to avoid them and are frightened when the young people introduce them. Nellis(1992, pp6–7) tells a familiar story from a project in which he took part in 1975:

The night after we arrived the children were doing some creative activities including painting . . . We, the Irish leaders, were told that everything was prepared. There were sufficient Dutch leaders and people specialised in arts and crafts to supervise the children and we weren't really needed for the activity so to relax upstairs and have a cup of tea for a minute. We

consented only to be called down in a short time to restore order, as some
of the kids were painting tricolours, others were painting union jacks, and
it had turned into a paint fight with some kids smearing each other with
paints. It was a good natured, almost slapstick comedy type happening
which was surprising considering the only time these children had met, if
at all, before going to Holland was when stoning each other over the
barbed wire between Unity and the Shankill.

Hosts often want to greet the group with flags. One host organisation had,
through experience, realised that both the Tricolour and the Union flag can
cause problems. They then rang up the organisers in Northern Ireland to say
they had found an answer. They had discovered there was a Northern
Ireland flag and they assumed everyone could identify with it. Unfortunately it is not that simple. Similar experiences have faced adult groups, as
we saw in the case of the Irish rugby tour of America. With young people
mistakes by the hosts can often be a useful opportunity for the group to
consider some of the underlying issues, if the participants are allowed to
explain their reactions and they are not avoided.

One such experience followed an invitation to a group to play football
against a local team: 'I remember we were all full of excitement as we sat
down to try to choose a name and there was no animosity trying to chose a
name. But we wanted to choose a name that was not particular to any one
group and I remember another group sat down and they made a flag and it
was half a Union Jack and half Tricolour and we went out and we won the
match.' (Nellis, 1992, p49)

Another incident occurred during a three week visit to a residential
centre. The participants came from all over Northern Ireland and none of
them had known each other before the visit. While the group was away from
the centre for a day, the leader of the group stayed at the centre and while
walking around he was surprised to find a Tricolour flying from the centre's
flag pole. One of the centre staff had obtained the flag thinking it would
please the group. The leader realised this might not be the case but the flag
was left up.

When the group returned one unionist was quite annoyed. It seemed that
he was not objecting to the Tricolour as such, but was more offended that his
tradition had not been included. He decided to rectify the situation personally, so he went into the workshop and started to paint a Northern Ireland
flag on a piece of wood. The other members of the group realised what he
was doing and also realised how he felt. One of them said that she realised
for the first time how much it meant for him that his flag should be recognised, so they joined him in the workshop. They were not sure of their
motivation but they said that they thought they wanted to show that they
understood what he was doing. Their offers of help were rejected. The boy
was quite possessive about his project and he said they could not paint the
crown properly and that they would splash red paint on the white background. The girls were quite relaxed about it, and in the end he had to get
help because he wanted it finished in time for a cultural night which was

being organised. The outcome was that the Tricolour continued to fly over the centre, but the Northern Ireland flag had pride of place at the front of the stage for the cultural night. The young man was able to have his symbol included, the Tricolour was not a problem in itself, and the others had learnt something of what a flag can mean to someone.

They may have seen much more conflict than was really there. But at the same time they may not have been aware of how much the group learnt about each other. It was an obvious incident for the local papers to seize on. They carried photographs of Protestants and Catholics together painting the flag. One paper reported it in this way:

> The underlying tensions are obvious, even among friends. Each side has its own view on which flag should fly over Northern Ireland, and last week a student from one side helped a friend from the opposite side to paint one of the flags.
>
> 'Don't tell them that back home!' the first student says. 'They'll kill me!'
>
> Later, [the leader] adds: 'She's not kidding, you know, about killing her.'

The hosts are probably not fully aware of what is happening in these situation.

Award Ceremonies

It is common in many societies to organise special ceremonies at which awards are given for achievement in various walks of life. It is a way of acknowledging the effort of those who have completed a course or demonstrated skill and ability. It is also a way of validating the importance of the programme of work or the event which has led to the award. As our society becomes more 'qualification conscious', award ceremonies are becoming more common, though many are now quite informal. Social functions, in the form of a meal, a garden party or a dance, are often a part of the programme.

However, the higher the achievement, the greater the wish to make the award ceremony a special event. People of distinction are asked to attend, make speeches and present the awards. Traditional rituals have become established which enhance the sense of the importance of the occasion and also symbolise the historic continuity of scholarship and the pursuit of knowledge. Even ceremonies which have been recently introduced borrow rituals from older traditions. For example at the award ceremonies for those completing some job training schemes in America, the trainees wear academic gowns and mortar boards to encourage greater self-esteem.

As at other special occasions the national anthem may be one part of the ritual, but its presence or absence is not normally a significant cause of controversy. One reason is that they are seldom public events. In many institutions, including schools, participants are usually part of the same social and cultural group and share similar attitudes towards the anthem.

In common with other areas of life, the custom of playing the national anthem has declined. For example one large school decided it was 'inappropriate' to play the anthem at its Prize Days apart from the senior ceremony, and there also, it is considering whether the practice should continue. It has never been part of the passing out parades for police cadets, which is perhaps surprising in view of the role of the police as a servant of the state. This may be an indication that the absence of the anthem is not necessarily a sign of a lack of allegiance. In fact it was suggested that 'it belittles the national anthem to play it on such paltry occasions.' The RUC march, the traditional Irish love song, 'The Young May Moon', is played, and it is said that it means a lot to new officers. It is a symbol which helps to create their bond to the force.

But it is still an integral part of many ceremonies, and the recent controversy in one institution, Queen's University, Belfast, has highlighted many of the complexities of such situations. Accordingly we shall look at it in some detail. The underlying issue is, as always, political, concerning allegiance to the state, but there is also the question of intellectual freedom and the relevance of national anthems in educational institutions. The situation is made more complex because the University is a significant public institution, and many people not closely involved in the university wish to influence the course of the dispute.

The procedure at Queen's is that at the commencement of the graduation ceremony the audience stands for the academic procession. At the end of the procession, everyone is expected to remain standing while the anthem is played on the organ. The Chancellor then invites everyone to sit and introduces the rest of the proceedings. In the afternoon there is a traditional garden party at which the Royal Ulster Constabulary Band normally plays, finishing with another rendition of the anthem.

For some time there has been opposition from some students, though a small number of staff members and others have also said the practice should be discontinued. Those who sit down during the anthem do it quietly, and do not otherwise disrupt the proceedings. Those on both sides of the argument agree that there are only a small number involved, though one unionist politician said he was 'appalled' at the number who sit down and Suzanne Breen (*Irish Times*, 12.1.1993) has quoted a figure of one quarter of the Catholic students. It is not clear if the small numbers is a good indication of the extent of the opposition to the anthem. Suzanne Breen also suggested that 'many' students boycott the ceremony.

There are aspects of the situation which may inhibit some people from sitting down. Since everyone is already standing, it is somewhat different from the more common situation when everyone is sitting and are then asked to stand for the anthem. One person described it as a gesture 'by commission rather than omission.' There is no warning of what is about to happen, either in the programme or by the Chancellor who is conducting the proceedings. Some people do not sit down immediately, but during the course of the tune they make up their mind and sit down. It is evident that many students have not thought about it in advance and there is not an orchestrated plan to sit down. One ex-student, incidentally from a Protestant background, said that he had decided in advance to sit, but he still found it difficult. He felt tense, and was very aware of his class mates who would disapprove of his action and might be offended. But he went through with the gesture, because it was important for him.

There is no visible reaction of disapproval from the rest of the audience, but one unionist said he has stopped going or he would complain and that would cause problems for the University administration. He also said that there was no evidence that anyone had ever been disadvantaged as a result of sitting down. Those who are strongly committed to the anthem watch keenly to see if there is any sign that the University is about to change its policy. In 1992, at the social science graduation, the Chancellor, Sir David Orr, went straight into his welcome and introduction without waiting for the anthem to be played. Later there were some complaints. It was alleged that the anthem had been left out because a guest from the Republic of Ireland had been present. In fact it was simply an oversight. One student was very disappointed because he was deprived of his one opportunity to make his gesture of disapproval by sitting down.

At the garden party the situation is even less clear cut, as it is quite a casual occasion. The guests are walking around talking and eating strawberries. Some people will already have left before the anthem. Others, without intending to protest, may be so busy talking that they have not noticed what is being played. Suzanne Breen in the *Irish Times* (12.1.1993) and an article in the *Belfast Telegraph* (12.1.1993) claimed that some students made a more explicit expression of their opposition by lying on the grass or humming 'The Soldier's Song' during the National Anthem. One student thought that the Police band would prefer not to have the engagement because of the level of security which is necessary. However, the RUC may well appreciate the invitation as a useful contribution to public relations.

While the conflict over the anthem has continued at a low level for some time, it became a more public debate at the beginning of 1993. On 12 January, the *Irish Times* and the *Belfast Telegraph* carried articles which reported that the national anthem and the invitation to the RUC band were under review. The Belfast Telegraph report said that the review 'follows criticism from nationalist students who complained they found the playing of the anthem was offensive and insensitive.' A spokesman for the University stressed that the arrangements were always kept under review, and so 'there's nothing new in this.'

A week later, David Trimble, the Unionist Member of Parliament for Upper Bann and a former student and lecturer at the University, reacted during a speech at a constituency meeting. He associated the issue with the proposal of the Community Relations Council to investigate current practice on national symbols, to identify any conflicts which arose and to explore how they could be resolved. He was reported (*Newsletter*, 18.1.1993) to say that the Community Relations Council's attitude 'provides ammunition for disloyal elements.'

Another week passed and the leader of the Democratic Unionist Party,

Ian Paisley, joined the debate by releasing a letter he had received from the Vice Chancellor, Gordon Beveridge. Dr Paisley condemned the 'much hyped and ill-informed reports' and said that the letter had reassured him that the anthem will continue to be played. However the extracts from Dr Beveridge's letter which were quoted did not refer to the future, but simply praised the contribution the anthem and the band had made to the graduation ceremony. He said (*Belfast Telegraph*, 26.1.1993) 'The playing of the National Anthem has been a part of our tradition for graduation ceremonies since the University was founded' and that 'The RUC band has provided the background music for the garden party for many years and the high standard of their music has added charm and grace to these occasions.'

These reports seem to have been stimulated by Unionist politicians alerting the public to what they saw as a threat to the anthem. They may not have been unrelated to a report which had been presented to the University Senate, on which some politicians sit. Employment Equality Services had been commissioned by the University to review the fair employment situation in the University. The Report, prepared by Beverly Jones and Fiona Cassidy, was confidential, but a few weeks later the *Irish News* (11.2.1993) printed a summary of its recommendations, based on a copy of the Report which had been leaked to it. The summary has not been denied. The anthem is only given a brief two-page reference in a substantial report on other matters, but it did keep the issue in the public mind. It also indicated that it was an issue which concerned staff as well as students by suggesting that the playing of 'God Save the Queen' may be discriminatory and a breach of the Fair Employment Code of Practice in that it does not contribute to a neutral working environment. We will return to this aspect of the subject in Chapter 6.

The Standing Committee of Senate considered the report, and according to the University newsletter, 'Update':

> reviewed the recommendation which deals with the university's aspiration to promote a neutral working environment. It is strongly of the view that the University must maintain and promote a neutral working and social environment, within which all staff, students and visitors can feel comfortable. It has, as recommended by Employment Equality Services, initiated a consultation on how this objective can best be achieved. As a first step, members of staff, students and bodies within, or associated with the University will be invited through *Update*, and by direct invitation, to submit their views on the matter to the Committee *by 30 June 1993*. The Committee is considering the means by which this evidence, and information resulting from other consultations, should be assessed.

The committee therefore did not make a decision on whether the University had a neutral working environment but affirmed its commitment to that goal. The University is satisfied that playing the anthem is not illegal and that it has got nothing to do with fair employment, but it still takes the matter very seriously as part of the general concern to ensure that the campus provides a 'social environment which all staff, students and visitors can feel comfortable with.' As an institution it does not have a view on what the outcome should be, but it is clear that it wants to be an equitable consensual result which is acceptable to all. However there are a number of factors which make it difficult to achieve that goal.

The Relevant Interests
The first problem is the number of interests which have to be considered. The number of people who work and study at the university, full or part time, are equivalent to a medium-sized town in Northern Ireland. Then the boundaries between the university and the wider community are very open or porous. Many people, including past graduates and politicians have an interest in one way or another. Politicians, as we have seen, have strong definite views, and some of them are members of the University Senate, which has the ultimate power to decide. As a public body the university is under public scrutiny and the politicians and other representatives on the University's decision making bodies are sensitive to opinion in their own constituencies and peer groups.

It is evident that there is a wide range of views, and it is difficult to balance all the shades of opinion. Should those who hold very strong views on either side of the argument be given more weight, either because they are most interested or because they care most strongly? If an accommodation could be made between the outspoken unionists and nationalists would that be an adequate resolution of the controversy? Should account be taken of those with no views, or those who have a preference but do not think that it is a matter of much consequence? Should those who work and study in the university every day have most influence? Should those who are about to graduate be given most consideration as it is a special day of celebration for them? The University is keen to listen not only to those of known views who represent a specific constituency, but to find a way to allow other views to emerge.

The dispute about the anthem has to be put in the context of the wider competition for influence in the University between unionists and nationalists, and this makes it a more important issue and more difficult to resolve.

The Context of Politics at Queen's
There are clearly identified unionist and nationalist interest groups in the University, especially in student politics. Because they are elected on different systems, the Executive of the Students Union tends to be nationalist in sympathies and the Students Representative Council (SRC) is more unionist in sympathies. Inevitably there is often a stalemate between them as the SRC will not accept proposals from the Students' Union.

The student body and the University administration often find themselves holding different views. Many of those in the University administration would see themselves as politically neutral in their work, but it has a unionist image. It is partly a historical legacy, but we have noted that unionist politicians are represented on the Senate, as indeed are nationalists, and others nominated to University bodies come from establishment and unionist backgrounds. The image has been reinforced by criticism of the University's record on fair employment, highlighted in 1992 by publicity about a number of appointments. The University stressed that these issues have been dealt with, but the perception will take longer to change.

The groups we have identified are very sensitive to attempts by their opponents to gain advantage, and at the same time they are looking out for issues in the University which they can use to challenge their opponents. Reference was made to the student who was disappointed when the anthem was not played as he was deprived of his opportunity to protest. We were told that he was genuinely concerned about the anthem, but his reaction suggests that from his point of view the anthem was also part of a wider conflict.

It is considered that there was a strong republican influence in student affairs in the early 1980s, but that it has declined, and student politics are now more broadly based. Someone from the centre of student politics said it is in the interest of the Unionist and Tory groups to promote the idea that the Students' Union is 'still a den of republicanism', in order to mobilise Protestants.

But some unionists do believe that republicanism continues to be a dominant force. One politician said that the objection to the anthem should be seen as 'part of the overall pro-republican campaign of the Students Union.' Other developments are taken as confirmations of that assessment. The Union's bi-lingual policy is one example and some people object to the presence of signs in Gaelic. Another is the refusal of a grant to the students supporters' club for Glasgow Rangers' Football Club, apparently on the grounds that it was sectarian. Unionists then ask why the GAA gets a grant. Perhaps the difference is that the GAA club plays sports, and the Supporters Club is mainly social. But other clubs, whose activities are mainly social, have been awarded grants.

The difficulty for the University is that they have to deal with the problem in this context. Whatever action one group takes, there will be a reaction from another. Each group does not understand what the other group wants and assumes it as part of a broader campaign. It is difficult to separate out genuine concern about the anthem, and its symbolic value as part of a wider conflict. This means that practice in other universities does not give much guidance.

The Practice Elsewhere

The anthem is played in about 24 out of 40 universities in the United Kingdom. The number may be falling because one person told us that two-thirds of them played it ten years ago. In some universities it is only played on special occasions, perhaps when a dignitary is present. At Cambridge it is a much simpler occasion with neither speeches or anthems, because it is a more private event in each college. In chapter two we noted that at the University or Wales at Aberystwyth a substantial number of students do not stand for the United Kingdom anthem. This also happens in Scotland, Stirling University being one example. As an example of how practice elsewhere is not a good guide, it was pointed out that an Irish student in England would have no grounds to complain about the anthem. Equally a Queen's student from the Republic of Ireland said in a radio interview that he objected to the practice at Queen's, but would have no problem with 'The Soldier's Song' at a Dublin university. Although we cannot draw direct parallels to the situation elsewhere, it does show that the national anthem is not an essential element to a graduation ceremony, and its absence is not a sign of disloyalty. And it does show that dissent can be tolerated. But in other situations, the anthem is not a sign or a test or an expression of the conflict between two sections of the community.

We can therefore look at practice elsewhere in Northern Ireland, including schools, the police and other institutions referred to at the beginning of this section. The other university in Northern Ireland, the University of Ulster does not play the national anthem, except at the installation of the chancellor. It was formed in 1984 by the amalgamation of existing third level educational institutions. Of the two largest, the New University of Ulster had played the anthem at graduation ceremonies but the Northern Ireland Polytechnic had not. The latter practice was adopted by the new institution with very little discussion, and national symbols are not an issue for the University. The garden party does not have music.

The Arguments

The main argument for the anthem is that it is traditional. It has been played since the University's foundation in 1908. It is part of the ritual which makes the occasion distinctive. It might equally be asked why wear a gown and mortar board, and, indeed, why have a ceremony at all. The degrees could be sent through the post.

For unionists its importance is as a sign of loyalty. They argue that the University got its name from the original college founded by Queen Victoria and it has a Royal Charter. If people chose to come to this University they should accept its allegiances. They are obtaining an education paid for by the state and so they should respect the symbols of the state. In any case they point out that very few people are complaining. It is also argued that the anthem is only played on a few days in the year. Graduation is possibly the only time a student may hear it. There might be more grounds for complaint if it was played every day and everyone was required to stand. It was suggested by someone from the political centre that signs like the Gaelic signs in the Union have the potential to be more intimidatory because they define a whole space and are there permanently. Finally the Employment Equality Report noted that it was suggested to them that to challenge the playing of the national anthem is offensive to members of both communities in Northern Ireland.

The counter argument is also put by the Report, that there is disruption and embarrassment when it is played at graduation ceremonies. It is offensive to some people. It is also suggested that it is an anachronism in the modern world. And it is inappropriate to a university which is a place which should be governed solely by the search for knowledge, and should avoid connections to the civil authorities. In response to the argument that the institution is financed by the state, it is said that the source of that money is the tax system into which students and their parents have paid. The Employment Equality Report noted the argument that regardless of traditions elsewhere, in the Northern Ireland context the anthem could damage the maintenance of a neutral working environment. This argument is considered in more detail in Chapter 6.

Others do not have strong views either way. For them the anthem does not have much functional importance, except perhaps as a marker of the start of the proceedings.

The Solutions

One solution is to continue with present practice. Alternatively, it was suggested by students, lecturers and others with no direct connection with the University that a University song should be written to take the place of the anthem. Other universities have their own song and it was suggested that the Composer in Residence should be asked to compose a University song. A third solution, suggested by the Employment Equality Report is to remove the Gaelic signs in the Students Union and the anthem from graduation, in a kind of trade off in which each side would give something up.

It is initially difficult to see a compromise solution. The University is clear that if it was ever decided not to play the national anthem, no other tune would be used in its place. It is not a choice between one anthem and another, in which each side could give up their preferred solution and agree on a compromise song. The choice is between the national anthem or nothing. Some of the opponents of the anthem were not really aware of how important it is for unionists. If it is not played, no other tune could be a substitute.

The idea of trading off the anthem against the Union's bi-lingual policy was described as a 'classic Alliance-Liberal plan but it would make more people angry that it would make happy.' Both sets of protagonists would feel deprived. The University itself questions a policy of avoiding all symbols. The absence of any music or signs with a cultural significance would create a sterile environment, and the question is asked if this is what is wanted, especially in a university which is assumed to depend on the cross-fertilisation and stimulus of conflicting ideas for its intellectual vigour. A more hopeful way to take account of all the interests could be based on gaining broad support for the application of the principle of freedom of expression (see chapter 7).

The Process of Resolving the Problem

As well as hoping to find an acceptable answer, the University is equally concerned to find a process for balancing all the views and taking the debate forward. Some state that it is not a question to be decided by consensus. There is a right answer which should be implemented. But the University does not take that view. It wishes to find a solution which satisfies everyone if possible. One person described graduation as 'a family occasion to celebrate the University's achievements with invited guests.' It is a high point in the lives of many students and their parents and the University wishes that the day should not be marred for any of them.

The difficulties of reaching such a resolution have already been referred to. The Standing Committee of the University Senate has started the process of collecting opinions. It now has to decide how to deal with the responses.' It is recognised that most views will come from those with an active interest. The question is being asked: 'Does this mean the University should be guided by the few who respond.'

Given the diversity of interests, an important step is to get maximum agreement on the process by which the dispute will be settled. Is it acceptable that the Senate makes the final decision, or would it be better in the light of all the circumstances to delegate its authority to some other forum? What criteria should be the basis of the decision? What importance will be given to different views? Will they be treated equally or will the views of the majority or those who have the strongest feelings carry more weight? Is there a need for some process of mediation with an independent facilitator? If this fails is there a need for a process of arbitration? An agreed procedure which deals with these kinds of questions would provide a mechanism for settling the controversy.

There remains the question of how important the issue is. It is clearly important for some people, but it was pointed out that there were no riots or demonstrations. One assessment was that the actions of a few committed individuals would determine if it would continue to be a problem. We considered that there were some grounds for thinking the dispute was only important because of the wider context, and if the other issues became less important, the concern about the anthem would become less. We were assured that this was not the case and one person said there would be objections to the anthem even if there were no other problems. There might well be objections but we are doubtful if it would become such a focus for concern. At the moment it is seen as a test of the University's intentions in other matters, and as a result the administration has found itself on the spot over a comparatively minor issue. In contrast, a ban on smoking was introduced recently into the University. It will have a big impact on the daily life of staff and students but there was little or no anxiety about the plan, because it was a discrete issue which did not have the same symbolic importance.

It is also true that an issue like this can drag on for a number of years without resolution, because it only comes to a head a few times each year. In 1994 one change was that the police band did not play at all of the garden parties. As with disputes about the routes of annual parades, once the event is over, there is less urgency and it may be left unresolved until the following year. The University seems concerned to avoid this happening.

Political Parties

Political parties are very much involved in many of the contentious public issues concerning national symbols. Their views are included in other sections of this report where relevant. But their own use of symbols is not normally a source of controversy between members as they share similar perspectives.

In Northern Ireland the unionist parties use the Union flag extensively in their literature and badges. Most of their literature uses the colours red white and blue. Both the unionist parties sing 'The Queen' at their meetings, but the Democratic Unionist Party also uses it at many public occasions, notably at election counts. The party leader is particularly fond of it and he has a good strong voice to lead community singing. He frequently adds hymns and other songs. For example he sings 'Oh God Our Help In Ages Past', and the short hymn known as the Doxology when some victory has been achieved:

> Praise God, from whom all blessings flow;
> Praise Him, all creatures here below;
> Praise Him above, ye heavenly host;
> Praise Father Son and Holy Ghost.

It is clear that the Doxology is a hymn of praise, and it was stressed that Dr Paisley sings it for this reason, and not as an anthem, but it is undeniable that it has something of the feel of an anthem. It has the same measured tone and it fulfils the function which anthems often have of giving a sense of completion and closure. One nationalist was critical of the amount that 'The Queen' is used by members of the DUP. To him they sing it at inappropriate times as a political song which belongs to them. So he would stand for the anthem on other occasions, but he does not think it is appropriate at an election count and so he would try to avoid it.

Sinn Féin, on the other side, incorporates the Tricolour and its colours, mainly in election literature and posters. Their theoretical magazine is called *The Starry Plough* after the flag. 'The Soldier's Song' is sung at various functions.

The Conservative party told us that they do not use the national flag, but that is somewhat disingenuous because the party has had a series of logos which use the colours of the national flag, and sometimes even part of the flag. The Scottish Conservative Party has a rather clever logo which uses part of the Union flag to make an outline map of Scotland. The Northern Ireland Branch use the United Kingdom logo of a torch with red, white and blue flames.

The Alliance colour is yellow, which is a conscious attempt at non-alignment with either tradition. But it is also shared with other liberal parties in Europe. There logo of a stylised 'A' is reminiscent of an arrow and a bridge. They asked if they were the only party which does not care about emblems.

Actually, the Social Democratic and Labour Party does not use any national symbols. It claims not to be symbol conscious and apparently it gained its logo by accident. At one election the set designers for the television coverage wanted to include the party logos. They rang up the party to find out what it was. The reply was that they did not think they had one. They had never thought about it. The television designers decided that they had better invent one for the occasions and made a simple shape based on two triangles. Later the party added their initials between the two triangles and coloured them green and red, and in this way the logo was created. However it is not an arbitrary design. The red is the colour of the socialist group in Europe and green represents Ireland.

Cultural Identity Organisations

A leader of the Orange Order told of an occasion when he was invited to the unfurling of the banner of an Orange Lodge, a typical function for someone in his position. The Lodge was in the Republic of Ireland. At the end of the proceedings the local person who was officiating announced that the meeting would now stand to sing the national anthem. While they were getting up he turned to the guest from the North and winked. 'I havn't said which anthem', he said, 'but I think they will know.' They proceeded to sing 'The Queen'.

The Orange Order is not a political party, but it is linked to the Ulster Unionist Party and it has strong feelings about national symbols. It exists to promote and protect the interests of the Protestant and unionist community in all its aspects, religious, cultural and political. It uses rituals, some of them secret, to bind its members together in a sense of brotherhood and shared commitment. In its private and public activities British national symbols play an important part.

There are other organisations which have some similar features. The Black Institution and the Women's Orange Order are companion organisations to the Orange Order. Also in the unionist community there is the Apprentice Boys of Derry, and among nationalist there are the Ancient Order of Hibernians and the Irish National Foresters. There are also organisations which promote cultural identity through more educational activities. One such is the Ulster Society, but it seldom uses flags or anthems at its meetings and lecturers.

The rest of this section will concentrate on the Orange Order. It is an influential body, though perhaps not as influential as in the past. The nationalist orders are much weaker in their community. The Orange Order as an institution puts great emphasis on national symbols, and lays down regulations on how they should be used. In contrast, the Hibernians do not have a very disciplined approach to flags. The Orange Order is also interesting because it is a broadly based organisation and therefore its members use symbols in different ways. To use the categories we identified in Chapter two, it is a place where respectors, grudging acceptors and confronters meet, and it is instructive to look at how the resulting tensions are managed.

The order has no written policy on symbols, 'but every good Orangeman knows how to honour his country.' The national anthem is played at almost all of its events, apart from the most casual such as a darts match. They expect members to treat the anthem with respect and stand to attention.

'The Queen' still finds favour in other jurisdictions. In countries such as Canada, Orange Lodges sing the Canadian anthem, but they also sing 'The Queen'. The story which introduced this section is an example of one occasion when it was sung at a meeting in the Republic of Ireland, but other information suggests that the Order avoids the use of either anthem.

The Orange Order gives the Union flag precedence and pride of place. It should be in the middle, in front of or higher than other flags. In principle other national flags should also be treated with respect. Perhaps the most important use of flags by the Orange Order, and certainly its most public display, is at its parades or demonstrations. The parade is led by a colour party. This will often consist of the Union flag, the Orange standard and the Northern Ireland flag. The flags of all countries which are represented by an Orange Lodge can be flown, and at the Belfast parade the second rank is made up of the flags of all the countries where there are Orange Lodges.

Scotland is represented by the St Andrew's Cross or the Rampant Lion, and England by the St George's Cross. It will be appreciated that the Republic of Ireland, where there are lodges, poses something of a problem. We were assured that senior Orangemen will respect the Irish flag, but they are not very keen to actually carry it. They therefore carry the Saint Patrick's Cross to represent the Republic of Ireland, but not the whole island as Northern Ireland is represented by its own flag. Another problem is presented at parades in the Republic of Ireland. For the Order the Union flag is the pre-eminent flag and they would like to fly it on all occasions. But under the Irish flag code they must display the Tricolour if they are displaying the flag of another state. Because they do not want to carry the Tricolour they use no flags, though it is noticeable some bands carry the Northern Ireland flag without any action being taken by the Garda Síochána. Incidentally one member of the Order said he would like parity in this respect between Northern Ireland and the Republic of Ireland, because this would mean that at events such as the republican Easter commemoration parade in the Falls Road, the Tricolour could only be flown if the organisers were willing to also display the Union flag .

Traditionally the Orange lodges, the local groups which constitute the Order, carried their large banners, but other flags were uncommon. The wider use of flags in parades is a relatively modern phenomena, introduced by the young loyalist bands. They are seldom actual members of the Orange Order, but they are hired to lead individual lodges in the parade. The style and culture of marching bands has changed radically. There are still many traditional bands, rather staid and 'respectable' with members of all ages. But there has been a marked increase in the numbers of rumbustious and aggressive bands made up predominantly of young people. It is not necessary to discuss them in detail here, and there are other interesting accounts of their activities (Bell, 1992). Their growth is a significant phenomena which is closely related to the display of flags and emblems.

The bands are loud, assertive and eye-catching, and they have become the dominant image of the parade in the eyes of outsiders. They often have a colour party of perhaps five or six flags. They give more impact to the band when it is in a traditional parade alongside the more conservative bands, and they provide colour at their band parades where there are none of the banners of a typical parade. It is also a way of expressing the allegiances of the band. The style and motif of the flag may indicate an affinity with a paramilitary group, together with the band's name, often printed on the flag, and the members uniforms.

Probably the flag carrying also has a social function. The band members are predominantly male, but the colour party is normally female. As well as making political statements with the flags, it is therefore a way to involve girl friends and potential girl friends. It was suggested that colour parties have been adopted by republicans from unionist practice. While the developments has not been fully documented, we would incline more to the view that it is a process of cross fertilisation. In the 1970s youth bands were a loyalist phenomena, and flags were uncommon. Republican bands then became established, adopting features such as uniforms and flags, which were evocative of paramilitary organisations. Loyalists bands incorporated these features themselves as they became more hostile to the British government. They are also reminiscent of the completely different tradition of American marching bands with bright uniforms and drum majorettes.

The Order is a very large organisation and the rules are not always complied with by everyone. Often flags on Orange halls and other property are left to become torn and faded. At parades the Union flag is often not given the pre-eminent place in the centre of the other flags. If only two flags are carried the Union flag should be on the right, but often it is carried on the left. This is true of the badges which some of the bands wear. Frequently, they incorporate crossed flags with the Northern Ireland shield in the middle. The Union flag is sometimes on the right and sometimes on the left.

The Saint Andrew's Cross is very common and it too is sometime given precedence over both the Union and Northern Ireland flags. There are also some unusual combinations. One Lodge at the Independent Orange Demonstration in 1993 was preceded by the American Stars and Stripes, flanked by two Union flags. To most people these may seem minor details, but the Order itself says that they matter. It may well be that members of local lodges are not well versed in flag etiquette, but one might suppose that they are instructed in the formal way to show respect to the national symbols and the reasons why the Order wishes certain flags to be ranked higher than others. In any case senior Orangemen seem to make the same mistakes. At the Independent Order's Parade in 1993 the colour party was led by the Orange Standard, flanked by the Union flag. This also happened at the County Londonderry Parade, when the Union flag was placed on the left of the Orange Standard with the Northern Ireland flag on the right.

Breaches of the flag code are not likely to cause public controversy, but in other ways flags have been one source of trouble at parades. Disputes about routes is a more important issue, but concern has been felt at the behaviour of some participants and followers of the parade. Flags have been waved provocatively and there has been some embarrassment when flags which resembled paramilitary flags were carried. The Order has ruled that the only flags which should be carried at one of its parades are the Union flag, the flags of the jurisdiction where the parade is taking place or of the Orange lodges present, the Orange Standard and identifying flags for lodges and band. These rules have two limitations. It is possible for a band to carry its identifying flag even if it is reminiscent of a paramilitary flag. Secondly, the Order concedes that it may be difficult to remove a flag which is forbidden if the band and other bystanders insist on its inclusion. The whole procession could be disrupted, and those in authority may themselves be ambivalent about the flag.

The procedure is that each lodge is expected to police its own members and the band it has hired. It should ensure that they know the rules and stick to them. If they feel they cannot take action at the time, they are required to discipline the offenders afterwards, and if necessary exclude them from future parades. But often this does not happen. There are differing views on how the rules should be applied. To some members it may not seem a very serious issue. There may be a degree of tolerance of the behaviour and perhaps even some sympathy for the attitudes expressed.

This is a clear example of a recurring theme in this study, which is not only faced by the Orange Order. People are prepared to tolerate behaviour in their own tradition which they would not tolerate in opponents. It is difficult to appreciate how people from another tradition feel about a flag associated with a paramilitary group or a flag which is used provocatively. Even when someone is unhappy about the behaviour of other members of his or her own tradition, it is difficult to challenge them for at least two reasons. He or she has some understanding of why they act as they do and that creates a level of ambivalence, and he or she is also aware of being open to the charge of disloyalty. Nevertheless the consequences of a group not exercising self discipline is increased community tension and damage to the group's reputation. It emphasises the importance of distinguishing behaviour which is celebratory from that which is confrontational, and deciding what limits are necessary. This problem often takes the form of a tension between the leadership of an institution and its followers and loose associates, and organisations like the Orange Order need to be sensitive to the implications of their response to the situation. The Order has recognised the consequences for itself and the community of not exercising self restraint and self-discipline, but of course that in itself does not remove the issue.

The Churches

Some years ago, a clergyman moved from a parish in the Republic of Ireland to a Shankill Road parish in the Protestant part of West Belfast. When the Twelfth of July came round, he was shocked one morning to discover that a Union flag had been hoisted over the church. He sent for the sexton and ordered him to take it down. As a result he almost had a riot on his hands and his parishioners decided he was 'disloyal.'

This incident demonstrates some of the issues which arise when flags and anthems are used on church property. It shows that practice varies from place to place. It reminds us that the church cannot be considered in isolation from the community which it serves. There are other relevant considerations. The most fundamental theological question which flags and anthems highlight is the separation of church and state, and church and politics. Is it appropriate that the church should be identified with governments or with political movements as happens when their symbols are used on church property, and does this interfere with their pastoral or religious roles? As one clergyman said perceptions become the reality.

We will look at these issues in relation to three main areas of church practices: flying flags on or in churches, church parades, and funerals, where the issues are raised most starkly.

Flags on churches
All the churches are All-Ireland institutions, but the churches follow consistent policies and practices in both jurisdictions. We have already noted in Chapter 2 that some Catholic churches are decorated with flags and bunting on occasions such as visits by the Bishop, during a novena and special anniversaries of the local parish, Saint Patrick's Day, the Feast of the Annunciation and other special days in the church calendar. National flags are seldom used, and even Saint Patrick's flag is not common. The Papal flag and the Bishop's flag are used, but coloured bunting forms the main display. It creates an informal festival atmosphere.

We also noted that the Papal colours of white and yellow are common and during a novena blue and white predominates, but all colours can be seen. Red white and blue are as prevalent as green white and orange. These occasions are said to be purely religious festivals, but in the past Saint Patrick's Day and the Feast of the Blessed Virgin, when the Hibernians paraded to the church may have provided a kind of surrogate opportunity to make an indirect nationalist statement.

The use of flags in the Protestant Churches is more formal. Though the traditional Orange song, 'The Aghalee Heroes', describes a more exuberant display perhaps we may have to allow for poetic licence:

Like the sons of King William we marched then
Till at length Lurgan Town we did view
Where the church it was there decorated
With the Orange and Purple and Blue.

Modern practice however, is very similar to public buildings: on public holidays a single flag is hoisted, often on the church tower if there is one. Although the practice of Protestant Churches is not dissimilar north and south of the Border, the national symbols of course change. There are also variations in the local conditions which make it more sensible to discuss separately the situation in each jurisdiction. We will deal with Northern Ireland first. Saint Patrick's flag is flown by some Anglican churches on the Saint's Day, and we know of one Anglican church which also flies it on the Twelfth of July. We noted in Chapter 2 that on the anniversary of the raising of the Siege of Derry, when the Apprentice Boys of Derry hold their service in Saint Columb's Cathedral before their parade, the Crimson flag flies over the Cathedral as it did during the Siege. Many churches, including Saint Patrick's Cathedral, Armagh, would never or rarely fly a flag.

In the Anglican and Presbyterian churches it is a matter for the local clergy and the committee or select vestry to decide whether the flag will be flown. There are a number of factors which influence the decision. Some churches have no convenient place to fly it. Some people feel it is not appropriate for a church to fly a flag. And we have already seen that local feeling is often a factor. We were told that in the Presbyterian Church local ministers must use discretion and respond to the needs of the local community. With regard to the Twelfth of July, some churches fly the Union flag either on the day itself or for about two weeks: 'Orange traditions are a very important part of local culture, a folk festival especially important in rural areas. The local church is not inclined to fight with locals. If flags go up the minister won't try to influence proceedings.' For Presbyterians, the local people are the church. An Anglican expressed the view that identity (and therefore the expectation that flags should be flown on the church) assumes greater significance as one goes farther away from the city.

The Churches recognise there may also be community opposition to the display of the flag, and in some areas churches feel it is prudent not to fly the flag. One church leader said his church would not be happy if the flag was flown in a tense areas in a way which was 'associated with provocation.' Questions are sometimes raised when the Union flag is flown in mixed areas. One church leader acknowledged that local people wonder if it is being flown in a sectarian sense or simply as the national flag. However, it is also necessary to understand that this distinction may be irrelevant to many of those who object, because they do not accept the legitimacy of the state, and for them any display of the flag is an act of identification with the state and therefore a sectarian act. As with the Hibernian church parade we mentioned earlier, opponents see an underlying sectarian meaning in the action. This does not in itself mean that either practice is wrong, but it is important to understand how it is perceived by others.

In the Irish Republic Protestant churches near the Border are unlikely to fly any flag. Farther away from the border Presbyterian churches fly the Tricolour on national occasions. For example, when the state President recently opened a leisure centre at Lucan , the Tricolour was flown.

Although decisions about flags is a matter for the local rector, the Anglican Primate insists that the Church in the Republic of Ireland uses the flag and identifies with the state. Uniformed youth organisations connected with the Church are also expected to use it. There may appear to be a contrast with Saint Patrick's Cathedral in Armagh where the flag is not flown normally. There may also be a contradiction here between expecting the Church to identify with the state and encouraging free expression of identity by each community. It was explained that the situation is less complicated in the Republic of Ireland because there is no conflict of national identity for Protestants. But what if Anglicans do not feel that they identify with the state? This is another situation where it is helpful to recognise that a distinction may have to be made between institutional and individual responses.

Some churches also hang flags inside the church. This is a practice founded mainly in the Anglican Church, and is rare but not unknown in the Presbyterian Church. They mainly hang historic regimental flags, which 'are pure history and the heritage of the people who use that church.' Only a few churches will have historic links with a regiment, but others may hold the British Legion flag. Many regimental flags are Union flags, with the names of the regimental battle honours sown on them. In this way Union flags are displayed in a number of churches in the Republic of Ireland. On the other hand Saint Patrick's Anglican Cathedral in Dublin may be the only church in the Republic of Ireland which displays the Tricolour. It hangs permanently in Saint Patrick's Anglican Cathedral in the south aisle above the memorial to Douglas Hyde, an Anglican and the first President of Ireland. In fact the President's flag, a gold harp on an azure field, might be more correct as it is there to honour the memory of the President. The Anglican church makes it clear that no party political flags or emblems are preserved in any church, though one exception might be the memorabilia kept in Saint Columb's Cathedral in Londonderry as part of its little museum of artefacts associated with the Siege of Derry.

Parades
Many organisations hold church parades: most obviously uniformed youth organisations, military personnel, the Royal British Legion, the Orange Order and Ancient Order of Hibernians. The participants parade to the church with their flags and banners and a church service is held in the church. The Hibernians and other organisations which parade to the Catholic church are unlikely to carry any national flag, most of the others will carry the Union flag. Youth organisations do not carry a national flag if they feel it will be contentious and cause problems for the young people. Some church parades by the Orange Order have been controversial, because they pass through areas where they are resented. In recent years church parades in Portadown and the Lower Ormeau Road in Belfast have led to public disorder. The churches deny that they are in any way responsible for the organisation of the parade and the behaviour of the participants. They are only responsible for what happens in church. It may be significant that in the case of one parade where there has been confrontation, the flags are not carried into the church, but at other church parades where there is no controversy they are carried into the church.

At the church the main flag of the organisations and the Union flag, if present, are carried ceremoniously to the front of the church and left in the sanctuary or similar position. These practices seldom cause problems. In fact only those involved are aware of the detail of the ceremony.

In the Republic of Ireland similar conventions are followed. The annual parade to Saint Patrick's Cathedral by the Dublin Branch of the Royal British Legion has a number of interesting features. Although the words 'royal' and 'British' appear in the title and the purpose of the organisation is to remember those who died fighting for the United Kingdom, the Tricolour is carried in the parade. The Union flag is not carried, but the flags of the local branches are present and they incorporate a small Union flag in the corner. At the Cathedral, the Tricolour and the flags of the Dublin district and the Women's Legion are carried to the front of the church and handed to the officiating clergy. So the Tricolour and flags incorporating the Union flag are carried together into the Anglican cathedral.

Church parades are one of the occasions when the national anthem may be sung. It is a hymn and is included in the hymn books of the Protestant Churches. Nevertheless when an organisation requests that the anthem is sung, the Anglican Church make a point of finishing the service with a blessing and then the anthem is sung. Similarly in the Republic of Ireland 'The Soldier's Song' will be sung on special occasions.

Funerals

Funerals give the Churches their biggest dilemmas. Death and funeral rites have both religious and social aspects. Most people, even many who are irreligious, find death a momentous event and a reminder of the mystery of life to which religion is able to respond. For most people it is also a time when relatives and friends wish to mourn, and also honour the deceased. The church is responsible for the religious observances, and the family and organisations with which the deceased was associated take responsibility for the civil elements. The two elements overlap, and sometimes they can also be in conflict.

Over the years conventions and customs have developed in the same way as other social rituals. Leaders of the state are given a state funeral and those who served its armed forces are given a military funeral. The procedures which should be followed in each case are governed by strict protocol. One custom is to cover the coffin with the national flag, and perhaps a symbol of office, such as a uniform cap. Another convention at a military funeral is a gun salute at the burial. Members of the Royal Ulster Constabulary can be given an official funeral, but some officers and their families do not want it, preferring a private family funeral. Some officers feel that they are serving the community and are uncomfortable with the military trappings. Some also feel they are best avoided if it helps to reduce tension.

Formal ceremonial has been adapted to other funerals on an unofficial basis. The civil authorities place very few restrictions on what is permissible at a funeral, provided the death is registered properly and the body is interred or otherwise disposed of in an authorised way. It is a matter for the family. David Martin, an ex-member of the Ulster Defence Regiment, who was killed in April 1993 by the IRA did not have a military funeral, but his coffin was draped in a Union flag. After Aidan McAnespie was killed in 1988 as a result of an apparently accidental discharge of a gun, while passing an army check point on his way to a GAA match, his coffin was covered with his GAA shirt. The flag or other items which had been on the coffin are given afterwards to the nearest relative as a momento and mark of respect.

Sometimes the deceased is dressed in a uniform or something of special value. In England it has become common in recent years for young people to be buried dressed in the shirt of their favourite football team.

The main restriction which is placed on funerals is the presence of anything which associates the funeral with an illegal organisation. Paramililtary groups wish to give members of their organisations a military funeral, including, a colour party, a gun salute, and, on the coffin, the flag, the deceased's gloves and beret. They explain this by saying that the member was committed to the organisation and the flag, and he should be honoured in this way. Part of the importance of these procedures for paramilitary organisations is they are rooted in long established rituals, sometimes originating in the conventions of their opponents, the British Army. Their adoption by a paramilitary group is another way of indicating that the organisation is an enduring and legitimate part of the long tradition of military struggle.

The authorities will try to prevent the beret and gloves being placed on the coffin and the gun salute as these are considered to be symbols of an illegal organisation. However, they do not object to the flag, especially in view of the repeal of the Flags and Emblems Act (see Chapter 5). The paramilitary groups have themselves changed their conventions in the light of circumstances. Loftus (1994) records that Belfast republicans cited the security risk as the reason for giving up uniforms and gun salutes, but she also suspects they wanted to give more emphasise to their growing political involvement.

The Churches all agree that they have no responsibility for what happens outside the church gate. At a public cemetery, a paramilitary group will avoid embarrassing the Church. For example a guard of honour would not appear and fire a gun salute until the officiating clergy have gone. On Church property, however, they expect that the funeral party will follow their wishes. Each Church has its own policy, and there may also have to be variations from that policy depending on the local situation and what is consider feasible at the time.

We will consider the official position first. There are less problems for the Protestant churches. At state and military funerals they have no objection to the use of flags and other symbols of the state. Paramilitary funerals at churches are uncommon. One Anglican said he could only remember two instances. There are a number of reasons for this. In the Protestant tradition in some areas in the past funerals took place from the deceased's home direct to the grave, and did not visit the church. In any case when a member of a Protestant paramilitary group is killed, the family often wants no mention made of the paramilitary connection. And many paramilitary members in the Protestant community have no church connections. One church leader said his Church would not encourage a church funeral. Where a paramilitary funeral is organised the security forces will already have forbidden the military trappings, the main reason why the church would object.

The situation is more complicated for the Catholic Church. We have seen that it is uneasy about the association of the church with national or military symbols, and this extends to approved official funerals. To give one example of how the Church has handled such situations, at the funeral of one Catholic policeman in Northern Ireland, the Union flag was not draped on the coffin as it was taken to the church. After the mass the coffin was taken outside, the union flag was placed on the coffin and the police band led the funeral procession from the church to the graveside. The Order of Christian Funerals (1991, mandatory Easter Sunday 1992, paragraph 38) states that 'Only Christian symbols may rest on or be placed near the coffin during the funeral liturgy. Any other symbols, for example, national flags, or flags or insignia of associations, have no place in the funeral liturgy.' There is a problem because the tradition of state and military funerals is strong and it is not easy to change this practice. The Church's initial concern is to stop the practice spreading. The Reverend Patrick Jones of the Irish Institute of Pastoral Liturgy has written in a personal communication that 'During the discussion before placing the new Order of Christian Funerals, the custom of placing the national flag and/or the flag of the UN in military funerals was noted. Also it seems the flag of the Life Boat Organisation is used at member's funerals. It is easy to see how many more exceptions – and often in very acceptable situations – could be added. It lessens the authority of the general norms and, of course, may be unhelpful in the stand which is taken on the occasion of paramilitary funerals and when symbols unrelated to the Christian status of the person (e.g. membership of a sports organisation) are requested to be used.'

Turning to paramilitary funerals, the Catholic Church faces a more complex situation. Most Catholic funerals include a requiem mass at the church, even for people who had lapsed in their faith. The Church considers it has a duty to carry out the funeral rites for any person who has died. The paramilitary organisation will want Church participation in the funeral because it may be the wish of the family and also it provides a measure of legitimacy for the armed struggle. The Church's position is laid out in a statement issued by the Catholic Press Office in 1988. It says that 'before agreeing to a funeral the parish priest insists on an undertaking that there will be no flags, emblems, political banners, paramilitary displays or similar manifestations in the Church precincts at any time while the body is in Church.'

It is not always possible to carry out the policies, and again the Catholic Church faces greater difficulties than the other Churches. The family of the deceased and paramilitary group may want a military style funeral and they may bring a good deal of pressure to bear on the clergy to allow the Tricolour to remain on the coffin when it is carried into the church. It may be brought in quietly and placed on the coffin when the church is empty.

In many ways the clergy are in a weak position. The priest is aware of the distress and vulnerability of the family, which also makes it difficult for us to describe specific incidents in detail. As well as immediate relatives, the extended family and the whole community are very involved, and some of them may act irrationally. Because there is a duty to perform the funeral rites it is difficult for a priest to refuse to officiate if the family and mourners are not willing to comply with his wishes, though it is possible for the funeral mass to take place at a different time from the funeral. A solution is needed immediately when there is a confrontation outside the church. It cannot be left until next week. On the other hand the Church is also aware that the situation is acted out under public scrutiny and it is criticised if it is seen to be colluding in paramilitary display.

The churches policy makes it clear that 'In arranging funerals priests of the parish will deal only with the next-of-kin, immediate family or undertakers, never with paramilitary organisations.' They will try to discuss the arrangements before the funeral, so that everything has been agreed. But still, priests are often placed in a situation where the Church feels that they have no alternative to making their protest and then continuing with the funeral rites to avoid a worse situation.

Normally the anthem is not played at funerals. The Orange Order gave an explanation for its absence at funerals for its members: it is not a 'religious' symbol in that sense, and it is not a 'political symbol'. It is a symbol of national pride.

Observations

A number of comments can be made on the practices of the different Churches. Firstly, there are clear differences between the Churches in their acceptance of flags. This seems to be a reflection of the culture of each Church, but it is hard to explain the reasons for the differences. One topic on which there is a range of views is the relationship between the Church and the State, and therefore the appropriateness of national symbols in churches. The Catholic Church has the most explicit opposition to the use of national flags, though in practice they are permitted sometimes. Protestants may be surprised that the Catholic Church adopts such a stance because they are very aware of the influence of the Church on social legislation in the Republic of Ireland. From the Church's point of view, its informal relationship with the state is satisfactory. The explanation may be that it considers itself the Universal Church separate from any state, and the attitude towards national symbols is not unique to Ireland. Given the prevalence of the flag in the United States of America, it is not too surprising that the Catholic Church there displays the flag.

The Anglican Church seem to use flags more than the others. Most church leaders seem to share that perception but a leading Anglican was quite surprised at the suggestion. If the assumption is correct, we could speculate that this reflects its origins as the state church and although it has been disestablished for over one hundred years, vestiges of its identification with the state may remain.

Views on these matters change with the changing social climate. Many church leaders have become uneasy about national symbols, military funerals and commemorations, because there is less support for the use of military force. One cleric made this point very strongly. He said the Church had become disenchanted with war and saw it for the horror it is. It should not be an object of glorification but of sorrow. A very public indication of the changing climate was the disagreement about the best way to mark the end of the Falklands War. The British government wanted a service of thanks-giving to God for giving the victory but the Church of England thought it was more fitting to have a service to remember the dead on both sides.

All the Churches agree that they have to be sensitive to the community and that they are limited in their ability to act against local feeling, as they cannot force people to accept their wishes, especially at funerals and other times when emotions are high. The responsibility for deciding practice on symbols lies with the church authorities and individual clergy, but church policy has to take into account the tension which can arise between the clergy and the community and in this way community opinion can deter-mine the implementation of church policy at local level.

This leads us to consider the practices and influences in the community. In the following chapters we shall consider the use of flags in the cut and thrust of every day life in the community and at the workplace, where it is more often the case that the purpose for using national symbols is to make a political statement.

Notes

1   i.e. schools managed directly by the Board and attended mainly by Protestants.

CHAPTER 4

Symbols in Everyday Community Life

At noon, in the dead centre of a faith,
Between Draperstown and Magherafelt,
This bitter village shows a flag
In a baked absolute September light.
Here the Word has withered to a few
Parched certainties
Tom Paulin

In this chapter we want to look at the informal use of flags in local communities. First we shall describe what happens in relatively homogeneous communities whose members are predominately from one or other tradition. Behaviour and practice are not regulated by any organisation or official body, as was the case in some of the institutions which we looked at in the last chapter. Group expectations and group pressure, guided by custom and convention, are strong influences, but loose networks within the community act as guardians of the traditions. These include local Orange Lodges in Protestant areas, local branches of political groups and informal youth 'gangs', the 'bearers of the culture' and 'guardians of 'tradition'' in Desmond Bell's (1992, p9) words. Not unnaturally these groups do not always agree on the form which local activities should take.

In the following two chapters we shall look at two types of situations where the two communities come into contact with each other, the street and the workplace. Wider issues then arise, because the activities of one community may have an impact on the others, and in these circumstances the law has intervened to regulate inter-group relations.

For many years, it has been common for unionists to erect flags and bunting at the main periods of celebration, the Twelfth of July in most areas, and in Londonderry, the anniversary of the lifting of the Siege of Derry in August. Individuals displayed a Union jack from their house and there was some competition to have a bigger, newer and brighter flag than the neighbours. A few people added additional features, perhaps a Northern Ireland shield on the wall or a short length of bunting from the upstairs windows to the front gate. It was also the time to brighten up the area generally and the front of the house was often painted and cleaned.

In addition to individual efforts the local Orange lodge organised the erection of an Orange arch and bunting in a prominent place, perhaps across the main road through a village, or at the entrance to a housing estate. The lodge collected money to cover the costs and the night when it was erected was a social occasion. Those not directly involved would come and watch. In those times it was quite uncommon to paint street furniture and kerbstones, though posts or pillars close to the arch were sometimes painted red white and blue as part of the overall effect. Murals were less common, perhaps only one in a district. The central motif was always King William in the characteristic pose, mounted on a white horse at the Battle of the Boyne. 'Red brick in the suburb, white horse on the wall', in the words of Maurice Craigs's poem. If a parade was scheduled to take place in the area, the preparations would be more thorough and elaborate than usual.

In the past the flags and bunting would only be left for the week or so around the celebration, and then removed. Some people only put out their flag on the Twelfth day itself. Since there was little painting, there would be few permanent signs of the street decoration left behind.

The social bonding and pride in the area, which was generated by these activities should not be underestimated. It is captured in memoirs or in anthropological and ethnographic studies such as Larsen's good descriptions of Twelfth preparations in a County Down village, and it is worth quoting at length. He describes it as 'a ritual expression of collective identity.' All the names are of course pseudonym:

> One evening, early in July, Sam Eakins starts to whitewash the front of his house. The next day the Hannas do the same. Then Sam gives the Boltons a hand with theirs, and while they are at it they give my house the same treatment . . . Inspired by all this activity, I give the door and windows a new coat of cherry-red paint.
>
> The neighbours and passers-by speak highly of my painting. They stop to admire the results . . . Windows are being cleaned, the beach (shingle) in front of the houses is being attended to. In short there is a constant hubbub of activity up and down the small street. At night we bring chairs out of the houses and sit around, admiring our work.
>
> . . . I regard it as straightforward maintenance work . . . Then, one night, little Elizabeth Eakins remarks casually, 'Daddy always does up the front with whitewash before the twelfth.'
>
> A whole new charter for interpretation is introduced. And during the days that follow more and more events fit into this new picture. The parents buy the children new dresses and new shoes ('They sure need something new for the summer'). The small ones compare the money they have saved up for 'the Twelfth'. All over Kilbroney there is activity. And then the music starts.
>
> Through the evenings the bands are practising . . .
>
> One night we start to decorate Sandy Row with bunting: red white and blue pennants, two or three faded union jacks. Mrs. McKee provides the outfit, Sam Eakins does the job. The other families stand around to admire and offer advice. (Larsen, 1982, pp278–9)

Larsen also described a darker side, when he notes that 'the celebration of "the Twelfth" breaks all the standards of "decent behaviour" ... that is to say, behaving in a friendly and cheerful manner and avoiding provoking the other side'. In addition to expressing group solidarity and shared identity, the display of flags and bunting together with the other elements of the celebration also communicated ownership of territory and dominance. Many people may not have thought of what they were doing in these terms. But we have seen that flags mark out territorial claims throughout the world, and the ability to display flags without hindrance indicates power and control.

In the Catholic community, there is not the same tradition of street decoration. We have already discussed the theory that nationalists are less concerned with national symbols than unionists. Whatever the reason, the Catholic community have mainly celebrated dates in the religious and church calendar, such as Saint Patrick's Day. Saint Patrick's flag and the papal flag were flown. Even then, it was on a much smaller scale than in the Protestant community.

There were few direct expressions of nationalist views until the 1960s. Travelling around the country, the Tricolour was not a common sight. If it was displayed it was quite probable that it would be removed by the authorities and the people responsible could be arrested. It seemed to be a tradition in some areas more than others. For example a single flag was often to be seen somewhere around Newry and there was usually one flying in a tree in the townland of Glen at the foot of the Glenshane Pass. We have already noted that the GAA flew the Tricolour at their sports grounds during matches, unless local opposition was such that the match might have been disrupted. Gaelic games provided another reason to erect flags. It became the custom to fly the county colours when the team reached the semi-finals or finals of one of the competitions and this was another marker of the religious composition of the district.

Bunting was erected in the town or village where a Hibernian parade was taking place, but not elsewhere. They were, and continue to be, fairly indifferent to the colour of the bunting and acquire it from any convenient source. About ten years ago they held a parade in Rasharkin, County Antrim, and borrowed red white and blue bunting from the Orange Order. Green white and orange were more common colours, but there were few displays of the tricolour, the Order treading a fine line between tolerance and opposition from the authorities, and overt expressions of political aspirations might have tipped the balance.

There were other customary uses of flags which did not have political significance, but indicate the different social and political climate before the present Troubles. It was normal to see a Union flag flying over an uncompleted house. It was put there by the builders, normally the bricklayers, as a sign that they were waiting for a bonus. As they finished the external work and were taking their ladders down they would erect the flag. They would agree to take it down for the owner, but he would have to pay them to put their ladders back up to get the flag, and so they would get a bonus. The origin of this custom is uncertain. One suggestion was that it came from Scotland, but it was prevalent across both the Protestant and Catholic community. The Union flag was always used, by workmen of all religious and political backgrounds, and it was an even more successful ploy in Catholic areas as the owner was more keen to get it down. The custom has completely died out in the last twenty years.

Street names in Irish are a way of promoting the Irish language, and their presence is a marker of the existence of a commitment to Irish national identity, in the same way as flags are expressions of the values of at least some of the residents of an area. It is therefore relevant to consider the policy in relation to Irish signs. Since the Irish language is not widely accepted in the Protestant community, street names have become part of sectarian politics in Ireland. The Report of the Project of the Churches on Human Rights and Responsibilities in the United Kingdom and the Republic of Ireland (Bailey, 1988) indicates clearly the implications of different perspectives on culture:

> Promotion of a community's culture can be used as a weapon in a political dispute, or it can be a genuine search for distinctive roots and identity. If the nationalist minority promotes Gaelic culture in Northern Ireland merely to wrong-foot the unionist majority it is not surprising that the unionists should react with hostility. On the other hand, any minority is entitled to ask others to respect its own culture and traditions.

In 1948 nationalist councils in Newry and Omagh erected Irish language street signs in some parts of the towns. The unionist government at Stormont opposed this development and the following year section 49 (i)(a) of the Public Health and Local Government (Miscellaneous Provisions) Act (N.I.) 1949 made it unlawful to erect signs in any language other than English. The Province of Quebec in Canada has a similar law prohibiting the use of languages other than French, but it goes farther and applies to any signs, including business notices and house sales signs. The offending signs in Newry and Omagh were not removed and some of them still exist, but the act curtailed the official erection of signs.

In the 1980s with the growth of interest in the Irish language, unofficial Irish street signs were erected in nationalist areas. There has been little Government interference in this practice, but one Sinn Féin member was arrested in Belfast for putting up signs. If local authorities were to erect signs the councillors could be surcharged for the cost because they would have acted beyond their powers.

Many people are proud of the use of the language in this way, but with the politicisation of the language issue, the erection of signs has been also supported by groups in order to make a political statement. At the same time there is greater interest in the language among Protestants, with a small number of unionists claiming it as part of their tradition. Chris McGimpsey, a leading member of the Ulster Unionist party has been quoted (*The Guardian*, 9.2.1993) as saying 'Irish is part of our tradition. It should be something we can all look at, a neutral thing. Irish has been abused by militant Republicanism in the past. The language should be removed from the political agenda.'

There has been a greater awareness of the importance of rights of cultural expression generally and the British and Irish Governments accepted some responsibility in Article 5 of the 1985 Anglo-Irish Agreement:

> The conference shall concern itself with measures to recognise and accommodate the rights and identities of the two traditions in Northern Ireland, to protect human rights and to prevent discrimination. Matters to be considered in this area include measures to foster the cultural heritage of both traditions . . .

This was taken to include Irish street signs and subsequently, the Anglo-Irish Ministerial Conference indicated that it was planning the repeal the relevant section of the 1949 Act. No action was taken and the situation has been somewhat confused. In fact in December 1990 a letter from the Private Secretary to the Secretary of State to Derry City Council made it clear that the Government was not prepared to move on the issue, but it was not clear why that policy has been adopted: 'The Secretary of State has asked me to say, however, that it is not Government policy to give Irish parity with English and that in the light of that policy has concluded, after careful consideration, that it would not be appropriate to amend the legislation governing the erection of street names.'

This decision can be compared to the situation in Scotland where signs can be erected in Gaelic, the Isle of Man where Manx is permitted, the Channel Island where Norman-French is used, England, where Chinese signs have been erected in Soho, and in Wales The Welsh Language Act 1967 protects the Welsh language and allows the erection of street signs in Welsh. The move from the earlier position which contemplated legalising the use of Irish language signs should also be considered in the light of relaxations on the flying of the Tricolour which is a more overt action, and the support for the language in other ways including grants to Irish language organisations and Irish language schools. It might be that a policy which allows councils to erect signs would make it less likely that the issue is politicised.

Some members of Derry City Council wanted to take a case to the European Court of Human Rights on the grounds of protection of cultural rights. However, a case could only be taken if someone had been prosecuted for trying to assert their rights. One suggestion was to create a test case by erecting an Irish language street sign to commemorate the Government's earlier announcement of its willingness to amend the law and one hundred years of Chonradh na Gaelige, the Irish language organisation. Since then the Secretary of State has said that he will be amending the law and the present situation appears to be that there is a draft order to repeal the 1949 Act which has gone out for consultation.

There have also been changes over the years in the practices associated with the display of flags and bunting for many reasons. In part it is a response to changing social norms and material conditions. For example there were closer ties between people in small side streets and it was easier to organise joint activities. It was also easier to string bunting between low houses near to each other, and there was less heavy traffic which might pull it down. The 'technology' and skills have developed. On the one hand materials and methods of electrical wiring and guttering have changed and buildings have fewer convenient attachment points for bunting. On the other hand the materials are better and synthetic fibres will last through the marching season and into the winter. If it is more difficult to mount streamers high enough to avoid traffic, it is also more difficult to bring them down, and so they are left. There is also more surplus capital to spend on decorations. In the first half of the century bunting would be carefully stored and used again in subsequent years. That is still the case in some thrifty communities. One person when asked why he was taking it down only two days after the Twelfth said 'well, its just a wee bit too dear.' Now extra flags and bunting can be bought each year and there are more and better materials to make Orange arches. Paint and brushes are more easily available for decorating walls and pillars, and the results last longer. Skills in mural painting have developed, and the painters are able to undertake a greater variety of styles and motifs, including non-political subjects.

Improved material conditions may also be a disincentive to street decorations. It is seen as a mainly working class phenomena. As people move up the social scale their political views may change, but regardless of politics they are less likely to erect flags and bunting. They have more outlets and interests and the social component of erecting street decoration has less meaning for them. When the flags are being erected in working class areas, they are more likely to be too busy or taking part in some form of sport or other recreation.

Bell (1990, p137) notes that responsibility for street decoration has fallen almost exclusively on young people and their bands: 'At one time in Loyalist neighbourhoods the decoration of the streets would have involved the whole community and would have been entrusted to the senior members of the community. Now, with the structures of Protestant working class communality considerably eroded, it is the young people who provide the manpower, and the bands the organisation.' Loyalist bands in particular have links with each other, and band parades are an important part of their informal social organisation. They take place once or twice a week during the summer, and each band takes turns to be host. They prepare their district by painting kerb stones and making the area look more loyalist. We have already commented on the influence of these bands on the use of flags in parades.

All these changes are significant, but equally important are the changes in the political situation since 1968. The inter-community tension has been expressed through increased displays of flags and assertion of group identity in working class areas and rural villages which are strongly unionist or nationalist. It was said that where communities feel threatened they put out flags 'in abundance'. In talking about the removal of flags from the workplace (see Chapter 6), a number of people said that unionists could compensate by decorating their local community. It is one way to answer back within the law, as one politician put it.

There has been a big increase in display in nationalist areas, often linked to political demonstrations which are more widespread. Republican Easter parades now take place in most towns with a substantial republican population. A number of people suggested that the change was in emulation of unionist practice, but that in itself does not explain it. Since the 1960s the nationalist community has asserted itself in many ways and challenged many aspects of society with which it was dissatisfied. The community has witnessed political action, street demonstrations and the use of physical force. By comparison, it has been easier to display the symbols with which the community identifies, particularly after the legal obstacles were removed. The increased use of flags and emblems is also a reflection of the general way feelings and opinions have become more focused and polarised so that people across the political spectrum are looking for ways to assert themselves. Overall it is still less than in unionist areas, and is noticeable in the nationalist community because of its relative absence in the past.

Flags are still not evident in all nationalist areas. The pattern is patchy. Areas like Newry which erected the occasional flag in the 50s and 60s are the same areas which now sport a profusion of decorations. Other areas such as parts of Derry, which are noted for strong nationalist views, continue to be comparatively bare of flags though wall murals and other emblems have become common. It seems that there may be a culture or tradition of flying flags in some geographical areas and not in others.

The impact of the various changes can be seen in a number of ways. In unionist areas there are discussions about whether the numbers of flags is increasing or decreasing. At one level it is a form of nostalgia, rather like comparing our present weather with the summers in childhood. At another level it is more important because people are trying to assess shifts in the commitment of the community to unionism and loyalism by changes in the decorations.

Whether or not the quantities of flags and bunting have increased, they remain up for a longer time. A single flag is often erected in a public place at a significant point in the political calendar, Easter for republicans and the Twelfth of July for unionists, and they are left there to get faded and threadbare until they are replaced next year. It has become common to erect the opponent's flag on bonfires which are then of course burnt . In the days before the fire, it flies vigorously on top of the piled wood and tyres looking like a proud statement and a symbol of the people who built the fire, and for a moment you might believe the neighbourhood has changed its political colours. Painting kerb stones, bus shelters, lamp posts and pillars in unionist or nationalist colours is more widespread. Slogans are daubed on walls, some terse and incomprehensible to the uninitiated, some amusing, some poetic, and many scurrilous and provocative. Some have developed wall murals into an art form (Rolston 1992). Flags are a common theme, and flag designers, anticipating that their flag may be painted on walls might want to note that it is more difficult to execute a reasonable representation of a Union flag than the three stripes of the Tricolour.

Not only has the form of display changed, but their meaning and impact has also intensified and changed. Their original function of self expression and building group solidarity remains. In fact as each group has felt more challenged, there has been a stronger need to assert group identity. The symbols and colours evoke a mixture of pride and aesthetic appeal for those who identify closely with them. Many people criticise the gaudy, sometimes untidy display of colours. Belinda Loftus (1994) records that the painting of kerbs, post boxes and other parts of the environment was decried in the 1970s by such republican sources as Maire Drumm and the Ballymurphy newsheet *The Tatler*. Many others feel that their drab environment has been cleaned up and enlivened.

Building group solidarity is what the display offers and there is often little awareness of the impact on others. One of us has noted elsewhere that at celebrations and political demonstrations 'there was quite a festive atmosphere and little awareness of how aggressive the action might appear to outsiders' (McCartney, 1991, p219) Even if they did think about it, as organisers of parades now have to do because of the threat that the parade might be banned, it is unlikely that these considerations would encourage them to change their activities, because they do have a message for the outside world.

We mentioned earlier that traditional displays were symbols of territory and dominance, and it is still an important element. Each community is marking out its territory and demonstrating its control. The prominent display of large flags on modern tower blocks of flats, as at North Queen Street in Belfast, are an assertion of territoriality, clearly visible over a considerable area. Party posters during elections also contribute to the definition of territory, since most political parties include the national flags and colours in their publicity material, and only put up posters in areas where they have substantial support. Northern Ireland is not unique in marking out territory in this way. Misha Glenny (1992, pp146–147) gives an account of Bosnia Hercegovina which is sadly reminiscent of Northern Ireland:

> The core of the Bosnian tragedy is to be found in the republic itself. By organising parties along national lines, all three communities bear responsibility for the country's appalling fate. Driving across Bosnia in 1990 just prior to the election afforded me a brief glimpse into the republic's miserable future. One village drowning in a sea of green crescents, which proclaimed the (Moslem) Party of Democratic Action (SDA), would give way to another where the sahovnica (denoting the Croatian Democratic Union – Bosnia Hercegovina, HDZ-BiH) was sovereign, or where every wall was covered with four Cs and the acronym SDS (the Serbian Democratic Party). In some villages, the western half was green while the eastern half was red, white and blue (Serbia) while in many towns it was easy to identify the predominantly Croat, Serb or Moslem districts. Many doomed settlements were a jumble of all three. This deeply entangled demography would ensure that if terror and war were to break out in any region of Yugoslavia, the pressure on the three communities in Bosnia Hercegovina to fight would be overwhelming.

In an editorial on the subject of murals the *Belfast Telegraph* commented 'Sectarian wall murals are an ugly manifestation of a sickness within Northern Ireland society. On both sides of the divide, they are designed to stake out territory and to intimidate those of a different view.' The markings of community are also a challenge to the other community and an expression of the rivalry between the communities. If flags and other displays are an assertion of oneself in relation to another group, they inevitably become a challenge to the other group and become provocative symbols. Another expression of the issue of territoriality is at the heart of much of the conflict about loyalist parades in areas such as parts of Portadown and more recently in the Ormeau Road area of Belfast. Flags are only a minor factor in these situations.

We may be able to learn something about the motivation behind the erection of flags if we consider how they are displayed. One person said that there seems to be competition in local communities as to who can perform the most dare devil feat in putting up a flag in an inaccessible place. Isolated flags are often to be seen at deserted rural cross-roads. These are clearly intended as a marker to passing motorists showing the political complexion of the area. In many places flags are left to disintegrate and blow away. This practice is not consistent with the conventions which indicate respect for the flag When a flag is left to become threadbare it does not suggest that it is being used as a symbol of group pride, and one could assume that it is being used to challenge opposing groups.

Some of those involved would not see the use of flags as a form of sectarian competition, however it appears to observers. Republicans for example argue that they are not directing their campaign at unionists but at the British Government, and the marking of territory as republican is a challenge to the Crown forces. The very act of flying a flag which the authorities want to remove is a form of non-violent challenge to the state, and as such one which the authorities cannot win. By forbidding the use of the flag, the authorities are offering their opponents an opportunity to protest. We noted earlier that Gandhi and the Indian Congress Party used this tactic when the British Raj tried to stop the use of the new Congress flag. It is perhaps surprising that the authorities did not learn any lessons from this when it came to dealing with the situation in Northern Ireland. An account in Purdie's (1990, p44) *Politics of the Street* shows the Irish Republican Army (IRA) understood this:

> The importance of such pageantry for the IRA in the early 1960s was underlined in a talk given in 1972 by Billy McMillen, commanding officer of the Official IRA in Belfast following the split with the Provisionals in 1970. He claimed that in 1961 the total membership of the IRA in the city was twenty-four and they were equipped only with two short arms. They did, however, have flags, and they were asked by the organisers of the Wolfe Tone bicentenary commemoration in 1963 to supply a colour party for the Belfast parade.

In the event the organisers withdrew the flag in the face of a Government

ban and the 'humiliation and embarrassment of the Volunteers was acute.'
Purdie continues, quoting McMillan at various points in his narrative:

> The following Easter there was no interference with the tricolour, but in
> October 1964 it was the focus of the Divis Street riots and in 1966, on the
> fiftieth anniversary of the Easter Rising, 'the Belfast staff saw . . . a golden
> opportunity to drive a coach and four through the notorious flags and
> Emblems Act' 'Thousands' of tricolours and 'miles' of green-white-and-
> gold bunting festooned nationalist Belfast . . . 'although no great material
> benefit accrued to the IRA . . . there was general satisfaction that progress
> had been made in dispelling the deadening apathy that had immobilised
> the people for so many years.'

The cycle of action and response continued into the 1970s. A good example
is the flag on the market house in the Republican town of Crossmaglen. The
local people liked to erect a Tricolour, and there was little possibility that
anyone in the neighbourhood would object, or even be annoyed by it. But
the army came regularly and removed it, even using a helicopter for the
purpose. It was simple for the local people to replace it. It became a game
for the local people and it made the local regiment look foolish. In West
Belfast Sinn Féin flew a Tricolour on its office near the peace line with the
loyalist Shankill area. It was fastened to a tall flag pole which made it easily
visible to loyalists. The Young Citizen's Volunteers, the youth wing of the
Ulster Volunteer Force, removed it in a midnight raid and for some time
there was a competition between Sinn Féin and the YCV with the flag being
removed and replaced.

Republicans also consider that their wall murals are part of the process of
political education in the communities, and are not sectarian in content. We
have already noted that flags do not feature significantly in the murals
because flags are simple images which make a simple political statement.
They are not capable of conveying a detailed political argument. None of
the parties in the Northern Ireland situation produce the long dialectical
statements which are found in wall posters in the Republic of China or the
ETA wall slogans in the Basque Country. The latter are so detailed and go
up in such profusion that they are like running pamphlets of political
thought and analysis provided free for the people. The difference in style
can partly be explained by the absence of inter-ethnic conflict in the Basque
Country and therefore the purpose of ETA's posters is only partly a challenge to the Spanish Government and is mainly intended to win more
support for their analysis from the wider Basque community.

Anthems in the community
The main focus of this chapter so far has been flags. Anthems do not play
such an important part in informal social life. They are played at specific
times and places, whereas a flag may be visible all the time. However, there
are some occasions when anthems are played which are appropriate to
mention here.

Anthems are played at many informal social occasions, including social clubs, dances, cultural events, pensioners' clubs and wedding parties. Any band or pop group which has pretensions to play for both unionist and nationalist audiences must be prepared to learn the chords and melodies of both 'The Queen' and 'The Soldier's Song', and in fact most performers have no problems with this.

The anthem is usually played at the end, sometimes presenting a strange contrast with the earlier part of the proceedings. Some social functions can be quite disorderly with copious quantities of alcohol consumed. There may have been fights and a good proportion of the audience may be very unsteady on their feet. The music for dancing may be loud and discordant. The whole air is irreverent and casual. But suddenly the band will break into the first bars of 'The Queen' or 'The Soldier's Song' and the whole company will manage to pull itself to attention, earlier feuds forgotten and they will sing along with passion. Afterwards they stumble into the night their patriotic duty completed. In nationalist areas of West Belfast there are different opinions on when 'The Soldier's Song' should be played. Some now play it at the beginning of the night when people are still sober, but others think this is wrong. Pensioners' clubs and many other meetings are much more orderly, but they do share the fervour with which the anthem is played.

This is mainly a working class phenomenon and is only really found in homogeneous groups where there will be no friction. It is not unknown to be played at dances and other functions organised by more middle class organisations, such as golf clubs. But it would not be a daily or weekly occurrence as it is in working class communities.

The practice would not be so common at similar function in most other parts of Great Britain or the Republic of Ireland. It has been retained in those communities where issues of identity are immediate preoccupations, and it has the same functions as the use of other national symbols in Northern Ireland. It reinforces commitment to group loyalties.

Anthems are used much less than flags, but there is more likely to be an incident if anyone is thought to have behaved in an insulting manner. There are clear expectations about how those present should respond. The location is usually a room where everyone's demeanour is obvious. It is more difficult to slip away. Almost everyone present is strongly committed to the anthem and standing in the appropriate manner. Sometimes many of those present have been drinking heavily. Anyone who refuses to stand will be the focus of all their anger.

In loyalist communities there has been fluctuating levels of concern about British policy on Northern Ireland, and there is concern that support for the British crown is being eroded. Therefore reactions to the anthem are watched to see who are half-hearted in their support. But even those who are losing confidence in the link with the United Kingdom do not insult the anthem directly, but stand with head bowed or otherwise indicate their lack of enthusiasm.

Sometimes standing is not enough. A typical incident happened at a wedding party. The guests were almost all Protestants and it was taking place in a loyalist club. A girl, a friend of the groom was a Catholic from West Belfast. There was a good deal of camaraderie during the course of the evening between the girl and the others at the same table. Differences were acknowledged and joked about. At the end of the dance the band played "The Queen" and everyone stood up, including the girl. One of the other women at the table looked at the girl to see if she was upset or annoyed, and they exchanged a rather weary look which could be interpreted as saying 'this is a bit silly but we have to put up with it.' Another person noticed the girl's expression. People who seem most absorbed by the anthem are also those who are quickest to notice other's behaviour. After the anthem she tackled the girl accusing her of disloyalty and others became drawn into the altercation on both sides. The girl was challenged about supporting the IRA. At first she argued back, but then became very upset and started to cry. It was a marked contrast to the earlier conviviality. Which was the truer reflection of the feelings at the table?

Issues

In this chapter we have been describing customs in areas which are fairly homogeneous in the sense that most of the population come from the same religious tradition. We might therefore assume that no problems will arise because most people accept what is happening. A loyalist said that national-ists can fly the flag in their own area, though he might draw the line at a flag he can see. A nationalist politician said that no one is affected: 'it just proclaims what people already know the residents to be.' The police would not intervene in such situations and if there are no objections they are powerless to act. If protests come from people outside the community, and they are likely to cause disorder by attempting to enter the area, they would be stopped and dealt with away from the local people.

Nevertheless there are some issues which we need to consider. Firstly, flags, slogans and other emblems can play a part in inciting hatred and sectarianism. We have seen that they contribute to building group solidar-ity. One way to do this is to encourage hostility to another group and its symbols, so that what happens within the community can have an impact on other groups. Incitement to hatred is, of course, an offence, but it would be hard to identify a specific incident, obtain evidence and bring a case in the kind of informal situations to which we are referring here. Nonetheless there is a responsibility on community leaders at all levels to be aware of the wider impact of derogatory gestures, slogans and statements which initially seem harmless because there is no one present who will be offended.

Abundant street decoration and slogans are in part to remind residents that they are living in a conflict and as such they increase the level of tension. One person caught this quality well when he recalled a holiday scheme in which he took part as a boy ten years earlier: 'It was free, relaxed there was no trouble, no pressures . . . It took all the pressure out, even if you'd met in Northern Ireland you still had the army running about and the police and you had sort of, the murals on the walls and the flag out, you were never going to get away from it.' (Nellis, p 38) In contrast when he was returning to Belfast from the airport after the trip 'you could see that once they hit Belfast and they started driving down and seen the murals and the flags out again and the soldiers, and you went, Oh my God, here it goes again you know but, ah, the nearer we got to the drop off point it got a wee bit more tense and sort ah, God its back to normal you know.' (ibid. p39)

There may also be those within the community who are unhappy with the way symbols are displayed. But a nationalist politician asserted that minorities have to accept the right of a majority to express itself. They have chosen to live in the area and have no grounds to object. Of course the community may have changed and they are being asked to tolerate behaviour which did not occur when they first lived there. It may also be the case that the majority of the community are not just expressing their identity and culture but are imposing it on individuals, and making them conform. They are not only being asked to tolerate it, but to join in.

They may be asked to contribute money to purchasing bunting or paint, or they can be ostracised or verbally abused if they do not put out a flag. Purdie (1990, p29) refers to one case which shows how far this pressure can go: 'In October 1966 a forty-six-year old man was jailed for nine years; he had threatened a Catholic householder with a revolver and warned him not to interfere with Twelfth street decorations that had been fixed to his house.' Members of minority groups are often the focus of displays. Flags may be put outside their house, either to annoy or intimidate them. One Catholic, living in a Protestant housing estate, said a pole was erected outside his house by the unionist council. He felt it had been sited there deliberately so that the local people would have a convenient place to hang a large flag at his door.

It is extremely hard to know what is the feeling of the majority in any community. There may be a small cohesive group who know exactly what they want to do and are not afraid to do it, and they become the most visible expression of what the community wants. On the other side there is an amorphous body of residents who may constitute the majority but they are uncertain and ambivalent and perhaps afraid to speak out. The small group, who are in all probability the people who want to decorate the area, will be able to go ahead and do what they want. Many influences will be at work. For example, attitudes will change, depending on the time of year:

> During parts of the winter decent private people were critical of [the activities of] young people, including painting wall murals and slogans . . . As the summer approached tough behaviour became focused on Orange celebrations, and this became legitimate behaviour in the eyes of decent private residents . . . At this time murals are painted openly, and residents were willing to provide paint. The collection of wood for the bonfire became an absorbing public activity. (McCartney, 1991, p155)

In these circumstances it is hard to find out what the community truly wants. This problem can also face large formal institutions and we noted one of the problems facing the Queen's University is the difficulty of finding a way to consult and balance the opinions of all those concerned.

The difficulties are posed most clearly by wall murals, and the press has been raising questions about whether they are really acceptable to the people in the area. The *Belfast Telegraph* (4.5.1993) reported on a mural in memory of Keith White, the only Protestant to be killed by a plastic bullet. It is near his family's home and the article said that his parents do not want it there. The article then went on to make a more general criticism of those who paint murals:

> These tribal signposts annoy a lot of people, very often including those whose property they are drawn on. Yet everyone seems powerless to prevent these slogans and pictures appearing. Property owners whose gable walls are defaced are afraid to complain. The authorities seem unwilling, or unable, to intervene.

The *Belfast Telegraph* has also reported controversy over a much publicised mural in East Belfast. It stretches along a considerable length of the Newtownards Road, where a wall joins the gable ends of three rows of pensioners' bungalows. The gables and walls have been decorated with a series of murals and slogans. One of the organisers of the project has said that the project, which is ongoing, is allowing the painters to explore their identity. He argued that an undeveloped community lacks ways to communicate and does not have lots of resources. But they have graphic skills and can draw their ideas on walls for others to see. The clergy have expressed their concern 'fearing that they put residents at risk of attack and have damaged the image of the areas.' (*Belfast Telegraph*, 13.4.1993) An Alliance councillor said 'they are put there to remind locals that they will be knee-capped if they don't abide by the rules.' The paper also quoted one man who did not wish to be identified: 'People are frightened to speak out or to remove the murals themselves – they feel helpless'. Since these statements many more murals have been painted in the area.

What should be done in these circumstances? In nationalist areas opposition to murals is often expressed by hurling pots of paint at it. This may be the worst of all worlds, which can please very few. The mural is defaced but is still there, and the whole appearance is now very untidy. On painted kerbstones, one nationalist politician was very sanguine because the 'rain and wind will take care of it.' Though here again there is a long period when the painting is untidy while it fades.

It clearly takes courage for someone to challenge a strong section of the community, even when they are from the same tradition. Support from the rest of the community is important and that may not be forthcoming if the situation becomes confrontational, and there are risks that hostility may be turned on the individuals who speak out. One community leader thought she had the confidence of her neighbours, but her house was vandalised and she had to leave the estate after criticism of the siting of a bonfire. People in this situation have been disappointed by the lack of help they received from the police, Northern Ireland Housing Executive and other authorities. Many of these issues can be illustrated by a specific incident.

'Paint in the gutters': a case study

This incident happened in a typical small town, fairly affluent and middle class. It is predominantly Protestant and unionist, with an Orange Hall and a well established band. Community relations were said to be good. There had never been any ill-feeling. 'People try to keep straight down the road and don't offend anyone.' Catholic families came out to watch Orange processions. In 1986 a 'kick the pope band' was formed by a group of recent arrivals in the town, who were considered to be rather undesirable by long-standing residents. The band organised a band parade in the town, inviting other bands to come. Local respectable bands were invited but declined to take part. One evening, just before the parade, the band members painted many of the kerb stones in the centre of the town red white and blue.

A number of local residents were outraged, though they were basically unionist and some were prominent members of the Orange Order. They thought the town was a 'nice wee place' and the painting would 'turn it into an eyesore.' One person said that kerbstones are meant to be grey and she would have objected to 'pink polka dots' or any colour. The police got lots of phone calls but were unwilling or unable to intervene. They tried to show that they treated all sides equally by saying they did not interfere with green white and gold markings in Strabane. This did not deal with the concerns of the residents. It treated kerb painters equally, but did not take account of people like them who objected to all kerb painting and who felt that they are the majority, at least in this town, if not in every community in Northern Ireland. The Department of Environment (Road Services) and the Borough Council were also approached but no one had a policy and no one would get involved. One explanation given was concern that their workmen could be victimised. It happened that the local community association was about to have a meeting and this may have provided a focus for action. It was agreed unanimously to buy battle ship grey paint and paint over the offending red white and blue.

The police were informed and their advice was that they were 'very stupid' in taking this course of action, but they would provide a presence. This turned out to be one car and the neighbourhood policeman. Word about the plan went round the community and about fifty people turned up to help with the job. They were mainly middle class, including two of the local clergymen. The band members also got wind of what was happening when they saw a couple of member of the association trying out the paint, so the clean up team was soon confronted by a number of people from the band.

The situation was 'hot and heavy' but the police did ensure that the clean-up group were not physically stopped, so the band members used other tactics. In a classic non-violent protest they lay down on the kerb stones and parked cars on the pavement to obstruct the painters. As they lay on the kerbstones, the band members remonstrated. They said that the painters were defacing the Queen's colours by painting over them. One response was that the gutter was not a very fitting place for the Queen's colours. The band members also took a video of what was happening. Later on in the night the band members tried to scrub off the grey paint without success.

A few days later they returned and again painted some of the kerbs red white and blue. They did not do as much as they had done before and it was noticeable that they seemed to concentrate on areas near the people who had opposed them. There the matter rested. It was a kind of stand off. The band had been able to paint some kerbs, but not as much as they would have liked. The rest of the community had been able to limit the amount of painting, but not able to stop it completely. Now a few years later the paint is flaking and fading. We will never know if the opposition to the painting stopped other slogans and murals being painted in subsequent years.

There were consequences for the anti-painting group. One thought 'they paid very dearly.' Two of the leaders of the group who were opposed to the painting had windows broken and a third had a car vandalised. There was other forms of intimidation. The UDA magazine later carried photographs of the group painting the kerbs grey. Members of the group received threatening phone calls. One person was told his premises would be burnt if he did not display a Union flag at the Twelfth of July. He reported the threat to the police who advised him to comply. Another who was a leading Orange man was jeered at when he took part in parades.

The band soon ceased to exist. A number were arrested after the attacks on their opponents, but they had to be released because the police could not establish a case against them, but the police continued to monitor their activities. At least one left the country and two have been arrested for offences connected to paramilitary activities. The band left controversy and bad debts behind it. They had not paid for their uniforms or bus hire to take them to band parades, and they had failed to award the prize in a raffle which they organised. The other members of the community felt that these revelations justified their stand against the band's activities.

There are a number of implications of this incident. Those who opposed the painting did not regret what they had done. One of them said, with an unintentional pun, 'We nailed our colours to the mast . . . No one has the right to deface [town] property'. They were also concerned that the incident could have damaged community relations, if no one had opposed it 'as it was totally offensive to lots of people'. But they were not sure they would do it again, because they now realise how much pressure and physical threat they might have to face.

They were disappointed in the support they received from the authorities. No agency was prepared to get involved. A borough councillor told one person that they were 'tangling with something you do not understand', apparently meaning that the band had a paramilitary group behind it. A contrast was made between the reaction in the present situation and an old practice of the police reserve, who carried a bucket of tar in their car and would paint over any slogans as they went around. In some areas there are arrangements where the authorities will work with local groups if there is agreement to paint over murals or slogans. This group was unaware of these arrangements and no one seemed interested enough to work with them to find such a solution. The police were not able to protect them from threats and although they arrested some of the band, they were not able to bring charges against them. It was not possible to get compensation for the damage to the car, because it could not be proved that three or more people were involved.

Friends and relatives were not much more supportive. Instead of being sympathetic, the father of one person told her she should have known what would happen. Many of the residents were unwilling to take farther action when they realised that they would have to deal with opposition and possible violence. Those who were most involved felt isolated. On reflection they think that they may have been naïve to expect more backing for their stand.

Although there was a clear conflict, the dispute was not about constitutional issues. Both parties support the link with the United Kingdom. The differences were about tactics, and how to express political opinions. There was also probably a class dimension. One person said that the band members always thought that mainstream unionists were 'not hard line enough'. Another person said that they thought that 'if you are not 102 per cent behind them, you are against them.'

This points to the heart of the matter. It is not particularly helpful to try to assess which party was right. More importantly, there was no mechanism to examine the matter and resolve it. The people who opposed the painting believed they had only two choices: to take direct action or else to tolerate the painting, even thought they thought it might have implications for community relations, and could be the start of much more provocative painting. The band members also believed they had only two choices: not to react when some people in the town painted over their handiwork, on the ground that they should not cause offence, or else to reassert their right to paint their symbols because they were an important expression of their identity. A way was needed to examine what was important for each group and if there was a solution which would satisfy everyone.

A basic requirement is that everyone is free to express their views on the subject without fear of intimidation, but in this case the authorities were not able to provide that reassurance. Intimidation is most effective if people are divided and isolated. In this incident the meeting of the community association provided a forum in which a substantial group were able to develop a unity of purpose which sustained them through the initial confrontation . But after the initial action it broke down as people felt threatened and tried to distance themselves from the conflict.

Removing the fear of intimidation from the situation does not resolve it. The question still remains. Is it acceptable to paint the kerb stones or should it be cleaned off? Who needs to be involved in the decision? Is it possible through discussion to reach a solution acceptable to everyone. This is the tone of the Community Relations Council's (1993, pp9–10) comments on handling celebrations and symbols in its recent report *What Can We Do?*

In the dispute we have been describing, one person thought that the issue was raised at a meeting of the community association to which the leader of the band came. Others have no memory of this, so the account of what happened is unreliable. It was suggested that the band leader came to complain about the action which had been taken to obliterate the painting done by the band. However he was not able to present his case very well in comparison to the others who were in the majority, on familiar ground, understood the rules of procedure and were more articulate. The decision to come and talk about the disagreement could be seen as a more positive approach than intimidation, but he went away dissatisfied. He could not compete in a meeting but he could compete in the cut and thrust of the street.

We therefore need to ensure that there is a forum in which everyone is satisfied that they are able to communicate, where there is no fear of intimidation and where no one will be disadvantaged because they are less articulate. This can be done. Practitioners in community development and mediation have developed methods and techniques of handling contentious issues in large groups. Recently a mediator facilitated such a discussion about a bonfire in North Belfast, involving about one hundred participants. To some degree the Conflict Mediation Network can act as a clearing house to link communities which are facing similar controversies with individuals and agencies which can assist in resolving the issue through dialogue rather than force. However more needs to be done to make people aware that this possibility exists.

One community leader in another area talked of his personal experience of dealing with provocation in his area. He said that if people put up a flag to provoke him, he would refuse to react and would affirm their right to put up the flag, as long as it was not on his property. He stressed that it was important not only to be tolerant, but to explain why you respected their right of free expression. He thought the best way to counter provocative behaviour is not to get annoyed, or at least not to show one has been annoyed. The people responsible for the provocation want to get a reaction and they will have failed and be disappointed. They may give up trying to cause annoyance, but another response might be to escalate the provocation. The dynamics of these situations are quite similar to the situations, where the Tricolour was used to challenge the security forces, as we described earlier in the chapter.

The same person also thought that community leaders from the majority tradition in an area can act to ensure that the majority do not interfere with the rights of those who are in a minority. He is a Catholic living in a mixed estate with a Catholic majority. He has defended a neighbour's right to fly the Union flag when others objected to it. He does not fly a Tricolour himself, but he hopes that protecting individual rights against intolerance in this way will one day create the climate of tolerance where he could fly a Tricolour if he wished and it would be protected by his Protestant neighbours. His aim would be for a local community to establish its own consensus on national symbols, through open discussion and taking account of different interests. United, it would be able to protect itself from outside interference from those who might try to disrupt the local equilibrium.

In this chapter we have looked at symbols in fairly homogeneous communities, and a number of issues have been identified. The situation become even more contentious when communities of the other tradition are involved. This is the subject of the next chapter.

CHAPTER 5

National Symbols, The Community and Public Order

Controversy over displaying flags and emblems goes back long before the Partition of Ireland and the creation of the Irish state. Recorded accounts may give us only the tip of the iceberg, and often the references to flags and emblems is almost incidental. One example from Boyd (1969) describes how on the Twelfth of July 1857 'Brigid Kane, an inoffensive Catholic who lived in Tea Lane in the heart of Sandy Row, heard prolonged cheering outside her house and, on looking out, saw a crowd of people waving flags and bunches of orange flowers and dancing around an immense effigy that was supposed to represent Dan O'Connell ... Next day when a friendly neighbour advised her to leave, she packed her belongings and found herself another house in English Street, in the safety of the Pound.'

The number of cases brought to court were such that they made a significant contribution to the case law on public order, one example being the case of Humphries v O'Connor in 1864 which revolved around the wearing of an orange lily by a Protestant in a Catholic area.

Until the 1950s the law governing the regulation of displays of flags and emblems was the common law on public order, under which the police authorities could intervene where behaviour was likely to cause a breach of the peace. This could include the display of flags and emblems or the singing of songs including the national anthem. Anthems are not a major factor in public order situations, as it is difficult for provocative singing to make an impact on the hurly-burly of street confrontations. However, it has played a part in some confrontations. Bob Purdie (1990) reports that 'a crowd of youths sang the Irish national anthem and a republican song, 'Kevin Barry', outside the courthouse in Derry during an election count in 1965, and had to be restrained from attacking a Unionist procession.'

Controversy over flying flags came more forcibly to public attention at the time of the coronation of Queen Elizabeth II as this was an occasion for the display of the Union flag in greater profusion and by many people who did not display the flag during the Orange celebrations and other more local events. The *Belfast Telegraph* at the time gave detailed descriptions on the decorations and bunting which was erected in each locality. Ironically this gave a focus to nationalist discontent (Moloney and Pollak, 1986).

In Cookstown the Unionist Council erected bunting which was torn down and then replaced. The Catholic population then threatened to put up Tricolours and the Council took the unprecedented step of meeting at

2.00 a.m. on Sunday morning to see what action they should take. They decided to leave up the bunting under police guard. In Newry the nationalist council refused to allow bunting to be placed on council property. Union flags were also burnt in other places, and a Coronation Day parade in Dungiven led to a confrontation, and was only allowed to proceed by protesting nationalists when, among other concessions, a large Union flag was removed.

Another incident at this time was particularly influential. At Derrymacash, a mixed but predominately Catholic area near Lurgan, two Protestant residents displayed the Union flag. Some neighbours objected, and some ten households expressed their disapproval by flying the Tricolour. The police were called in and were presented with a situation which might escalate if they tried to remove the Tricolours while protecting the Union flag. As a result they proposed the compromise that all flags would be removed, and this was in fact done.

These incidents caused some agitation in the unionist community which felt the national flag had not been respected and protected, and this controversy was given a forum by the Stormont elections of that year. The Prime Minister, Lord Brookborough promised 'that the Union Jack will fly in any part of this country.' The result was the Flags and Emblems (Display) Act (N.I.) 1954. The act is less than two pages long and has only 5 sections, yet it became the focus for much of the opposition to the Stormont administration among nationalists. Section one made it an offence to prevent or threaten to interfere by force with the display of a Union flag by someone on his or her own land or property. Section 2 permitted a police officer to require the removal of any emblem whose display might cause a breach of the peace, or to enter and remove it himself if the person responsible is unwilling to comply or cannot be found.

It should be noted that the act did not refer directly to the Tricolour, nor did it make it an offence to display emblems in all circumstances. The Minister of Home Affairs, G.B. Hanna, in announcing the legislation said that he could not ban the Tricolour outright as this was a matter of foreign policy reserved to Westminster (Moloney and Pollak, 1986).

One Unionist told us that in this respect the law was a moderate and sensible measure which on the one hand protected the flag of the state and on the other only restricted the use of other flags in specific circumstances where a threat to public order existed. From his reading of the cabinet papers on the subject he understood that the main concern of Lord Glentoran and other Ministers had been to avoid giving the police too extensive powers and they had been steadily reduced at each discussion. There was the possibility of one other limitation on the exercise of the discretion which the Act gave to individual officers. The RUC at that time was a small and centralised force, and headquarters would have had to be consulted about any sensitive decisions such as the removal of flags. He also stated that he RUC also tightened its own practice on flying Union flags on police stations at this time.

One might ask why section 2 of the Act was necessary at all. Prior to the act, action could be taken under the existing public order law where the display of a flag might cause a breach of the peace. This also applied to the Union flag, and it could be argued that section 2 of the Act could also have been used against the display of the Union flag in spite of the protection in Section 1, but this was never tested in practice. The only change was that police powers to enter and remove a flag were strengthened. The situations which arose at Derrymacash and Cookstown gave an explanation. It was realised that there was the threat of a new opposition tactic of erecting Tricolours in considerable numbers. It would not have met the demands of the unionist community if the display of the Union Jack, though protected by law, could be challenged by the display of numerous Tricolours. Therefore the inclusion of section 2 seemed necessary. This may be an example of the idea that it is not advisable to legislate unless it is necessary, and ironically the result of combining the protection for the Union Flag and limitations on the display of other flags had the result 25 years later that when demands to remove the limitations was met, the whole act was repealed and the protection of the Union flag was also repealed. It is not certain that a campaign against the right to fly the Union flag could have been sustained.

The passage of the Flags and Emblems (Display) Act did not end the controversy. Not long after the passage of the Act a new Irish Republican Army military campaign began. In one incident a Tricolour was found flying on a windmill at the disused Cluntoe Aerodrome at Arboe, County Tyrone. A police officer went to remove it. It was a booby trap, and he was killed in the explosion; a cynical use of the flag, which was presumably destroyed in the blast.

Incidents were not a daily occurrence, but over the years the list became substantial. In his book *Politics in the Street*, Bob Purdie (1990) comments 'One of the principal causes of communal conflict was the provocative use of flags and emblems. Sometimes this resulted in violence, sometimes not, but in all cases what was involved was a very symbolic assault on the other community'. He provides a long list of more recent incidents (p29):

> an Orange arch over the Coleraine-Dungiven road was burned in July 1962. At the same time three Royal Air Force men were beaten up for interfering with an Orange arch at Lisnarick, County Tyrone. As these cases show, such provocations were by no means confined to the Protestant community. In July two Catholic girls were arrested for singing a republican song during the Twelfth celebrations and a Union flag which had flown near the entrance to Moira Demense in County Down disappeared. This followed a dispute caused by a request from the management of a local poultry-processing factory for the removal of a Union flag from the roof of the plant, where it had been placed by a section of the workers. In June 1964 a trainee nurse was bound over in Belfast for producing an Irish tricolour pennant during an Orange demonstration. In November a County Donegal motor mechanic was also bound over after having 'forgotten' to remove a tricolour from his car before crossing the

border. The same month a tree in Bessbrook, County Armagh, from which a tricolour had been flying, was felled in an explosion, and there was a debate in Stormont about the fact that a Union flag had been flown over a school which was being used as a polling station. In March 1965 a youth was jailed for failing to pay a fine imposed after he had set fire to a Union flag at a demonstration in Clonard in Belfast. In June another youth was fined for having set fire to some red-white-and-blue bunting in Portadown, County Armagh. In July forty-seven employees of a reli-giously-mixed Belfast linen mill walked out after the management re-moved flags and bunting put up to mark the Twelfth. In March 1966 two youths were fined after a gang had gone into a Protestant area waving Irish tricolours and singing republican songs. In October a forty-six-year old man was jailed for nine years; he had threatened a Catholic house-holder with a revolver and warned him not to interfere with Twelfth street decorations that had been fixed to his house. In Stormont, Austin Ardill, Unionist MP for Carrick, felt it necessary to scotch a newspaper report which claimed that Girl Guides were prohibited from carrying the Union flag in Keady, a mainly Catholic town in County Armagh.

Section 2 of the Flags and Emblems Act was applied repeatedly, but, argues Bob Purdy, with 'remarkable inconsistency'. The police prevented the tri-colour from being carrying at 1964 election meetings in Enniskillen and Coleraine, and the previous year they had prevented the flag from being carried at a parade in West Belfast for the bicentenary of the birth of Wolf Tone. But no action was taken against the display of the Tricolour at a republican march along the Falls Road in 1964 or when it was displayed in the window of the republican headquarters in Newry. Both these incidents happened within a few weeks of an incident with a different outcome which received much publicity and which helped to bring to public attention the subsequent leader of the Democratic Unionist Party.

This was the controversy over the display of a Tricolour in Divis Street, Belfast in 1964. Ian Paisley has always identified closely with the Union flag as can be seen at his rallies and DUP election material , and he has equally strongly opposed the display of the Tricolour. In 1964 during the Westmin-ster election campaign, republicans placed a Tricolour and the Starry Plough, the flag of James Connolly's Irish Citizens Army, in the window of their election headquarters in Divis Street. Mr Paisley announced that he would lead a demonstration to the area and remove it if the police did not. The police had taken no action until this point. According to Moloney and Pollak (1986) a conference was held in the RUC City Commissioner's Office and it was decided to act. According to Purdie the decision was taken by the Minister of Home Affairs, Mr Brian McConnell. He also acted under the Public Order Act (NI) 1961 to restrict a planned parade by Mr Paisley to an area around the City Hall. Paisley decided not to march, but held a meeting instead.

The removal of the flags was followed by rioting. The flag was replaced, to the accompaniment of the Irish National anthem. (Boyd, 1969, p180) The police broke the window and removed the flag and farther rioting ensued. Purdie states that nationalists, republicans and Protestant liberals were all angered because they argued that the flag was in a solidly Catholic area and could have provoked no one. 'Paisley it was argued had gone out of his way to draw attention to this particular flag in order to provoke just the kind of conflict which had occurred.' (Purdie, p30.)

It is further reported by both Purdie and Moloney and Pollak that the situation was escalated to strengthen loyalist feeling and to secure the election of the Unionist candidate, Jim Kilfedder. It may therefore be an example of how national symbols can be used to focus and simplify issues.

These incidents indicate some of the problems which faced the police. Under the common law on public order they had a discretion as to what measures they should use to keep the peace. The Flags and Emblems (Display) Act had limited the discretion. They should act to remove flags if they consider a breach of the peace is likely, but how should their performance be judged? If they acted the same in every situation it would appear that they were not exercising any judgement. If they reached different conclusions in apparently similar circumstances they were open to the charge of 'remarkable inconsistency'. The police would also stress the importance of communication and negotiation with those concerned and often a solution could be found. At this distance it is difficult to find out about such details and to judge any specific situation. But there was a presumption that the Union flag would be protected. One County Inspector said in 1965 that 'they would never try to interfere with people who were carrying 'the flag of this country" (*Belfast Newsletter*, 19.4.1965, quoted Purdie, 1990).

The Divis incident provides a clear example of one dilemma which might face the authorities. The display of a flag might not provoke anyone in the immediate area and therefore might not seem likely to cause a breach of the peace. However people elsewhere might take exception to the display and threaten to use violence in order to have the flag removed. In these circumstances what causes the greater threat to the peace: is it the initial display of the flag, or the subsequent hostile crowd? Whatever the rights and wrongs of the issue, the authorities were likely to chose to remove the flag or emblem as the easier option, especially in view of the wording of the Act.

With the escalation in community conflict from the late 1960s, hostility towards the flag which was supported by one's opponents was farther entrenched. However, the public order implications of the display of flags and emblems became one element within the wider issues. If a parade was causing controversy there were likely to be many elements of which the use of flags was only one factor.

This did not mean there were no incidents which were specifically related to flying flags. In Chapter 4 we mentioned Crossmaglen as one place where there was a test of strength between the army and the local people to erect a Tricolour, but it is not unique. One particular incident, attracted a good deal of public attention. In 1984 the flying of a Tricolour on Whiterock Leisure Centre seemed initially to have created a rather similar situation to the Divis Street incident of 1964, but it took a very different course (De Baróid,

1989). Whiterock was the latest leisure centre to be completed by Belfast City Council, and was due to be opened officially on 12 September. It was in a strongly nationalist and republican area, but the local Member of Parliament, Gerry Adams, was not invited because he was a member of Sinn Féin. On 10 September the local people organised their own 'People's Opening', at which Mr Adams unveiled a plaque in Irish and the Irish Tricolour was hoisted over the building.

There was strong reaction from Unionist Councillors at the Leisure Services Committee the next day and George Seawright , councillor and member of the Northern Ireland Assembly, said it would be better if the Centre 'was closed or burned down.' However, no action was taken and at a special Council meeting on 8 October, Cllr Seawright called for the Centre to be closed until the plaque and Tricolour were removed. He could find no seconder for the motion and so he took action himself. Early on 18 October he and two other men forced their way past security staff at the Centre, climbed up and removed the Tricolour. There was extra controversy because Cllr Seawright was carrying a gun, albeit a legally held weapon. Immediately afterwards the Tricolour was replaced by three others.

At some level both sides seemed to feel that their honour was preserved. Loyalists were satisfied because they had taken a symbolic gesture to show that they could take action to remove the Tricolour, but the local people were also satisfied because they were able to continue flying the flag. It is replaced at important dates in the Republican calendar such as Easter, and then left until it is blown threadbare.

The leisure centre has also been a source of less dramatic controversy in a mixed small town as it is the venue where each part of the community has tried to assert its identity. Each in turn put up their flag to have it taken down and replaced by the flag of the other section of the community.

To move forward in time for a moment there was a sequel to the Whiterock incident which indicates some changes. George Seawright was later shot and killed by the Irish National Liberation Army, and his wife, Elizabeth was elected to his seat in the Council. She was an active promoter of community groups and eventually became chairperson of the Leisure Services Committee responsible for managing leisure centres. Her husband's visit was remembered when she visited Whiterock Leisure Centre.

Typically, Mrs Seawright diffused tension over the incident, immortalised in loyalist folklore, with a joke: 'I told them that George had left his wallet behind on his last visit and that I'd come back to collect it ... They respected me for visiting a republican district . But as chairperson of the community services committee, I was only doing my job (*Irish Times* 6.5.1993)

Returning to the 1980s, the Flags and Emblems (Display) Act (NI) still rankled with nationalists. The Act itself had a symbolic importance, partly because of misunderstanding about what it actually said. It was assumed on all sides that it banned the Tricolour, and there was some grounds for that assumption because the application of the act was such that in practice, objection to the flag meant that it would have to be removed. It was not only Nationalists who recommended the repeal of the Act. The Standing Advisory Commission on Human Rights and the Project of the Churches on Human Rights and Responsibilities in the United Kingdom and the Republic of Ireland (Bailey, 1988) supported this action.

Eventually a commitment to deal with the issue was included in the Anglo-Irish Agreement: 'matters to be considered . . . include . . . changes in electoral arrangements, the use of flags and emblems . . .' The repeal was proposed as part of the Public Order (NI) Order 1987. In December 1986 the Northern Ireland Office produced an Explanatory Document on the Proposal for a Draft Order in Council. It referred to the misunderstandings which existed about the operation of the Act, some of which resulted from the way the act had been applied, and explained why the Government thought the Act was unnecessary.

10. The Act is widely but wrongly believed to protect any display of the Union flag from interference and to make the flying of the Irish tricolour illegal. Neither of these assertions is correct. Section 1 of the Act makes it an offence to prevent or threaten to interfere by force with the display of a Union flag on lawfully occupied land or premises. However, a person interfering with the display of a Union flag on private premises anywhere in the United Kingdom would be committing at least one of a range of offences, such as conduct likely to lead to a breach of the peace and criminal damage, so the law already protects the peaceful display of the Union flag in such circumstances. Moreover the Act only applies to displays of the Union flag on private lands or premises: it confers no protection on displays in public places or at work or by marchers; and it is in fact an offence under existing public order legislation (Article 6 of the 1981 Order) to display any flag (which includes the Union flag), in a public place or at or in relation to any public meeting or public procession, in a manner likely to cause a breach of the peace and such behaviour could also be an offence under section 9 of the Criminal Justice (Miscellaneous Provisions) Act (Northern Ireland) 1968.

11. Section 2 empowers a police officer to require the removal of any emblem other than the Union flag if he believes its display may cause a breach of the peace, and authorises him to enter premises to remove such an emblem if necessary. The Act does not therefore make the flying of the Irish tricolour illegal in itself in Northern Ireland but only if its display would be likely to lead to a breach of the peace. Police officers already have available other public order powers to require or effect the removal of a tricolour, or any other flag if they believe its display would lead to a breach of the peace.

12. The Act is therefore in practice redundant and its repeal (which has been recommended in the past by the Standing Advisory Commission on Human Rights) would have no practical legal effect. However, it is seen

by many groups as a piece of legislation which is discriminatory and offensive to certain sections of the community in Northern Ireland. Those who see it in this way believe that the effect of the Act is to protect displays of the Union flag even where these are clearly being used simply to assert domination of one section of the community over another, rather than to encourage respect for the national flag. There is a strong case for repealing the Act so that the law on the display of flags and emblems in Northern Ireland can be on the same basis as in the rest of the United Kingdom. Repeal of the Act would make no change whatsoever to the position that the Union flag is the official flag of Northern Ireland as it is of the United Kingdom as a whole; and as such is the flag which is flown from public building on public occasions.'

The repeal of the act meant that again the law on the protection of the national flag was the same in Northern Ireland as in Great Britain, but, as has already been noted, this was different from the normal practice in other jurisdictions. The repeal may have had no practical legal effect, but it had an important psychological effect. A republican said that the Tricolour was still not treated as a legitimate emblem because of the opposition and hostility of the police and army.

Even if it had removed a source of resentment for one section of the population, as is often the case in Northern Ireland, it left another section, the Unionists in this case, feeling that their concerns had been ignored. A unionist said that the repeal of the act was symbolic, but it gave the message that limitations had been placed on British sovereignty. In a pamphlet issued at the time, *The Public Order: Equality Under the Law?*, the Joint Group of unionist MPs objected, partly because they saw the repeal of the Act as evidence of the influence of the Irish Government through the Anglo-Irish Conference. They considered that the new order meant that 'the flying of the Union Jack would now appear to be an offence where there are enough opponents of that flag to threaten disorder.' One unionist said the *only* effect of the repeal of the Act was to remove legal protection from the Union flag. The pamphlet also addressed the question that the law was now the same as in England and argued that flags form an important element of the Northern Ireland problem and therefore there should be different provisions for Northern Ireland. Unfortunately for this argument, the rest of the pamphlet argued for parity of legislation between Great Britain and Northern Ireland.

At one stage there was a possibility that the English Act might have put limitations on the use of the Union flag, which might have had major implications if it had been applied to Northern Ireland. The Government White Paper *Review of Public Order Law* (Cmd 9510, paragraph 6.4) devotes one paragraph to the question:

In the course of the review of public order law it has been suggested to the Government that the use of the Union flag should in some way be restricted. This suggestion reflects concern at the use of the national flag by extremist right-wing groups. The Government considers this use of the flag deeply offensive, and believes that most people share this view. But it has proved impossible to devise a provision which defines satisfactorily those organisations or individuals who should be allowed to use the flag or those occasions on which its use would be permitted. Accordingly the Government has concluded that it is not practical to try to legislate to control the use of the flag.

It should be noted that the decision not to impose restrictions was based on the difficulty of defining the circumstances to which the ban should apply, and not on the grounds of any principle such as freedom of expression. It should also be noted that it was assumed that the ban should apply to organisations and not to the way it was being used in specific circumstances. Presumably this means that a restricted organisation would not have been able to use the flag in any circumstances, while other organisations could use it as they wished.

Of course the way flags and emblems are used may constitute an offence under the general provisions of the Public Order (NI) Order . For example they may constitute behaviour which falls with the provisions of Part III of the order, 'Stirring Up Hatred and Arousing Fear'. Card (1987, p120), writing of similar wording in section 19 of the Public Order Act 1987 which applies in England, says 'Written Material includes any 'sign' or 'other visible representation' (s29) . . ., with the result that displaying a racially inflammatory picture or holding up a racialist banner or wearing a racialist badge is caught if it is displayed in the prescribed way. Other examples would be posting a fly-poster on a wall or spray-painting graffiti on a bridge or road sign. (p102)

There are also specific offences under the Order which can relate to the ways flags are displayed. For example under section 19, which deals with provocative conduct in public, 'a person who in any public place or at or in relation to any public meeting or public procession (b) displays anything or does any act; or (c) being the owner or occupier of any land or premises, causes or permits anything to be displayed or any act to be done thereon, with intent to provoke a breach of the peace or by which a breach of the peace of public order is likely to be occasioned (whether immediately or at any time afterwards) shall be guilty of an offence'.

It is important to note that under the Order the display of a flag or emblem, or the playing of a national anthem would not in themselves be offences. An important restriction on the possibility of an offence is the manner in which the actions are done. In section 19 and in other sections the action must be accompanied by an intent to cause a breach of the peace, or there was the likelihood that a breach of the peace would occur. In fact one view would be that the restriction in Part III to 'threatening, abusive or insulting words or behaviour ' is too restrictive. Card, writing about the equivalent sections of Part III of the Public Order Act 1987 makes the point that

The present requirement is a major limit on the offences, since, if views are expressed in an apparently moderate or reasoned manner (i.e. with-out overt threats etc.), they cannot result in a conviction, however upsetting they may be to a racial group, and even though they were intended or likely to stir up racial hatred. It may be that the main effect of the criminal law here is not to reduce the amount of incitement to racial hatred but simply 'to change the style of racialist propaganda, make it less blatantly bigoted, and therefore more respectable'. (Macdonald *Race Relations; the New Law* (1977), p139. It is arguable that it is over-restrictive to limit the offence to threatening, abusive or insulting words etc since the gist of the offence is incitement to racial hatred and if words etc have that effect it should not matter how they were expressed. Moreover, it has been said that racist propaganda is probably most effective when expressed in apparently moderate terms rather than abusive or insulting ones. (p100)

The repeal of the Flags and Emblems (Display) Act (NI) has not therefore substantially changed the legal situation. One jurist has suggested that the Union flag may still have greater protection than other flag because of the emphasis on **provocative** behaviour. The presumption would be that the display of the constitutional flag of the state is not provocative and it is probable that the display of the Tricolour would be more readily considered to be provocative. Of course the use of the Union flag could be provocative under the law, as, for example, when it is taken into a strongly nationalist area and waved about.

The police consider they have adequate powers under the Public Order (Northern Ireland) Order and the common law. In some ways the change in the law has allowed them to exercise their discretion more flexibly and take account of the sensitivities of the situation, and the wider issues. They would prefer to resolve situations by mutual agreement and they would try to negotiate and work with local leaders and the parties concerned. They would hope to build contacts through the neighbourhood police and members of the Community Police Liaison Committees. They would not lay down rules but would highlight the problems, perhaps suggest how they might be avoided, and indicate the consequences of pursuing different courses of action. Much of this communication is not obvious to the general public.

If there is a question of taking police action, the central consideration is how the display would have given offence. For example they might treat differently a flag flown in an interface situation from one flown in the heart of a homogeneous nationalist or unionist community. In fact if a flag is displayed in an area where there is no objection, the police have no power to act. If a situation arose similar to the Divis Street incident where a hostile march was threatened, the two elements of the display of the flag and the counter march could more easily be dealt with separately, and either could be considered likely to cause a breach of the peace and treated accordingly.

A recent incident took place under the eyes of the media during the Twelfth of July celebrations in 1993. The parade in Dungannon passed the nationalist Ballygawley Road estate. There had been calls for the parade to be re-routed and there was a heavy police presence. Some people in the estate attempted to display a Tricolour from the window of a house at the side of the road. The police acted swiftly and entered the house and force-fully removed the flag, before there had been any reaction from the people in the parade, as far as one can tell. There were some scuffles between local residents and the police, both inside and outside the house. The police clearly felt they had sufficient powers to remove the Tricolour which they saw as a potential cause of a breach of the peace. Another question is whether a flag should be permitted in such circumstances, and we will consider that point in the final chapter.

The police stress that the display of flags is not the subject of many complaints. Individuals occasionally phone in to object to a Tricolour flying at the roadside, but there are seldom grounds to remove it. Flags can be a minor element in wider controversies over paramilitary funerals, parades and other sources of intercommunity tension. We have already discussed the Churches' position on paramilitary funerals, and noted that they take no responsibility for what happens outside church property. The police are responsible for the public order implications of the way the funeral is conducted. The police's main concern is the display of paramilitary uniform contrary to the Public Order (Northern Ireland) Order, and they judge that on the whole appearance of the cortege. So they would insist that the deceased's uniform gloves and beret are not placed on the coffin, but would not object to the flag.

More controversy surrounds parades and, while flags may be flown, the problems will be about issues such as the route or the timing. When the police are trying to deal with these situations by negotiation, various ar-rangements are possible which allow the organisers of the parade or meet-ing to achieve their main purpose, but it is done in a way which causes least offence. For example, a change in the route may be acceptable, or a band parade may agree not to play at a particularly sensitive spot, as was pro-posed for one Orange parade in the Ormeau Road, Belfast, in July 1992. The use of flags can be an element in these discussions as was evident in the Coronation parade in Dungiven in 1953, when the parade was allowed to continue when a Union flag was removed. This kind of agreement may not always satisfy both sides, and it may break down because the organisers and leaders on both sides may not be able to maintain strict control. A band may break an agreement not to play. One individual can undermine the delicate balance by a provocative gesture or by waving a flag and in the heightened atmosphere the consequences can be serious.

From the perspective of the police their discretion allows them to act flexibly and sensitively. From another point of view there is a concern that they are not fully accountable for their decisions. If there are principles and criteria which govern how the police will apply the law, they are not known to the public, and there may be implicit unconscious assumptions which influence their exercise of discretion. If they give advice or exercise their discretion consistently in line with a set of underlying assumptions, in time, through custom and practice, these assumptions will create new law without any public debate. The Public Order (Northern Ireland) Order is one example of the trend in law making. Statutes lay down wide general powers which are then made more explicit through the exercise of administrative discretion by the institutions responsible for implementing the laws: a form of administrative law making.

There are four reasons for concern. Firstly in making judgements we all need to be aware of the factors which influence us, and if a institution is making judgements these factors need to be made explicit and agreed in order to ensure consistency. Furthermore it is difficult to train individuals to carry out their duties, if the basis for making these judgements is not clear. From this point of view it is in the interest of the Police to have internal guidelines.

Secondly there may be public misunderstanding about the police's opinion on specific situations. As a result people may be unnecessarily cautious in their action. The police may be criticised for imposing restriction when they have not done so. Or they may be criticised for not responding to a complaint. For example there may be a presumption that in general flying the Union flag is unlikely to constitute an offence, but that carrying it into a strongly nationalist area might well be an offence. Or there may be a presumption that the police would not act to remove a tricolour in a nationalist community. If these presumptions were made explicit there could be discussion of their acceptability and there would be less criticism of the police if it was clear why they did not respond to specific complaints.

Thirdly, the assumptions, which are determining how the law is applied, might not be an interpretation of the law which would gain widespread public support. But without knowing what the guidelines are there is no means of discussing and debating the issues. For example if the police suggest some restriction on a proposed action it will be difficult to test the correctness of police advice, unless we know its basis. The only way to do this would be to ignore the advice and test the situation in court if a prosecution is taken. This is a very risky step to take.

Finally, we want our institutions to be accountable, and the courts are prepared to review administrative discretion in related areas. For example, in 1991 *McCullen J.* ordered the police to reconsider its decision in relation to a march, and after the *Marchioness/Bow Belle* boat disaster the court stated that they had the right to review the Director of Public Prosecution's decision not to bring a prosecution.

But the court's authority is very restricted. In the Court of Appeal in the case of *Re Murphy* which concerned a public procession in Pomeroy, the Lord Chief Justice said:

> the court will not intervene to set aside the decision unless (the onus of proof being on the applicant) the person making the decision has failed to consider matters which he was bound to consider or included in his consideration matters which were irrelevant or unless the court considers that the person making the decision has abused the exercise of the discretion given to him and has come to a decision to which no reasonable person could have come.

For the courts to exercise this jurisdiction it is necessary to know the basis on which judgements are made.

Consequently there is a view that the police should publish a code of practice or guidelines which governs their use of their discretion. This would allow public discussion and comment on the guidelines and it would allow the public to see when the guidelines are not followed.

CHAPTER 6

National Symbols in the Work Place

They're raising banners over by the markets
Whitewashing slogans on the shipyard walls,
Witch doctors praying for a mighty showdown
No way our holy flag is gonna fall.
Paul Brady

The display of flags and bunting in factories has been common place from at least the nineteenth century. In her book on linen mills Betty Messenger (1988) describes typical features of the phenomenon.

> In some [work] rooms where those with Unionist (Protestant) sympathies predominated, 'celebrating' might begin as early as the first of July and extend until the twentieth of the month. Machines were festooned with red, white, and blue flags or streamers, which action in itself caused no trouble. But celebrants, carried away by the spirit and significance of the impending event and by party songs sung too early and freely, might turn to more physical means to express their sentiments.
>
> An incident which occurred in 1916 in the reeling loft of a mill located in a mixed area in Belfast serves as an illustration of what could happen. There, fourteen Catholics, out of a total of sixty reelers, walked off their jobs and out of the mill after being tormented by the waving of small Union Jacks in their faces and being chased with brushes used to clean the reels. In this instance, management stepped in to settle the dispute ... During the same period women in the spinning rooms and, presumably, elsewhere in the mill worked on as usual. (pp200–1)

She also notes the limitations on Catholic or nationalist display. The Fifteenth of August, Hibernian day, was not marked, though Catholic workers stopped early. On St Patrick's Day at many mills in the Falls Road area of Belfast 'it was customary for girls to go to work that day with blouses and hair ribbons of green. Where a firm (especially in Belfast) was located in a 'mixed' ... area, the wearing of the green by the workers was tolerated if they also donned a bit of red, white, and blue.' (Messenger, 1988, p190)

The process lasted for a few weeks, from the collection of money for the bunting to the joint work of putting it up. It was mostly instigated by the work force, but it was treated benevolently by employers. From their point

157

of view it created a good atmosphere and increased morale, in a similar way to Christmas activities. Some employers facilitated the decoration of the factory, either because they had strong political sympathy, or because it was an easy way to identify with the work force.

Depending on your point of view, it did not cause many problems. It was a kind of a folk festival and had the same qualities of shared enterprise and expression of common identity which we have seen in displays of bunting in the community. We quoted (pp148–9) the assessment of the anthropologist, Larsen (1982) and noted that he also described a darker side to those celebrations, communicating ownership of territory and dominance. This quality is also evident in the example quoted by Ms. Messenger, and all the reports of community conflict are agreed that 'right from the earliest days of industrialisation in the North of Ireland the workplace has been a major focus of sectarian conflict and communal politics' (Finlay, 1989) .

The cause of conflict often was related to external tensions, and the workplace was a natural meeting place, where work mates exchanged views and opinions on current events. There was little room for dissent, especially in a segregated work force, and it was an environment in which feelings grew and hardened. The result might be action on the street. Many work places were partially segregated in that some departments might be identified with one section of the community, and they would often be unaware of what was happening in other parts of the factory.

It is also important to consider the implications of these celebrations for workers who did not share the sympathies of the majority of the work force. It was often said that all workers, Catholic and Protestant alike, were happy to share in these activities, contributing money and working together to erect the decorations. And the brighter 'holiday' atmosphere may have been infectious after the routine of the rest of the year. But it would not have been easy for an individual to object when the overwhelming mass of the work force was united in assuming that this was the natural and right thing to do.

For many years the problems were overlooked. There are few recorded examples of bunting being removed though Purdie (1990, p29) reports that in July 1962 a dispute was 'caused by a request from the management of a poultry-processing factory for the removal of a Union flag from the roof of the plant, where it had been placed by a section of the workers' and 'in July [1965] forty-seven employees of a religiously-mixed Belfast linen mill walked out after the management removed flags and bunting put up to mark the Twelfth.' However, the prevailing assumption on all sides was that a worker had to accept the dominant ethos of the workplace. This can be seen in the report of an incident in the British Army in 1913. A Catholic soldier stationed in Fermoy, County Cork with the Shropshire regiment, wore a sprig of shamrock in his hat on Saint Patrick's Day. Although it is now the custom in Irish regiments of the British Army, he was ordered to remove it by a superior officer, and was charged with mutiny when he refused. The general in command cancelled the charge.

The interesting feature is the newspaper comments. The report in the

Irish News (23.3.1913) quotes an article in the *Daily Independent*: 'If the British military authorities wish to popularise the army in Ireland, and to secure recruits, they should make it clear to officers that Irish soldiers must not be insulted in this way.' The *Irish News* had little sympathy for this 'pathetic' concern for 'the popularisation of the army.' Instead it took the view that 'the able-bodied Irish youth who prefers service as a 'Shropshire' soldier to honest work in his own country must not be astonished if insults and contumely are his portion at the hands of officers.'

Whatever one's opinion about the desirability of the Irish being made welcome in the British army, in the long run the *Daily Independent* is closer to current thinking in its recognition of the importance of making the workplace acceptable to all workers, though now the way that is achieved is by removing flags and symbols. Some companies have never had flags and emblems, but it is only in the last ten years that this thinking has become widespread. Most employers, trade unionists and the Fair Employment Commission agree that to all intents and purposes it is no longer an issue. There are very few workplaces where sectarian symbols are to be seen.

There has also been something of a change of attitude. The new situation is accepted widely, though not universally as we will discuss below. And there has been some recognition that it is not just a question of meeting the requirements of the fair employment legislation. To a degree it has been recognised that a minority in any situation needs to be respected, and the display of flags and emblems can be an unreasonable imposition on a worker who has other views and attitudes. This is not intended to deny the common desire to express identity through symbols. One nationalist politician emphasised that people are still free to erect flags at home, and a unionist politician said they should make a point of erecting flags on their houses to show how they felt.

The change has been so complete and has occurred so quickly that it is instructive to try to understand how it has come about and see if there are lessons for other area of social life. In fact because a neutral work environment has become the accepted standard, this chapter does not dwell on the arguments in its favour and on the feelings and rights of those who have had to work in conditions where they feel intimidated by flags and bunting, important though they are. As a case study of how attitudes to the use of symbols has changed, we have focused more on the reasons for resistance to a neutral working environment and the influences which have encouraged changes in that direction by managements and workers.

A few companies banned displays at the beginning of the Troubles or in the 1970s. One manager has said that his company had taken immediate steps to remove them in 1968/9, and explained the reasons to the work force. He believed that the decisive steps taken then contributed to the awareness of employees that sectarian behaviour was unacceptable, and as a result they have never had any trouble either in relation to flags or any other aspect of inter-communal relations.

However, generally attitudes towards sectional displays of flags and emblems did not change until the issue of discrimination became a matter of concern in the late 1970s. There were a number of reasons for this. Sometimes people had simply been unaware of the bunting. We might call this phenomena 'cultural blindness' meaning that something is so much part of the culture that we take it for granted and do not realise what the impact may be on those who do not share this outlook. In the light of the clear policy it is perhaps surprising to find that some people continued to hold such attitudes until the 1990s. One firm in a nationalist area only removed flags in 1992, and, according to the personnel manager, 'that was really ignorance on the management side of it: not seeing that as sort of harassment.'

Some may have taken for granted the presence of bunting, and others were prepared to turn a blind eye, as, from a company point of view, there was no point in risking the possibility of an industrial relations problems until they had to. But when they had no alternative, they dealt with it positively and quickly.

Even when it began to be accepted that employers were responsible for ensuring equality of employment, it was not immediately understood that flags and emblems might be part of the 'chill factor', those practices which might discourage applications from one or other section of the community, or might induce employees from one community to leave.

Firstly it was argued that bunting and flags were traditional and harmless. It was said that they were erected as an annual commemoration to the many people from Ireland killed at the Battle of the Somme on 1 July 1916, and this could not be seen as a political action. In fact unionist politicians believe that the objections were politically motivated, and people were not really offended. 'The whole object was to question British sovereignty' as one of them said.

Secondly it was argued that it was an activity of the work force and had nothing to do with management. In fact management in some companies went so far as to say that they were powerless to intervene and any attempt to change practices might lead to severe industrial action. Thirdly it might be argued that the display of flags had no bearing on recruitment practices, and should not be taken as implying any limitation on the acceptance of anyone into the work force.

It is interesting to consider a newspaper report of the reaction of a managing director as late as 1986 in response to an allegation that there were emblems on the shop floor. It is probably very different from how he might respond now following the implementation of the Fair Employment Commissions Code of Practice, and for that reason it is only fair not to identify the person or the source of the quotation:

'there are one or two emblems in an isolated area, but nothing that the public can see,' he said ... There were no Eire flags or Union flags on display. Asked if he would order the republican emblems to be taken down in a similar action to that of the Shorts management [he] said, 'We have a different situation ... The Shorts management issued the order because of intimidation at the factory. We have no problems like that here ... On the question of the religious make-up of his work force [he] said: 'I have never asked them, but I get the impression that most of them are Roman Catholics'

In the last ten years there has been a dramatic change, and these arguments are seldom heard. How has this happened? Many situations have been handled by negotiation between the work force, management and unions, and there has been little or no outright confrontation and public dispute. In some cases the bunting was taken down while the factory was cleaned and redecorated and it was never put up again. In one situation the company changed the design of its protective clothing and introduced a code of practice on wearing the company overalls, including a regulation that no emblems or badges of any kind could be worn. One reason for this was to strengthen the company image but the question of sectarian badges was also resolved. Public health issues may also provide an opportunity to change practices. In 1985 loyalist workers in a food processing factory were angry that they were not allowed to wear poppies. The factory had a rule prohibiting staff from wearing emblems or jewellery to avoid the risk of fragments falling into the food products. This may have been the management's only concern, as the concept of a neutral working environment was only beginning to be clarified at this time, but the workers argued that the policy had not been enforced previously, and so there must be another motive.

Sometimes change happened in stages. In one factory flags and bunting were displayed throughout the year. One year it was agreed with the workers that it should be restricted to July, and in the next year there was no display at all. Sometimes it was agreed that the Union flag would be flown officially by the company, perhaps together with the company logo and the national flag of the parent company, where appropriate. One trade unionist said that there has only been difficulty in the east of the province, perhaps because the population is more evenly balanced in the west and there is greater sensitivity to others' opinions and feelings.

Occasionally unusual problems arose. Near the beginning of the Troubles, employees in one company put up balloons at Christmas, some using the colours red white and blue, the others green white and orange. In another case an electrician was working with a reel of cable which had a small union jack sticker attached by the manufacturer. He took it off and stuck it on his helmet. The union complained and he was asked to take it off, which he did. Shirts in the colours of football teams and other personal apparel, tattoos, shamrock at Saint Patrick's Day and badges have also been the subject of criticism and invariably the management have the offending items removed or tell people with tattoos to keep their sleeves turned down so that they cannot be seen.

In the discussion about the theatre in Chapter 3, we have already referred to *Facing North*, the play by John Boyd (1982), as a rare example of a play using disputes about flags as a theme. The play is about the changing relationship between a factory owner and his son, whose more pragmatic approach seems better suited to the modern world, and this is demonstrated in the flag incident. In the present context the play is interesting because when it was first produced in 1979 it foretold how some of the disputes in the workplace would develop in the following years. The son had removed the flags from the workers' machines in a blunt and insensitive manner and in the play some of the workers come and argue their case for erecting the flags. While the father does not feel that the son had acted wisely in the first place he feels that to reverse the decision would seem to be a climb down by the management and would weaken their position. The son is willing to put the matter to a vote of the work force as a way to resolve it and comes up with a proposal which was to be widely used in subsequent real cases. He suggests that a large flag should be erected officially by the company but that individual workers should not decorate their work areas. This compromise is accepted by the workers in the play so that we do not see how the situation would have been resolved if the workers had voted to retain their flags as this would have brought the company into conflict with the fair employment legislation.

The Fair Employment Acts (Northern Ireland) 1976 and 1989 reinforced the informal arrangements by placing statutory responsibilities on employers. It is considered to be part of the duty of employers to ensure equality of opportunity and promote a supportive, neutral and harmonious environment free from material or behaviour likely to be offensive, provocative or intimidating or in any way likely to cause apprehension to any employee. As Livingstone and Magill (1990) have commented

> The Standing Advisory Commission on Human Rights has observed that the Fair Employment Agency interpreted section 3 to mean that equality of opportunity was denied if practices adopted by employers operated to exclude members of a community under-represented in the work force or discouraged applications from that community. Such practices include those now described as 'indirect discrimination', e.g. word of mouth recruitment. But the Agency's interpretation seemed to go farther. It included practices, such as allowing sectarian displays at workplaces . . . which had the effect of discouraging applications from [the under-represented] community.

The Fair Employment Commission (which replaced the Fair Employment Agency under the 1989 Act) has also statutory functions, notably the duty under section 7 'to maintain a code of practice for the promotion of equality of opportunity 'and to 'take such steps as they consider necessary to encourage employers . . .to adopt the policies and practices recommended in the code.'

Section 5.2.2. of the Code of Practice refers to flags and emblems directly.

5.2.2 To promote equality of opportunity you should:
  promote a good and harmonious working environment and atmosphere in which no worker feels under threat or intimidated because of his or her religious belief or political opinion: e.g. prohibit the display of flags, emblems, posters, graffiti, or the circulation of materials, or the

deliberate articulation of slogans or songs, which are likely to give offence or cause apprehension among particular groups of employees

If an employer is deemed to have acted in a discriminatory manner, a case can be taken to the Fair Employment Tribunal by the individual. In principle the Fair Employment Commission can itself initiate an action, but it would be only likely to do this at the end of a chain of actions which include an FEC enquiry under Section 11 of the Act, the issue of an FEC direction to the company and the employer's failure to comply. It is unlikely that most cases would reach this stage without being resolved. Under the Act, the Code of Practice must be taken into consideration by the Tribunal in considering the case. The Code is therefore authoritative but it is not mandatory. The only clear direction on the law are the findings of the Tribunal or the finding of any appeal.

The first, and one of the few cases, concerning flags occurred in the days of the Fair Employment Agency. It was brought against the firm of James Mackie in West Belfast and the presence of flags was found to be discriminatory and the company had to pay compensation and change its practice (*Sunday Times*, 17.5.1987). It was a clear signal that the display of flags could be construed as discriminatory practice, and companies would be held responsible . Other employers were not keen to have a case brought against them.

There are few examples where the minority in the work place have made an actual complaint about flags, but we have seen that this would not be an easy thing for them to do. Complaints seem to have been more likely after the company had removed flags and stated that it was now company policy that flags were prohibited. Then if an isolated flag appeared it would be brought to the attention of management, often by a shop steward.

Perhaps the situation which attracted the most attention was the East Belfast aircraft manufacturers, Short Brothers. It is the biggest manufacturing employer in Northern Ireland and as in many other issues such as equal pay or relations with trade unions, it became the seminal example which was watched by others and used as a guide. The work force was predominately Protestant and the presence of bunting had been accepted in the past. It seemed likely that the work force would oppose strongly any attempt to change this or other employment practices, and they were a powerful group, being mainly skilled engineering workers, the elite of the trade union movement. But there was a powerful force on the other side because the company relied on American orders and it was coming under increasing pressure to meet demands from America to achieve a more balanced work force.

The company had adopted a comprehensive policy on equality of opportunity, which included a commitment to remove flags and emblems. At the end of 1985, the *Sunday World* newspaper carried articles that the work force were not complying with the policy. It should be noted that this was shortly after the Anglo-Irish Agreement signed in November 1985 and the unionist community were very sensitive to any challenge to their way of life. Notices were displayed towards the end of January 1986, warning workers that they could be disciplined for displaying sectarian or political emblems and holding illegal marches in the factory, but on 12 and 26 January the *Sunday World* reported that the notices were removed and replaced by posters opposing the Anglo-Irish Agreement. It also claimed that no action was taken by management.

The issue came to a head in July 1986, and on 22 August 1986 the workers received a notice in their pay-packet reminding them that flags and emblems had to be removed. It was believed generally that the company's action was in part a response to intimidation of Catholic workers and an editorial in the *News Letter* (23.8.1986) went so far as to say 'the blame for the total ban on flags and political posters belongs to those responsible for tampering with clock-in cards and threatening workers of a different religious or political viewpoint.' The Orange Order and the Democratic Unionist Party became involved and there were threats of a strike. On 27 August about 1000 men walked out, apparently in relation to another problem which, in the heightened atmosphere, had become entangled with the flags controversy. Next day the company chairman sent a letter to all employees which, among other points, defended the company from the charge of disrespecting the flag and said 'so that there is no misunderstanding on this issue, the Union Flag will henceforth be flown every day on our headquarters.' The issue seemed to be defused, but it resurfaced again the following year.

The workers felt that there had been an agreement after the dispute in 1986 that they could display flags in 'designated areas' and that the management would be 'sensitive' to workers' feelings about the matter. The management denied that such an agreement had been reached or was even possible under the Fair Employment Legislation and the *Belfast Telegraph* (1.7.1987) reported that Peter Robinson of the DUP said that his recollection was that the DUP continued to press for designated areas but the company resisted. The workers walked out when management took the flags down and the management closed the factory. At a meeting between the management and the representatives of the unions, the Confederation of Shipbuilding and Engineering Unions, the management was assured of union support for its position and on that basis the company's plants were reopened on Monday 6 July. At first many workers still stayed away, but the remainder returned on Wednesday and the factory closed for the holidays on Friday.

The outcome here and also at Gallaghers Tobacco Company, which had similar features, were the watershed and clarified the boundaries of acceptable conduct. It also gave a signal of the willingness of management to deal with the issue. At Shorts a powerful group of workers who felt strongly about the issue had accepted a policy which removed flags from the workshop. Other groups of workers who might have resisted change were uncertain about what they could do. Politicians may have been more cautious in getting involved in subsequent disputes. Their intervention in the Shorts and Gallaghers situations had limited impact on the policy and farther involvement in other situations was unlikely to benefit their public credibility. The outcome of the situation at Shorts is also thought to have influenced the development of the new Fair Employment Code of Practice.

If the work force is mixed, there is more opportunity for confrontation but at the same time greater efforts may be made to avoid it. A trade unionist said that where the population is more balanced there is greater sensitivity and care on all sides. But particular problems arose in a clothing factory in County Armagh where the work force was mixed. Nationalist workers went on strike because the management were flying the Union flag over the factory. It seems that the management were flying the flag during July under pressure from the Protestant employees. The company was an English company and the local management were told by the head office to remove the flag. They did this and the nationalist employees returned, but the unionists went on strike. Management replaced the flag and again the situation was reversed with the unionists back at work and the nationalists on strike. This continued for some time until the management went to take the flag down in August. At this point the unionist employees surrounded the flag pole to prevent the flag being removed. This meant that all the work force was out of the factory so the management locked the factory. It was decided that the work force would only be allowed to return if they accepted a clause in their contract banning flags, emblems and intimidatory behaviour. A meeting of the work force was arranged, and the work force had no choice but to comply. It was what the nationalists wanted so it was not difficult for them to agree, but it was more difficult for the unionists to agree. On the next working day about 80% of the unionists turned up for work, but over the next few days they all came back.

In another factory in County Tyrone, the dispute between the different groups of workers led to the factory being closed for much of the summer. As in other similar cases, commercial considerations may have meant that closure at this time did not create problems for the company. One compromise was proposed which would allowed the flag to be flown for the two weeks around the Twelfth of July and then taken down. The employees were able to take staggered holidays and it was suggested that nationalists who objected to the flag should take their holidays at that time. This compromise would not fall within the spirit of the FEC advice that it might be acceptable to fly the flag on official days or all the year, but not specially on politically sensitive occasions such as the Twelfth of July. Nevertheless the Catholic workers were willing to accept this arrangement, but it was not acceptable to the unionist employees. They wanted the flag still to be there on the next Monday when the workers who were on holiday would return. It would appear the unionists not only wanted to express their identity, but they wanted the Catholic workers to have to work with the flag flying above for at least one day. One observer described this as 'a brutal example of what the issue really means'. He said that it showed that the question of the flag represented the issue of control of territoriality and the need for that control to by symbolically accepted by the other community. In this case the nationalist workers were not willing to comply and so the stand off continued.

There have been few problems with national anthems in the workplace, because they are seldom used. Only two examples were identified. One company held an award ceremony for those who were completing their training. At the end 'The Queen' was played. As part of their drive to create a more balanced work force they invited a wider range of people to the ceremony, including the principals of the local maintained schools. One of them was aware that playing the anthem might discourage recruitment from the Catholic community. He quietly pointed this out to the management who had not thought of it, and in subsequent years it was decided it was not a necessary part of the ceremony.

Reference has been made in Chapter 3 to the controversy over the playing of the national anthem at graduation ceremonies at Queen's University, Belfast, and here we want to focus on the fair employment aspects of the problem. As the issue was discussed both within the University and outside, the fair employment implications became apparent and they were articulated in Employment Equality Services' report to the University on its employment practices. The Report, prepared by Beverley Jones and Fiona Cassidy, was confidential but according to leaks in the press which were not denied

> the report quotes an earlier tribunal finding, Grimes v Unipork Ltd. to support its belief that the playing of *God Save the Queen* may be discriminatory. In that case the tribunal ruled that no conduct should be allowed 'which has the potential to disrupt the harmonious working environment or to intimidate or embarrass any worker because of his religious beliefs or political opinion.' The Jones-Cassidy report, drawing on this finding, says 'It has been suggested to us that to challenge the playing of the national anthem would be offensive to members of both communities in Northern Ireland. However, it is the case that there is disruption and embarrassment when the national anthem is played at graduation ceremonies. We therefore believe that this tradition irrespective of whether it is followed in other United Kingdom universities may in the Northern Ireland context amount to conduct of the nature identified in 'Grimes." (*Irish News* 11.2.1993)

The argument is that playing the national anthem has the same potential to make the work environment intimidating as Irish signs in the Students' Union. One Unionist politician argued that the graduation ceremony is not a work place, whereas the Students' Union is. This view might not be shared by a tribunal. More fundamentally a Unionist lawyer questioned the premise that the Grimes case was relevant to the Queen's situation.

The National Anthem raises a particular problem because there are behavioural conventions associated with it. As we have seen it is normal custom to stand in respect for the anthem and the state it represents, while a refusal to stand is an expression of one's opposition to that state or some aspect of that state. If someone walks past a flag it is not easy to judge their opinions from their manner. They may not even have noticed it. Therefore on the occasion of Queen's graduation senior officers are present and could make assumptions about staff's opinions from their behaviour. There is always a possibility that this might be taken into account in future job applications or promotion panels. One unionist said that there was no evidence that they would be disadvantaged, and in any case he could not see how this would apply to graduating students who had just passed their final exams and were leaving the University.

We noted that the National Anthem is played at graduations in over half the universities in Great Britain, but it is argued that the possibility of discrimination is greater in Northern Ireland. It is not only a question of the University's obligations under fair employment law. It should also be considered in terms of what is appropriate in that particular setting. We shall return to a discussion of the merits of the different arguments later, but in the meantime the controversy has become a public issue which makes it more difficult to find a way to satisfy all interests.

These examples are only a few of the many negotiations which have taken place. We want to stress that most were resolved with little controversy or rancour. In many cases an acceptable compromise was possible, and some examples of these have already been given. It is possible to identify some factors which led to the change.

Employers were determined to deal with the issue. This may have had as much to do with the employer's fear of prosecution, or the threat of lost orders in some cases, as a reflection of deep conviction on their part. Employees in turn recognised quickly that employers were committed to implementing the policy and many of the early confrontations were a testing out process to see if the employers were really determined.

It was easier to handle the issue where there were already good communication between management and workers and where there were systems of consultation already in place to deal with other issues such as new working practices. It could then be dealt with through these normal procedures. The role of the trade unions was important. It has already been noted that the ideal of a non-sectarian workplace fitted with their overall commitment to equality for all workers. In many cases they took the lead and, when the issue was first beginning to be recognised, seminars were organised for shop stewards. This was one place where attitudes and opinions about the merits of the changes were discussed and the reasons for the changes were examined. The unions were often better able to handle the negotiations between the different groups of workers and between the management and employees. But one manager pointed out that shop stewards were in a difficult situation because they were elected by the work force and had no authority apart from that vested in them by the work force. However, the union could often bring in a full time official, who had not been previously involved and who did not have to continue to work in that situation afterwards.

The same considerations also apply to foremen. One foreman had his car blown up not long after he had removed a Union Flag from company property on the orders of management. The company decided that in future they would not ask members of the work force to remove flags or emblems.

Union officials and supervisory staff live in the same communities as the rest of the work force and they are more accessible than management to the attacks of paramilitary groups or others who object to changes which make the work place more neutral. There is some disagreement about how much pressure should be brought to bear on companies. We have seen that in some cases it was convenient to use the threat of external pressure to justify making changes. And in some cases it has been easier for a company to respond to private advice as happened in the example of playing the National Anthem at the trainees' graduation ceremony. It is important to think of the implications if the controversy becomes public, as has happened with the question of playing the National Anthem at Queen's University graduations. It is more difficult to make concessions in public. People will be more aware of the issue, other interests take sides and try to bring pressure to bear, and there may be more opposition to change. In many cases there were opportunities to resolve the situation before it became public and it is in management's interest to face up to the issue then. One person said this could have happened in the Queen's University controversy.

A common approach would be based on the principle of least contest. It is better to start negotiations with a low level of confrontation because it is possible to escalate the level of conflict if no movement takes place. However, it is more difficult to move from a high level of conflict to more co-operative negotiations. The FEC's experience is that a low key approach has often had no impact and has only delayed the process of change. For example the Commission wrote in the draft of a report of an investigation of a public body that it thought it should remove pictures of politicians from the security hut where they were visible to everyone as they arrived. The management accepted the comment and said they would deal with it. But they asked the FEC to remove the reference to it in the report as it might bring it to the attention of the workers and perhaps the politician concerned, and there would then be more opposition to the change. The FEC agreed but for many years nothing was done even though it was mentioned at all meetings between the FEC and management.

It was important to try to treat all sides fairly and to keep politics out of it, as far as possible. In one case a meeting was arranged for the whole work force and the Protestants walked out because of the attendance of a party worker for the Social Democratic and Labour Party (SDLP). He said he had been asked to advise the workers, but the union representative asked him to leave because it was a union issue, this was a union meeting and the union would advise the workers. This was some reassurance for the Protestant workers. It was probably that they were going to have to agree to the flag being removed, and it would have been even more difficult to accept if it had seemed that they had been forced to make a political climb down in the face of SDLP pressure.

A number of people stressed the importance of not being vindictive or triumphant over those who had to remove their bunting: 'Don't rub their noses in it'. For example, after the Protestant work force in one factory backed down at the end of a dispute, the union official, from a Catholic background, suggested that it might be helpful to agree to allow a photograph of the Queen to remain and to allow the Union flag to fly over the factory The FEC, who had been involved in the negotiations, accepted that this was probably within the legislation. It was suggested that it would be more fitting to properly mount the photo of the Queen and hang it at reception. The effect of this would also be to take it out of those areas where all staff had to go. Neither the picture or the flag on top of the building could be seen easily. However it was a way to show some respect for the employees' feelings, given that they had already accepted the principle of removing bunting.

In this context it is relevant to look again at the situation in the factory in County Armagh (p193) where each section of the work force went on strike at different times. After the situation had been resolved and the Protestants had accepted that the flag would not be flown, the Catholic employees claimed compensation for the wages lost during the strikes, apparently at the suggestion of a local SDLP party worker. The case was settled and a payment of £2000 was made to each of the Catholic workers. It was suggested by an observer from a Catholic background that this was doubly hard on the Protestant workers as they too had lost wages and they had also had to accept the loss of the flag.

A situation like that in County Armagh is difficult. Under the law the employees who feel discriminated against are entitled to claim. It would be hard to advise people on low wages to reject the opportunity of compensation. Initially it appears that the Protestants were uninvolved in the early stages and only got involved when the management took down the flag as a result of the Catholic strike. But in fact the Protestants had persuaded the management to go against company policy and fly the flag, so in that sense they had been involved directly from the beginning of the dispute.

Change of attitude was seldom an important factor leading to the removal of bunting. One exception is the type of situation we have called cultural blindness. For example one manager worked in a factory where unionist bunting was all pervasive. By chance he offered to show a new recruit from a Catholic area to the place where she would be working. When she saw the flags and decorations hanging everywhere she said that she was not willing to work in that environment and left. For the first time the amount of bunting registered with him and he took steps to remove it immediately.

Arguments based on the intrinsic merits of fair employment or equity were seldom raised and such arguments would have carried little weight during a confrontation. On occasions the argument has been used with the work force that either it was acceptable to have all emblems and flags, unionist and nationalist, or else none. The work force has been unwilling to allow their opponent's emblems to be displayed so they have accepted eventually that there would be no bunting.

In most cases the work force was faced with the practical reality that the company would suffer if the bunting was not removed. The seminal case of Shorts was perceived as a problem of maintaining orders and therefore jobs. Shorts stressed that they had come under no pressure from Government nor were threatened with the withholding of Government grants. The management presented the case for removing flags in terms of equity and good employment practices, but a letter to the employess from the chairman pointed out that 'how our customers and business partners see us is of prime importance in obtaining orders', and probably workers were more influenced by this concern and specifically the need to satisfy American customers. Overseas customers was not an issue for many companies, but nevertheless assumptions about the Shorts case set the tone for the future.

In subsequent cases management was able to say to the employees that they had to obey the law and to ask the work force to help them regardless of their personal feelings. It may have been easier to accept something which seemed outside the control of the company, and which did not demand a change of opinion. Although changes were often accepted grudgingly, a few years later, many workers and politicians accept that it is not particularly appropriate to have political displays in the workplace (though there is some disagreements about what constitutes a political display and how disputes should be resolved). This seems to support the conclusions of Raab and Lipsett (1962) writing about race relations in America: 'our feelings and conceptions – our attitudes – do not necessarily *precede* our behaviour . . . In brief, behaviour typically shapes and alters attitudes.'

It would be wrong to assume that everyone is happy with the present situation and that no problems remain. Some employers find these issues an irritation which they would prefer to ignore. As one business man said fair employment is another area like VAT where the employer is required to act as the agent of government, but the effective industrialist may not have the necessary education, skills or experience to do this additional task sensitively and thoroughly.

While most employers feel that there is an acceptance of the situation in the work force, they keep a close eye. A number of managers concede that it is very difficult to ensure that flags are never displayed, and they put most emphasis on ensuring that even small emblems are removed immediately, not least because they believe the number of flags would quickly escalate. One manager in a mainly Protestant firm told a story somewhat against himself. During a visit by a school group he was explaining the company policy on equal opportunities and he said that they did not allow flags and emblems, at which point one of the school boys said he had just seen a Union flag in a hallway.

Unforeseen circumstances will always arise which revive the arguments. For example on 3 June 1994 the *Belfast Telegraph* reported that there had been a walk out by 270 Shorts employees because the management had refused to allow the Union flag to be used at a lunch to commemorate D-Day. In fact the management had ruled that their normal policy applied and all flags were banned from inside the building. The participation of Ireland in the Soccer world cup in 1994 led to at least one incident where a worker in a mainly Protestant firm wore a football shirt. The company policy is that workers can wear football shirts unless someone objects, and in this case the Tricolour was part of the shirt design and complaints were made. The worker was asked to remove it and eventually was subjected to stage one disciplinary proceedings. He later apologised, but both these incidents show that flags can still cause problems.

There are also criticisms of the present policy and its implementation, mainly expressed by unionist politicians, though there is no reason to assume their complaints do not reflect feelings in the unionist population. It is important to understand these views, though it is also important that they are put into the context of the general acceptance of the overall policy.

Most unionist politicians are now willing to accepted that political bunting is not appropriate in the workplace, but they find it hard to understand why the Union flag cannot be flown. They do not consider the Union flag to be a political symbol.

Some problems were caused by the campaign in the Sun newspaper at the time of the Gulf war, when they printed a large picture of a Union flag and asked readers to pin it up in the workplace or other locations to show that they were supporting British troops. Workers in different places took the newspaper's advice and pinned it up, but invariably management said that it had to be removed. One manager found it a little hard to deal with, because when it was removed the workers said 'Well, it's the flag of the country in a time of war. Why not? They're doing it all over Britain.'

The FEC has described three sets of circumstances which explain why flying of the Union flag may be a breach of the Code of Practice. It can be a direct example of discrimination if it is flown in a partisan way, as opposed to being used as a symbol of the state. Some loyalists and republicans from their different perspectives would argue that this is a false distinction, because the conflict is about the boundaries of the state, but an example of the former could be a company which only flew the flag at the Twelfth of July celebration. Secondly the FET is able to infer if discrimination is more likely to take place on the basis of the circumstances in the work environment, and in view of this it may be better not to have flags. *Duffy v Eastern Health and Social Services Board* was an example of a Tribunal adopting this approach. There the person making a staff appointment had photographs of politicians in her room. Their presence could have made it more easy to infer that she might discriminate. Thirdly the presence of Union flags may make it more difficult for employers to fulfil their statutory duty to create a neutral work place. For these reasons it would not encourage an employer to fly any flags, even the Union flag over the factory.

But the Commission acknowledges that the Union flag is the official flag of the state and therefore has a special place. Otherwise there would be no circumstances in which they would find it acceptable. It is hard to draw that line in a way that everyone accepts, though, the FEC's position is actually very close to the position that many Unionists adopt. The FEC's recommendation is that the flag should only be flown from an official company flag pole and either on the recognised official flag days, or all the year. They stress that these arrangements could be challenged before a Tribunal, but they would be unlikely to support such an action, if there were no other sources of complaint.

Unionists and Protestants have similar feelings about the wearing of the poppy at Remembrance Day. One unionist said that a factory in his constituency had a photograph of the Princess of Wales opening the factory, but that was probably not allowed under the policy.

The underlying criticism of the policy is that it seems to oppose any expression of identity or loyalty. Unionists are unhappy about the level of restrictions placed on them. In most cases it was unionist bunting which was removed because unionist bunting was much more widespread, but the examples given earlier show that restrictions have also been placed on nationalist symbols.

Employers have also been concerned about how to deal with little badges which say 'Jesus Saves' or a Sacred Heart of Jesus Badge. One employee of a national chain of retail stores was asked not to wear a necklace with 'Rangers' written on it, but she was supported by her trade union. The aim of the policy seems to be to completely 'sanitise' the workplace. At first sight this seems at odds with the policies of other organisations, including the Community Relations Council, to encourage sharing of culture and acceptance of difference. Even some non-unionists feel that there is a danger that the policy could become discredited if it objects to things which are quite innocuous. Yet in carrying out this study it is clear that almost anything can have a symbolic significant in a highly charged situation like Northern Ireland. Employers in the main have preferred to restrict any emblem however trifling, because they fear that minor emblems might lead to bigger emblems until displays were again pervasive.

The FEC is also of the view is that it would be preferable if no emblems of any kind are displayed. The working environment should be neutral and from that point of view they do not apologise for aiming to sanitise the workplace. They argue that we are living in a society where there is conflict, and displays of symbols can intimidate people. It causes less confusion to draw clear boundaries and to discourage all displays of flags and emblems. Any display could be a breach of the duty to promote a work environment which is free from anything which might cause apprehension to any employee.

But they believe that the law would not get involved with small issues such as lapel pins, unless there were other causes of concern in the company, because they would be considered relatively minor grounds for complaint, and the legal maxim 'De minimis non curat lex' would be applied: the law does not deal with trifles. This does not mean these emblems were necessarily trifles to those who wear them and those who object to them, but simply that the law would not intervene where minimal or no damage has been caused.

Unionists complain that the present procedures are too rigid. They feel that situations should be resolved at a local level between the management and the work force. If those directly concerned are happy with the arrangement then there should be no outside interference. We noted that one company does not put restrictions on football shirts as long as no staff member complains. However a note of caution is sounded when we recall the situation in earlier times when the minority may have been offended, but they did not object because they were afraid to. They needed outside support and protection.

Unionists see the whole policy as one of appeasement of nationalists and their supporters in America. They resent the pressure from Americans to limit the use of the Union flag when Americans fly their own flag regularly and proudly. One unionist politician stated clearly that he hoped that the legislation will be repealed, and he hoped a future legislature in Northern Ireland would do it.

The Fair Employment Commission was criticised not only by unionist politicians but also by some employers. Some of the criticisms were very sweeping and damning, which makes it difficult to respond to them. For example one unionist politician said that it makes 'atrocious decisions.' It is important to remember that most, but not all, of the critics are hostile to the fair employment policy in general. It is becoming more difficult to express such views as there has been growing acceptance of the principle of the right to equal opportunities to employment. In these circumstances the Fair Employment Commission may be an easy target for more general opposition to the policy. It is very closely identified with the policy, which is not surprising given its central and very influential role in maintaining the Code of Practice, advising individual employers, and supporting cases before the Fair Employment Tribunal. Some of the critics are mainly concerned about other aspects of fair employment such as recruitment procedures, and comments about the Commission and flags and emblems need to be considered in this wider context. It is not appropriate to try to deal with all the ramifications of these broader issues here, but with these reservations in mind it is still relevant to indicate the areas of concern.

The Commission was accused of being too narrow, biased and cautious, and at the same time was said to give a wide interpretation of the scope of the law, so that any displays were condemned.

The criticism partly relates to different perceptions of what the Commission is doing when it gives advice. Its comments and suggestions are on the basis of what is best practice, and it tries to indicate what the good employer should be doing anyway even if there was no legal sanctions.

Another factor in some of the criticism may be that the critic has come to a different conclusion from the Commission. For example one person who criticises the Commission for interpreting the law too widely gave as an example the action of the Commission in issuing a general advice on displaying pictures of royalty and politicians, following the Tribunal finding of discrimination at Purdysburn Hospital in the Duffy case. He argued that the case did not depend on the presence of photographs and the Tribunal did not comment on them. The FEC should not therefore have given the advice it gave on the basis of the Tribunal's ruling. It is true that the case only refers to the pictures in passing, but, as explained in our earlier discussion of the case, the Commission takes the view that this is a relevant consideration which it should bring to the attention of employers, because the FET is able to infer if discrimination is more likely to take place on the basis of the circumstances in the work environment, including the presence of photographs.

More generally, the Commission was said to take a subjective view of what constituted offensive displays: if someone felt offended it was offensive. From the Commission's point of view the important consideration is the basis of the Tribunal's judgement and that is a reasonableness test: 'something such that a reasonable worker would or night take the view that he had thereby been disadvantaged in the circumstances in which he had thereafter to work'[1]

Allegations are also made by unionists that the FEC is biased in a number of ways, or at least blinkered in its concerns. These charges are denied by the Commission. It was said that it is much more strict about Protestant bunting than nationalist. It was suggested that there are places where the Tricolour is allowed to fly without hindrance and one factory on the Border was mentioned by different people. Not long after the initial controversy at Short Brothers the unionist morning paper, the *Newsletter* (29.8.1986) carried a story about the display of republican emblems at Belleek pottery in Fermanagh. Whatever the practice at that time, as far as we could ascertain there are no emblems displayed now. It was also said that the FEC was very concerned about unionist bunting, but seemed unconcerned that in other workplaces there were no Protestants because previous Protestant workers had been shot and there was a fear that any others would suffer the same fate.

There were also complaints about the Commission's style of working. It was criticised for being confrontational, interfering, vague in its advice and for a lack of accountability, and these comments were not restricted to unionists. It was said that the staff were not considered to be sufficiently experienced in industrial relations matters in general and they could be rather heavy-handed and rigid. There was also a feeling that not sufficient recognition had been given to the shift which many Protestants had to make in giving up customs and agreeing not to display what they regarded as the legitimate symbol of the state.

The FEC said that it could be argued that they go too far the other way, and were too patient and tolerant. They had given employers too long to comply, on the ground that they needed time to gain the support of the work force. In the case of the politicians' photographs in the security hut, which has already been discussed (p169), nothing was done for many years, because the company was given repeated opportunities to resolve the situation co-operatively and diplomatically.

Some employers have been dissatisfied with the Commission's advice on the grounds that it was vague and unhelpful. The Commission would question if this complaint arises on those occasions when the advice given is not what the employer wants to hear. Sometimes employers want to know if there is a way round the regulations, and this applies more to recruitment practices than flags issues.

Finally there is the concern that the Commission is a very influential body, but is not fully accountable. It is able to give directions to employers which is at the end of a formal statutory process. It can also give advice through its advice officers and even this informal advice carries a great deal of weight.

For its part the FEC would want employers to see the advice as simply the Commission's opinion on the law – nothing more than that. They are ad hoc responses to situations as they arise. The general advice it distributes are not set out in a very formal document with very attractive presentation for this reason. But the Commission's opinion will carry weight whatever its formal status. Employers are not keen to be found guilty of discriminatory practices by the Fair Employment Tribunal. It is therefore much safer to follow the directions or advice of the FEC. If the employer thinks the advice is wrong, he or she could ignore it and wait for an employee to bring a case before the Fair Employment Tribunal, but the risks of such a strategy are clear. Therefore the Commission's directions and advice tends to be the basis of established practice, but there is no mechanism for any formal scrutiny of its conclusions or requirement for consultation. It does not seem difficult to create some procedure to obtain a second opinion on the correctness of FEC advice and interpretation of the legal position. The Commission's view is that employers can obtain a legal opinion if they wish, but that still leaves an element of risk.

This is somewhat similar to the concern about the impact of the role of the police in dealing with street parades and other public order situations, and the lack of oversight of their deliberation. It contrasts with the procedures required in order to change the Code of Practice under the Fair Employment Act (Northern Ireland). The Commission must consult with the Standing Advisory Commission on Human Rights, employers and workers organisations. The revised code is then sent to the Secretary of State for his approval and he lays it before Parliament. If it is accepted by Parliament the Code comes into effect. There are alternative provisions if a local Northern Ireland administration exists. This procedure allows scrutiny and debate, but it is cumbersome. At present the Commission prefers to work within the existing Code which is relatively new and broadly satisfactory and to avoid revising the Code.

We have acknowledged the existence of a number of criticisms and concerns about the policy and the role of the Commission in relation to the policy, but the staff of the Commission say that they do not receive many complaints. It is necessary to conclude with a reminder that, overall, flags and emblems are no longer an issue in the work place. Practices have changed dramatically from 1984 until 1994 and attitudes have also changed so that most people now accept that the display of flags and emblems can be an unreasonable imposition on workers who come from a different tradition.

A Final Case Study: The Prison Service

In the description of current practices and problems we have not referred to prisons, and instead we have decided to give them a separate short section.

Their experiences have been relevant to various sections of the study. A prison is a work place for the staff and the prisoners. It is a home and community for the inmates. It is an institution with all that implies. It is in fact a total institution in that it encompasses the total life of the inmate and is the context for all aspects of their existence: sleeping, eating, working, playing and socialising (Goffman, 1968). It therefore incorporates in microcosm all the situations we have discussed in the previous chapters and it seemed useful to draw together the different elements in this final case study. The prison situation is also worth focusing on because it is more sensitive and complex as a result of the close proximity of people with conflicting militant views.

We will look at three aspects of prisons; their organisational ethos and policy, the Service's expectations of how officers should behave and the regulations governing prisoners.

Organisational ethos

There are two main elements of the service's organisational ethos which are relevant to a consideration of flags and anthems. Firstly it is a Crown Service. The symbol of the service, which is worn on the cap badge of officers, consists of the letters ER (Elizabeth Regina) surrounded by the words H.M. Prisons and surmounted by the Crown. Prisons are called Her Majesty's Prison, Maze and so on. We understand that most members of the Service are very proud of their association with the Queen and would not want to lose it.

The service also demonstrates its allegiance to the state in familiar ways. Each prison flies the Union flag on the prescribed days, but it is in the nature of the layout of a prison that the flag pole is not visible from many parts of the prison. It is usually inside the prison, where it cannot be seen by the public, or in the administrative area where it cannot be seen by most prisoners. The Service also takes Remembrance Day seriously. There is a formal ceremony, conducted by the chaplains, the Service pipe band is in attendance and the roll of honour is remembered. It has particular meaning for the Service as a number of members have been killed as a result of the present 'Troubles'.

At the same time the organisation takes pride in being a neutral Service for the whole community, and it feels it has made significant progress in that direction. As stated in the Prison Service's Aims and Purposes, the 'overriding purpose is to serve the community by protecting it through holding securely those committed to our charge. . .', and one of its objectives is to 'treat prisoners as individuals regardless of their religious beliefs or political opinions and to offer them the opportunity to serve their sentences free from paramilitary influence.' There may be some tensions between being a Crown service and neutrality in the context of the politics of Northern Ireland. The issues were clearly presented by the Northern Ireland Association for the Care and Resettlement of Offenders in an undated pamphlet, *Justice Safety and Openness*, which was itself a response to the Prison Service strategy document, *Serving the Community*, which was launched in

June 1991. It is worth quoting the relevant section of this document at some length:

> 'We shall treat prisoners as individuals regardless of political opinion or religious belief . . .' announces the Strategic Plan. This is one of the statements to which, we feel, the leadership of the Prison Service has the greatest commitment. In itself, it is a bold declaration of adherence to the principles of non-discrimination but which will require a huge amount of work to implement. The history of the prisons over the past two decades, the religious composition of the Prison Service, the sectarian attitudes that are found in some parts of the Service, as well as amongst the prisoners, *the uniforms, emblems and symbols* associated with prisons here – all these form formidable obstacles to the implementation of this commitment.
>
> Clearly, there is a need to confront these issues in the initial training of officers and in greatly extended in-service training . . .
>
> From another point of view, there are dangers in the individualisation of treatment aim. It has to be recognised that quite large groups of prisoners firmly believe that it is society that should be rehabilitated, not them. In these circumstances, individualisation of treatment can be seen as an attack on their political principles. (p10, emphasis added)

In response the Service has tried to maintain a balance which maintains commitment to its status as a Crown Service but avoids over-emphasising it. For example in 1990 the Controller of Prisons announced in the *Northern Ireland Prison Service Annual Report 1989–90* (p2) a 'new corporate image for the Service and a Code of Conduct for staff are intended to increase the sense of identity and purpose of all staff.' Part of the aim is to distinguish the Service from the disciplined security forces. We will remember that the RUC also wants to enhance its image as a servant to the community. One aspect of the new image is a new corporate logo alongside the existing royal symbol. The new logo is part of the trend to geometrical shapes and is a diamond pattern with no obvious contentious significance. It is now more widely used than the crown badge, the latter still used on uniforms.

It believes that in implementing the objective of creating a neutral service it has gained more acceptance from the prison population and the wider community, and conflict with prisoners and paramilitary groups has been diffused over the last few years. It has also made the service more congenial for Catholics to join, but the numbers are still very low.

Expectations of staff behaviour
Staff have an important part to play in all aspects of the way the Service operates, including creating the neutral image. Encouraging professionalism at all levels is taken very seriously. The NIACRO document (p19) foresaw that 'anti-sectarian training will come to be seen, we are sure, as a necessary part of the curriculum for new and serving officers.' The Service is satisfied that it has a programme well in hand. New recruits are made

sensitive to the possibility of allowing bias and prejudice to influence behaviour and they are made aware of the kind of messages that prisoners are receiving from the attitudes and manner of staff. It is also planned to include a compensatory module into in-service training to introduce longer serving officers to the same concepts and ideas.

The Service has also made clear its expectations of officers. In relation to flags and emblems they are not to display any national or political symbols. They are only allowed to wear Prison Officers' Association long service badge, the badge of members of the dog section and a Butler Trust Award badge, which is given in recognition of distinctive and outstanding work by those working in prisons. Other uses of symbols is also not acceptable, including a mug with the badge of Rangers Football Club. The picture of the Union flag published in the *Sun* during the Gulf War cropped up in prison as well as in other work places. Officers pinned it up in the visits area of H.M. Prison, Maze. They were told to remove it. Management thought the coverage was very jingoistic, but it is probable that they would have wanted a picture of a flag removed in any circumstances. The regulations help to ensure a neutral working environment as defined by the Fair Employment Code of Practice. In the context of prisons they have a wider function. They ensure that the officers do not display emblems which the prisoners are forbidden to have. It also sets a standard of what is acceptable behaviour for prisoners.

The regime for prisoners

The Prison Service is concerned that prisoners do not act in ways which could precipitate conflict between prisoners. There is clearly a potential for friction when people who hold conflicting militant political views are held in close proximity to each other for long periods of time. The Service has accepted some level of segregation in practice in some parts of the prison system, but it is determined that it should not be extended. It wishes to avoid anything which might exacerbate the situation and where one group might provoke the other. It wants to reduce the risk of prisoners or officers being injured. Restricting flags and emblems is one aspect of that. No badges, clothing or banners which might have political significance are allowed. The Fianné is acceptable as a badge of educational attainment.

Prisoners have more freedom to possess emblems when there is no risk of them being seen by political opponents, applying similar principles to the public order law in the community. There is more latitude on what prisoners are allowed to have in their cells, and, for example, pictures of football teams are quite common. There are segregated blocks in H.M. Prison, Maze, which allows a more tolerant attitude to emblems. It was vividly demonstrated in the film of life in the prison made by Peter Taylor. He showed loyalist prisoners making band uniforms and regalia out of paper and other materials. They then marched up and down the corridor at the time of the Twelfth of July celebrations in the community outside. This event was not likely to cause problems for the good order in the prison because the republican prisoners could not see it. The film showed other prisoners watching through the gate of another wing. It would have been easy to assume from the film that they were republicans, but in fact they were other loyalists. It is interesting to speculate what would have been the response if republican prisoners had organised a band.

The restrictions on emblems are applied very firmly in neutral areas of the Maze and especially the visits area, as is the case in all the other prisons. Traditionally the prisoners themselves have kept the visits area neutral for the sake of their families. It was not permitted to display a pictures of the Queen and a Glasgow Celtic team pennant. The fact that the officers pinned up the Sun picture of the Union flag in the visits area made it even more problematic, and ensured that it was removed speedily.

The rules are fairly obvious, but it is more instructive to consider how they are enforced. They are very strictly adhered to and the service is unlikely to relax them in special circumstances. Staff are concerned that such requests are often made as a way to test the rules to the limit, and to disrupt the system. At the same time, the staff believe that most prisoners want to know where they stand, and want clear rules without exceptions.

A recent controversy over Remembrance Day poppies illustrates the point. In 1992 in H.M. Prison, Belfast, the Free Presbyterian chaplain organised a Remembrance service for the prisoners, who asked if they could wear poppies. The Governor did not allow the request because it might have created tension between loyalist and republican prisoners and led to problems in running the prison. We were told that copies of the football shirts of the England team are also banned because the red rose badge is thought to look like a poppy.

Politicians, including Ian Paisley were very annoyed and argued that the poppy was not a sectarian symbol. A request was made for a judicial review of the governor's decision, and the judge accepted that he was acting within his powers in making the decision. The Prison Service thought the review had been a good thing in the circumstances because it had upheld the Governor's decision. Loyalists were less happy. They thought the judgement rubbed salt in the wound, because the judge compared the poppy to the shamrock.

It is possible to think of arrangements which might have allowed the prisoners to wear the poppy without causing offence. Perhaps they could have been issued to the prisoners as they went into the service and taken back as they came out. But the authorities thought that for the good management of the prison it was better to keep the regulations simple. It was felt that wearing poppies in this context would be a statement of some kind, directed at political opponents, and there was no point in accommodating the request given the risk of trouble and extra supervision involved.

It is unlikely that such a restrictive attitude would be acceptable in dealing with flags and anthems in the community outside prison, but other prison services adopt a similar stance and in some cases go farther. In state penitentiaries in California for example, visitors to prisoners are refused entry if they have any visual signs that they are identified with a gang and this can include their hair style.

The specific issue of poppies has cropped up in the English Prison Service. A headline in the *Sun* of 8 November 1993 read 'No Poppies in Jail, It Might Offend the IRA'. It reported that prison officers had been banned from wearing poppies in the category A unit of Belmarsh Prison in south east London. It was said that the prison governors were concerned that poppies might offend republican prisoners and lead to rioting. According to the report a prison officer said that the ban on poppies was 'an insult to all those who died fighting for Britain', and a spokesman for the Royal British Legion was quoted as saying 'Irish lads served with us in the war so it's ridiculous to say a poppy can offend. The warders should say 'stuff it' and wear the poppy with pride.' This is another example of how the emblem is a symbol of an underlying memory or ideal or entity which is the thing that is really important to people. For this reason it has both the power to offend and the power to evoke pride.

Notes

1   This test is taken from *De Souza v Automobile Association* [1986] IRLR 103, and was quoted in *Magill v Fair Employment Agency*, Recorders Court, 10.7.1987.

CHAPTER 7

Where do we go from here?

The shamrock, rose and thistle and the lily too beside
They do flourish all together, boys, along the Faughan side
(Traditional, Irish)

The previous sections of this study have reviewed the practice of using national symbols, both in Ireland and elsewhere and both in the present and in the past. We have seen that currently in Northern Ireland there is not a standard approach which is used in all situations. Different practices are found in different social situations. They can be set out on a continuum as in figure 7.1 from absence of symbols to complete freedom of use. For each stage along the continuum, we have identified an approach, described its principle characteristic, and suggested one type of situation where it is a normal response to potential or actual problems.

The first option is to avoid all symbols as far as possible. This is the option that is chosen by some sports bodies and by other social groups who are particularly concerned not to cause offence. Many pubs have a policy of not allowing football colours to be worn. As a public policy option it is most clearly seen in the workplace, where the intention of the Fair Employment laws is to remove all symbols if possible. Exceptions to this are accepted only with reluctance.

The second option is to look for neutral alternatives. This is most often found in sport where it is recognised that songs and flags are valuable as an

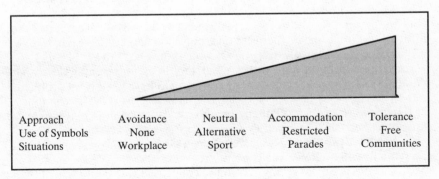

Approach	Avoidance	Neutral	Accommodation	Tolerance
Use of Symbols	None	Alternative	Restricted	Free
Situations	Workplace	Sport	Parades	Communities

Figure 7.1   A Continuum of Approaches to Symbols

encouragement to team spirit, but divisive songs and flags would undermine morale. In these circumstances other songs or flags are used, either existing or specially created alternatives. It is an option which has been adopted voluntarily and informally and it has not been applied as a public policy stance. However, we have seen that it could become important as part of a new political accommodation, when more cohesive symbols might be required.

The third option is to accept some display of symbols, but with regulations to ensure that it does not lead to more problems. The best example of this is related to public demonstrations where in public policy terms it has not been considered desirable to ban symbols generally. However limitations are placed on display, on the grounds of the need to maintain public order. If the display may cause a breach of the peace it is forbidden.

Finally there are situations where any display is permissible. This occurs in homogeneous groups where no one is likely to be offended or provoked. Public policy does not feel it can interfere in these situations which are mostly to be found in local communities, and local institutions such as social clubs and in the home. Some people would seem to want to reverse this continuum. During one dispute over the removal of flags from the workplace it was pointed out that some of those fighting hardest to keep them in the factory did not fly a flag from their own homes.

The most contentious area is the line between regulated use and free use. When does a situation become too contentious to be left to individual choice? Should more situations be brought under regulation or is there too many areas where limitations occur? Is self restraint better than regulation? These debates arise most notably in relation to parades in areas where they are not welcome, and the concerns are much wider than the display of symbols. Nevertheless the issues are demonstrated very starkly. We have also seen that it arises in relation to murals. Even in homogeneous communities some residents may be unhappy about some displays but are powerless to prevent them. Does free expression of negative attitudes among likeminded people have an impact on behaviour outside that group?

There are ways in which the present practices seem limited. They seem to denying the importance of symbols of identity for people. The message seems to be 'Fly them if you must but do it in the privacy of your own home. And it would be better if you did not want to fly them at all.' We talk of accepting the different traditions in Northern Ireland, but that includes those parts we do not like. We are not really accepting people if they have to act like us.

This seems to be in tune with a recurring theme in the interviews that national symbols do not cause many problems. There have been problems in the past, but they have been dealt with. If problems still arise there is a legal framework to deal with them. In any case flags and anthems only cause difficulty where they are used as a focus for the expression of more important underlying problems. As one republican said, solve those problems and the symbols will no longer be contentious, and people may lose interest in them. Current practices seems to be more concerned with containment than with responding creatively to people's identification with flags and symbols.

To some degree the analysis is correct. Flags and anthems are not fundamental. 'You can't eat a flag' is a common expression which reminds us that
material issues may be more important. Symbolism may also mean very
little without the substance. At the twentieth anniversary anti-internment
rally a huge banner was carried with a statement along the bottom: 'Though
they promise us work and our flag we will not rest until we are free.'

We can ignore symbols and hope they will go away. But the study has also
shown that symbols are important and their use is connected closely to some
of our basic needs of identity, security and self expression. Many of those
interviewed, on all sides of the community divisions, were quite nonchalant
about flags in general, but there is a point where they care very much about
what is done to symbols which they value.

The present situation does not satisfy everyone. Maybe that is never
possible, but can we be content with a situation if the worries of large
sections of the community are ignored? This does not seem to fit with the
idea of respect for all traditions which is espoused in the rhetoric of all the
political parties and is of course the philosophy of the Cultural Traditions
Group. The aim is 'to find solutions that others can accept and solutions
which do not cause offence to others with different aspirations', as Joe
Clark, the Canadian Minister for Constitutional Affairs put it at the constitutional conference in Toronto in February 1992 to consider the constitutional options in response to the issues of identity and rights in Canada.

Some people, mainly Unionists, are concerned that the policy of minimis-
ing the use of symbols seems to be denying their heritage. Recognising their
feelings does not mean tolerating the use of symbols provocatively without
consideration for others, but it does mean understanding and responding to
the underlying motivation.

Perhaps communities will always have those needs to a greater or lesser
extent, and many societies much less troubled than Northern Ireland still
value highly their flags and anthems. From this perspective it may be more
productive to consider how we can use flags and anthems to satisfy our
needs, but in a non-controversial way. Might it also be possible that, as
happened with the Different Drums Project, the use of flags and anthems
could address the wider issues symbolically and in resolving these problems,
a contribution could be made to solving the wider issues, so that different
traditions and their symbols can 'flourish all together'?

Such an approach is not a system of rules which covers every situation,
but Maurice Hayes (1993, p8), in his pamphlet *Whither Cultural Diversity,*
points us to a standard against which we can measure our attempts to deal
with difference in society. Not for the first time he draws our attention to the
insights of earlier generations, which are still relevant today, when he quotes
from a 1917 pamphlet by Æ (George Russell) *Thoughts for a Convention*:

The more richness and variety prevail in a nation, the less likelihood is
there of a tyranny of one culture over the rest. We should aim in Ireland at
the freedom of the ancient Athenians who, as Pericles said, listened gladly
to the opinions of others and did not turn sour faces on those who

disagreed with them . . . We should allow the greatest freedom in respect
of cultural development in Ireland so that the best may triumph by reason
of superior beauty and not because the police are relied upon to maintain
one culture in a superior positions.

This needs to be dealt with at a number of levels and the rest of this section
outlines a synthesis of some of ideas presented to us and our own reactions.

Framing the debate

Firstly we need to consider how the arguments are framed. We have seen
how different arguments are used to justify different positions, and how
often we use different standards to judge other people's behaviour than we
apply to our own group. Some say we should respect some symbols because
they represent the state. Others say they are outmoded and anachronistic.
Others say they are offensive, provocative and intimidatory – usually referring to opponents' symbols. Sometimes we try to stick to a set of rules which
we hope are neutral. We saw how this can lead to misunderstanding, as in
the recent debate about practice at rugby internationals.

All these arguments can be valid, but underneath them all is often a
political argument because the symbols in the context of Northern Ireland
are political artefacts. This element of the debate is often not articulated,
but it is often recognised. Certainly we are much quicker to understand the
underlying political argument being used by opponents, than to acknowledge them in our own rhetoric.

We must also recognise the importance of the power relationship in our
reaction to other symbols. At a personal level it makes a difference to our
feelings if we have free choice in respecting another person's symbol. It also
makes a difference if we may be penalised in the future if we do not respect
that symbol. And at a broader community level, we are assessing what will
be the impact of our actions on the ongoing power relationships in society.
Will we weaken our position if we respect our opponent's symbols or make
a concession to his preferences?

We were struck by how seldom people, especially politicians referred to
these kind of issues directly, even though other arguments lead to contradictions and non-sequiturs. It would be helpful if debates about symbols included more explicit statements of the political arguments on each side.

The issue is more complicated because the Union flag, the Tricolour,
'The Queen' and 'The Soldier's Song' are at the same time political and
non-political symbols. They are the symbols of two sovereign states, one
of which exercises jurisdiction over the territory of Northern Ireland.
Sometimes the flags are used in this way, as national flags are used throughout the world. Sometimes they are used as the political slogans of competing
sections of the community. Often they are used as both. And of course
the existence of the state and the question of sovereignty are political issues.
It may be fruitless to disentangle the different motivations, yet we may have
to try.

An effort has been made with the Union symbols, as we have seen in the areas of Public Order and Fair Employment, though the situation is not fully understood. Some Unionists thought that the Union flag should be given formal protection, arguing that the threat to it was greater in Northern Ireland. A nationalist said that if it is necessary to put special safeguards in place to ensure a flag is respected, that leads to disrespect. Although there is no legal protection for the Union flag, it is less likely to be considered provocative than other flags and it can fly as the official flag over a workplace. We have also seen how some nationalists who do not approve of the present constitutional arrangements are prepared to respect the symbols when they are used in this formal way. The Union flag therefore does seem to have some special status, but the situation could benefit from clarification.

On the other hand the Irish flag and anthem are seldom accorded the status of the symbols of a neighbouring state. The American consulate flies the Stars and Stripes every day with no objection, because it is not seen as a threat. Similarly the Tricolour is flown along with other flags of the European Country or over Irish offices overseas when appropriate – but not in most parts of Northern Ireland.

We would suggest that the Tricolour should be treated in the same way as other national flags. The difficulties that this would pose for some Unionists are well know and not very different from the difficulties some nationalists would have in accepting the presence of the Union symbols in the way suggested in the previous paragraph. However it might create a better climate if we could come to accept the presence of both sets of symbols in a limited way on appropriate occasions, and more importantly accept the legitimate right of the other part of the community to express its identification with the state that the symbols represent. We understand the strength of the feelings which are evoked by the opposing symbols, and it would require quite a change of attitude. It would not require either community to give up its commitment to its own constitutional solution, but we recognise that such a change could be taken as a weakening of the resolution of each part of the community to oppose the state of which they disapprove. One might ask how strong that commitment is if it could be undermined so easily. These changes could come about by example from influential figures in the community. There remains the question of how we deal with the overtly political use of symbols.

Freedom of expression

It has been suggested that the right to freedom of expression is the basic principle which should guide our approach. Rather than trying to contain and disapprove of the display of symbols we should try to ensure that people can express themselves through symbols if they wish. Of course there are always limits to free expression, and we will return to them in the following sections, but within those limits we would see merit in this approach.

In principle we uphold the right to free speech, and we uphold the right for people to express their identity. On one side John Hume has talked of a society where Catholic, Protestant and Dissenter can live together, and on the other the principles of the Orange Order and Unionism are based on basic human rights. However, in our conflictual society we have hedged these rights with so many qualifications that we fall far short of the ideal. The presence of the other side is tolerated, but it would be better if they conformed to our way of life and aspirations.

There are difficult issues in working out how freedom of expression and other rights can be exercised in our society but it is not completely unknown territory. Philosophers and jurists such as Ronald Dworkin have analysed the problems and we could benefit from a wider airing of their ideas in the debate in Northern Ireland.

We noted in Chapter 2 the difficulty of limiting behaviour because it is offensive. There needs to be additional grounds before behaviour should be curtailed by law. We must also bear in mind that those who wish to restrict freedom of expression may themselves be acting provocatively and for sectarian reasons. They have an equal right to express their views, but they do not have the right to limit the free expression of others. We have also seen that it is sometimes (thought not always) more effective to ignore offensive behaviour than to react to it.

We are therefore recommending greater tolerance of other peoples' display of their symbols. It may be helpful to apply this logic to real situations. If we refer back to Chapter 5 and the example of the Orange parade in Dungannon in 1993 when the Tricolour was displayed in a window, in the same way that the Orange Order asked that their parade is tolerated as an expression of their identity, perhaps they may also have to accept that someone else can display a flag from his or her window during the parade as an expression of a different identity. Applying it to the decision of whether to play 'The Queen' at University graduations, the authorities are clearly within their rights to play it. But those who object are equally entitled to sit while it is being played. Each side should respect the other's right in this matter, even if they find it offensive. If however someone is discriminated against in some way as a result of his or her action, that action is illegal and can be dealt with accordingly. The discrimination which causes damage is an issue, but not, in a human rights sense, the freedom of expression which causes offensive. However this does not mean that we should be complacent about behaviour which is offensive.

Exercising restraint

Rights need to be set along side responsibilities. We may have the right to express ourselves, but we also have a responsibility to exercise that right in the least offensive way, bearing in mind the sentiments of opponents. When people are uncertain of their rights they may try to use them aggressively. If they are clear about their rights they may be ready to think about the impact of their behaviour on other people.

There are examples of this happening in practice. The Orange Order has begun to think about how they can exercise their rights with the minimum of offence, perhaps aware of the possibility of the authorities imposing controls on them. A unionist politician conceded that there are circumstances where the symbols may be regarded as provocative. The GAA has considered itself circumspect in flying the Tricolour at some of their grounds if it might cause offence, though perhaps also aware that it might result in violent confrontation. To apply this concept to the actual issue of the Queen's University anthem controversy, it might suggest that the authorities are entitled to play it, but that they should consider if it might be better not to play it in the circumstances.

It was suggested that local arrangements can be made and sometimes an outside person has been able to help groups to think more thoroughly about the issues, as in the example of the bonfire, discussed in Chapter 4.

Finding alternatives

Within the context of freedom of expression, it is possible and desirable to find alternatives which will gain wider support. There was support for new symbols when a group had little power and were talking about changing their opponents' symbols. There was little support for changing one's own symbols when one had a greater measure of control. Thus Unionists saw little need to change the national symbols used in Northern Ireland and Nationalists saw little need to change the national symbols used in the Republic of Ireland. Other states have changed their symbolism often to achieve greater cohesion, and this makes the opposition to change in Ireland more worthy of note.

Within the community we have noted that other songs are used. Co-operation North attempted to find an alternative anthem and arranged for one to be tried out at a rugby international. The words were handed out to encourage full participation. Roy Arbuckle has devised a project to hold a competition to find a new anthem. He presented it to the Ophsal Commission (Pollak, 1993, p345), but as yet still needs sponsorship.

It would appear that no community in Ireland is ready to give up the present symbols. Symbols give a sense of permanence and continuity which is not easily replaced, though the potential for such a change could be explored in more detail. However there is scope to create patriotic flags and songs which would not replace national anthems and national flags, but would express a shared heritage and shared identity. Foster (1989, p11) has argued that all the people of Ireland share a sense of identity with the land, and that might provide a basis for such shared symbols. They would serve a useful purpose for groups which want an alternative, and could also be used alongside the official symbols. If in time they seemed part of an enduring tradition and acquired the status of public institutions, they could be formally adopted by popular demand.

It would be relatively easy to do this for the whole island, but the implications would be more complex in Northern Ireland What geographical area would the symbols represent. Some would want it put in the context of the province, others would want to relate them to the present Northern Ireland and some would object to the whole concept.

Limiting freedom

Even in the most hopeful scenario, voluntary restraints on the expression of freedom are unlikely to be sufficient. Legal limitations will be required to avoid excesses which interfere with some greater good and in particular with the rights of others, where 'freedoms collide' in John Rawls' striking phrase. One Unionist was clear that there are times when no limitations would be justified. He argued that there were appropriate occasions on the basis of well established custom when the display of symbols is always legitimate. We were not certain that a consensus can be established on what all those occasions are, in view of the different customs in different parts of the world and the speed with which customs are changing in this area.

The two most obvious situations where limitations are necessary have been identified and are widely accepted: where the freedom to display symbols can infringe the right to work free from intimidation and where it can threaten public order.

Dealing with these situations within the concept of freedom of expression, has a number of implications. Most obviously a clear code of practice is necessary so that decisions to restrict freedom are open to public scrutiny. It is possible to be categorical about the circumstances in which some behaviour is unacceptable. These restrictions should be clearly laid down and made public. However this is not always possible, and discretion has to be left to make a judgement in the light of specific circumstances. The criteria on which such discretion is based should be laid down and the person or body which can exercise that discretion should be clearly identifiable. We have suggested in Chapter 2 that the most appropriate criteria are behavioural, based on not imposing on the free will of others. With these safeguards, it is then possible to review decisions and to hold to account those who do not exercise their discretion according to the code laid down.

This system exists in relation to fair employment, though aspects of it may be open to criticism. In the area of public order the basis of decision making is much less clear and there is a strong argument for greater openness about the exercise of discretion.

If the perspective described in this chapter was applied more widely with all its implications at different levels, then it is to be hoped that a greater consensus could be achieved which would allow the display of symbols in a more positive way without causing harm and offence

BIBLIOGRAPHY

Allison, R. and Riddell, S. (1991) *The Royal Encyclopedia* London: MacMillan.

Anderson, W. and Damle, S. (1987) *Brotherhood in Saffron: the RSS and Hindu Revivalism* New Delhi: Vistar.

Bailey, S.D. (ed.) (1988) *Human Rights and Responsibilities in Britain and Ireland: A Christian Perspective* London: MacMillan.

Barraclough, E.M.C. (1971) *Flags of the World* London: Warne.

Bell, D. (1986) 'Acts of Union: Youth Sub-Culture and Ethnic Identity among Protestants in Northern Ireland' in *British Journal of Sociology*, Vol XXXVIII No 2.

Bell, D. (1990) *Acts of Union: Youth Culture and Sectarianism in Northern Ireland* London: MacMillan.

Berger, P. and Luckman, T. (1967) *The Social Construction of Reality* Harmondsworth: Allen Lane, The Penguin Press.

Boyce, G. (1991) 'Northern Ireland: A Place Apart?' in Hughes, E. (ed) *Culture and Politics in Northern Ireland 1960–1990* Milton Keynes: Open University Press.

Boyd, A. (1969) *Holy War in Belfast* Tralee: Anvil Books.

Boyd, J. (1982) *Collected Plays, 2* Belfast: Blackstaff Press.

Bruce, S. (1992) *The Red Hand: Protestant Paramilitaries in Northern Ireland* Oxford: Oxford university Press.

Buckley, A.D. (1984) 'Walls Within Walls: Religion and Rough Behaviour in an Ulster Community' *Sociology* Vol.18, No.1, pp19–32.

Card, R (1987) *Public Order: The New Law* London: Butterworth.

Caulfield, M. (1965) *The Easter Rebellion* London: Four Square Books.

Community Relations Council (1993) *What Can We Do: A Practical Guide to Community Relations in Northern Ireland* Belfast: Community Relations Council.

De Baróid, C. (1989) *Ballymurphy and the Irish War* Dublin: Aisling Publishers.

Devlin, P. (1981) *Yes, We Have No Bananas* Belfast: Blackstaff Press.

Diffly, S (1973) *The Men in Green, The Story of Irish Rugby* London: Pelham Books.

Enloe, C. (1986) *Ethnic Conflict and Political Development* Langham, Maryland: University Press of America.

Finlay, A. (1989) *Trade Unionism and Sectarianism among Derry Shirt Workers 1868–1968* London: University of London, Ph.D. dissertation.

Fish, S.E. (1980) *Is There a Text in This Class? The Authority of Interpretive Communities* Cambridge, Mass.: Harvard University Press.

Glenny, M (1992) *The Fall of Yugoslavia* Harmondsworth: Penguin.

Goffman, E. (1968) *Asylums* Harmondsworth: Penguin Books.

Gutierrez. J. (1992) 'The Olympic Games and the Ethnic Conflict in Catalonia' in *Conflict Resolution Notes*, Vol 10. No 2, p 11.

Hammond, P. (1993) *The Concept of a National Music* Dublin: RTE unpublished radio talk.

Hayes-McCoy G.A. (1979) *A History of Irish Flags from Earliest Times* Dublin: Academy Press.

Hayes. M. (1993) *Whither Cultural Diversity?* (2nd. ed.) Belfast: Community Relations Council.

Jefferson, A. (1986) 'Structuralism and Post-Structuralism' in Jefferson, A. and Robey, D. *Modern Literary Theory* London: B.T. Batsford.

Joint Group of Unionist MPs (undated) *The Public Order Order: Equality Under the Law?* Belfast: Joint Group of Unionist MPs.

Larsen, E.E. (1982) 'The Glorious Twelfth: a Ritual Expression of collective identity' in Cohen, A.P. *Belonging : Identity and Social Organisation in British Rural Culture* Manchester: Manchester University Press.

Livingstone, S and Magill, A. (1990) 'Religious Discrimination' in Dickson, B. (ed.) *Civil Liberties in Northern Ireland* Belfast: Committee on the Administration of Justice.

Loftus, B. (1994) *Mirrors: Orange and Green* Dundrum: Picture Press .

McCartney, C. (1991) *The Politics Of Intransigence* Coleraine: Unpublished D. Phil Thesis, University of Ulster.

McGuigan, B., Cullen, G. and Mullan, H. (1991) *Barry McGuigan: the Untold Story* London: Pobson Books.

Messenger, B. (1988) *Picking Up the Linen Threads: Life in Ulster's Mills* (2nd ed.) Belfast: Blackstaff Press.

Moloney, E. and Pollak, A. 1986) *Paisley* Swords, Dublin: Poolbeg Press.

Nellis J.J. (1992) *The New Lodge Tigers*: Londonderry: Unpublished M.A. Thesis, University of Ulster.

NIO (1986) *Proposal for a Draft Order in Council: Public Order: Explanatory Document* Belfast: Northern Ireland Office.

O'Casey, S. (1963) *Autobiographies*, volume one London: MacMillan.

O'Casey, S. (1974 edition) *Juno and the Paycock & The Plough and the Stars* London: MacMillan.

O'Malley, C. (1988) *A Poets' Theatre* Dublin: Elo Press.

Osmond, J. (1988) *The Divided Kingdom* London: Constable.

Pepys, S (1953) *Diary* Everyman Library Edition London: Dent.

Pollak, A (ed.) (1993) *A Citizen's Inquiry: The Opsahl Report on Northern Ireland* Dublin: Lilliput Press.

Potter, J. and Wetherell, M. (1987) *Beyond Attitudes and Behaviour: Social Psychology and Discourse Analysis* London: Sage.

Purdie, B. (1990) *Politics in the Street: the Origins of the Civil Rights Movement* Belfast: Blackstaff.

Raab, E. and Lipset, S.M. (1962) 'The Prejudiced Society' in Raab, E. *American Race Relations Today* New York: Doubleday and Co.

Rolston, B (1992) *Politics and Painting: Murals and Conflict in Northern Ireland* London: Associated University Presses.

Scottish National Party (1993) *A Short History of the Scottish National Party* Edinburgh: Scottish National Party.

Shehadeh, R. (1988) *Occupier's Law: Israel and the West Bank* Washington, D.C.: Institute for Palestine Studies.

Stewart, A.T.Q. (1977) *The Narrow Ground: Aspects of Ulster 1609–1969* London: Faber and Faber.

Sugden, J. (1993) 'Political Football' in *Fortnight* May 1993 No. 317.

Sugden, J. and Bairner, A. (1993) *Sport, Sectariansim and Society in a Divided Ireland* Leicester: Leicester University Press.

Todd, J. (1987) 'Two Traditions in Unionist Political Culture' *Irish Political Studies*, 2, pp1–26.

Todd, J. (1990) 'Northern Irish Nationalist Political Culture' *Irish Political Studies*, 5.

Turner, J.C. and Giles, H. (1981) *Intergroup Behaviour* Oxford: Basil Blackwell.

Zimmerman, G-D. (1967) *Songs of Irish Rebellion: Political Street Ballads 1785–1900* Dublin: Alan Figgis.

Statutes

Flags and Emblems (Display) Act (Northern Ireland) 1954 c. 10.

Northern Ireland Public Order (Northern Ireland) Order 1987 No. 463 (NI7).

Fair Employment (Northern Ireland) Act 1989 c. 32.

APPENDIX 1

A – People Interviewed

Roy Arbuckle	Different Drums Project
Douglas Archard	US Consul General
Gordon Beveridge	Vice-Chancellor, Queen's University
Jack Boothman	President-elect, Gaelic Athletic Association
Joe Bowers	MSF
Keith Brown	Fair Employment Commission
Brian Carlin	Director of Resources, Shorts
Fionna Cassidy	Equality Employment Services
Brian Carlin	Bombardier Shorts
Robert Cooper	Chairman, Fair Employment Commission
Ray Coyle	Manager, Derry City Football Club
Prof. Brice Dickson	Dept of Law and Public Administration, University of Ulster
Nigel Dodds	Secretary, Democratic Unionist Party
Nigel Dummigan	Clothing/Textile Section, GMU
Robin Eames,	Archbishop of Armagh
Sean Farren	Social Democratic and labour Party
Guy Fetherstone	Albion Clothing Company
Christina Fisher	Northern Field Development Officer, CBSI
David Ford	Secretary, Alliance party
Ken Gillespie	Chief Scout
Dennis Godfrey	Fair Employment Commission
Peter Gwynn-Jones	Lancaster Herald, The College of Arms
Ronnie Hannah	Ulster Society
Peter Hartley	Secretary, Lord Chamberlain's Office
Denis Haughey	Social Democratic and Labour Party
Helen Honeyman	Harmony Community Trust
Stephen Hull	Young Alliance, Queen's University
John Hunter	Secretary, University of Ulster
Alan Hutchinson	
Rev Samuel Hutchinson	General Secretary, Presbyterian Church in Ireland
Ken Jamieson	Director, CEMA 1967–1970 and Arts Council 1970–1990
Francis Lagan	Auxillary Bishop of Derry
Kevin Lamb	Northern Ireland Council for Integrated Education
Brian Lampkin	Vice Principal, Lagan College
Belinda Loftus	Down Arts Centre
Ken Maginnis, M.P.	Ulster Unionist Party
Frank McArdle	
Eugene McCamphill	Ancient Order of Hibernians, Gortrighey Division 385

Maeve McCann	Dept of Anthropology, Queens University
Supt. Roy McCune	Operations Branch, Royal Ulster Constabulary
Dick McColgin	Secretary, Northern Ireland Commonwealth Games Committee
Brendan McGrath	National Executive Board, CBSI
Mr. McIlvenny	Training and Management Development Manager, Harland and Wolff
Alistair McLaughlin	Northern Ireland Bankers Association
Declan McLoughlin	
Paul McMenamin	President elect, Students' Union, Queen's University
Mr. Mulryne	Principal, Methodist College, Belfast
Gearóid Ó hEára	Sinn Féin
Colm O'Malley	
Mary O'Malley	Founding Director, Lyric Theatre
Pearse O'Malley	Founding Trustee, Lyric Theatre
George Patton	Executive officer, Grand Orange Lodge of Ireland
Mary Peters	Chairperson, Ulster Games Federation
Lawrence Price	Different Drums Project
Jim Quinn	Counteract
Representative	Northern Ireland Scout Council
Representatives	Shankill Historical Society
Representatives	Short Brothers Plc.
Resident	East Belfast
Rev Hugh Ross	Ulster Independence Movement
Alan Shannon	Controller of Prisons
Alan Thomas	Plaid Cymru
David Trimble, M.P.	Ulster Unionist Party
Sammy Wilson	Press Officer, Democratic Unionist Party

B – Organisations and Individuals who Provided Information and Materials

Belinda Loftus
Brice Dickson
Committee for the Administration of Justice
Counteract
F.A.I.T.
Fair Employment Commission
Northern Ireland Curriculum Council
Plaid Cymru
Scottish National Party
Short Brothers Plc
Women's Institute

APPENDIX 2

Songs Referred to in the Text

A NEW SONG FOR IRELAND

We share the tears
We all have shared the sorrow
We've looked and found
No future in the past
It's time to change
Now time to build tomorrow
We'll start afresh
Old quarrels must not last.

Chorus
We'll free our land from hatred
There's a better way
We'll free our children from
The conflict's curse
We'll free tomorrow from
The chains of yesterday.

Let's think peace first
And bring our land
A better day

We share this land
This life, this hope, this future
It's time to learn
To live, to work, to laugh
So much to lose
So much to build together
It's time to choose
    The future or the past.

INDEPENDENT ULSTER ANTHEM

Raise thy banner, Sons of Ulster,
'Neath its shadow we will stand,
As we call to God in heaven,
For His blessing on our land.
And our God enthroned in glory,
He will hear our earnest cries,
And the ancient land of Ulster,
Shall with new-born strength arise.

Raise thy banner, Sons of Ulster,
Pledge again thy heart and hand,
To be ever true and loyal,
In the service of our land.
Soon will come the dawn of morning,
Soon will end the night of pain,
And the ancient land of Ulster
Be a nation once again.

A COUNTRYWOMAN'S SONG

1. Gold of the whins on the Mournes and the Sperrins,
   Silver and green in the west,
   Pink foam of orchards, white spray at the causeway—
   Who shall say which is the best?

2. Hearts in the country are friendly and kindly,
   Nights in the country are long;
   Dark hours are shorter when we are together
   Singing our countryside song.

Derry and Antrim and Down, Fermanagh, Armagh and Tyrone,
Six Counties women all working together, and every one proud
   of his own.

FREEDOM SONGS

We watched our fathers fighting in the street,
We watched the nights burn from gold to green,
I saw my mother try to keep a home,
Still watch my people stand alone.

Freedom songs
Freedom songs we sing.

We watch the soldiers kick in our doors,
Drag away our fathers; call our mothers whores.
In the hope of justice we would kneel and pray.
Come Irish justice in an Irish way.

Freedom songs
Freedom songs we sing.

Of all the things we hope to achieve,
We watched them come and now we watch them leave.
Men in black say turn your cheek,
As an Irish body bites an Irish street.

Freedom songs
Freedom songs we sing.